KARLO BR

MEETING

the

PROTESTANT
RESPONSE

HOW TO ANSWER
COMMON COMEBACKS TO
CATHOLIC ARGUMENTS

Catholic
Answers
Press

All Scripture citations taken from the Revised Standard Version Second Catholic Edition.

Published by Catholic Answers, Inc.
2020 Gillespie Way
El Cajon, California 92020
1-888-291-8000 orders
619-387-0042 fax
catholic.com

Printed in the United States of America

Cover design by eBookLaunch.com
Interior design by Russell Graphic Design

978-1-68357-281-7
978-1-68357-282-4 Kindle
978-1-68357-283-1 ePub

To all Protestants, whom we acknowledge to be fellow members of the Mystical Body of Christ

Contents

I
Peter and the Papacy

II
The Sacraments

III
Mary and the Saints

IV
Scripture and Tradition

V
Salvation

Acknowledgments

Writing a book for Catholic Answers Press is *never* a one-man show. Whatever praise this book may receive is a direct reflection of the hard work that our team here at Catholic Answers put in to produce this book. This being the case, I must express my gratitude. First, I would like to thank the *entire* Catholic Answers team because *everyone* is involved in some way or another—whether it's my fellow apologists, the marketing department, or sales. Second, our team of editors, Todd Aglialoro and Drew Belsky, is simply amazing. I can't thank them enough for the long hours and in-depth thought they've put into this book. Third, I am very grateful to Jimmy Akin for the *many* hours that he put in helping me construct the arguments in this book, some of which are original to him. His generosity is most appreciated, beyond what words can capture. Finally, and most importantly, I am grateful to my wife, Jacqueline, and five kids—Dominic, Savannah, Elijah, Catherine, and Nathaniel, for their support in this project.

Introduction

When I travel to give talks, I often meet people who are just beginning to discover the joy of apologetics. Usually for them it involves giving a *biblical* defense of the Catholic faith in conversations with Protestants, and they readily share with me their excitement in learning to wield Scripture verses that support Catholic teachings.

Sometimes it's Matthew 16:18–19, where Jesus makes Peter the rock and gives to him the "keys of the kingdom"—the interpretative context of which is Isaiah 22:22, which speaks of the royal steward in the Davidic kingdom whose authority was symbolized by the "key of the house of David."

Scripture and Tradition? They're ready for that one, too, having on hand Paul's clear teaching in 2 Thessalonians 2:15: "Stand firm and hold to the traditions which you were taught by us, either by word of mouth or by letter."

Other times, the excitement comes from learning that Jesus gave the apostles the authority to forgive sins when he said, "If you forgive the sins of any, they are forgiven; if you retain the sins of any, they are retained" (John 20:23), or that the only place in the Bible where the words "faith alone" are used, the words 'not by' appear in front of them (Jas. 2:24).

The most excitement, perhaps, comes when such a person shares his discovery of the biblical evidence for the Eucharist. "Jesus said, 'This is my body, not this *represents* my body,' they learn to say with confidence. And it's often added, "In John 6, Jesus says six times in six verses, 'eat my flesh . . . drink my blood.' Surely, he wasn't speaking metaphorically."

That average lay persons are learning these biblical arguments is remarkable in itself. Such arguments were known and employed throughout Catholic history, but they were reserved to the writings of early bishops and theologians—writings that weren't really accessible to the average Catholic. These arguments took on special relevance in the early days of the Protestant Reformation (early sixteenth century) when churchmen and theologians such as St. Thomas More, Cardinal Thomas Cajetan, St. Robert Bellarmine, and others battled early Reformers like Luther, Calvin, and Zwingli.

Early twentieth-century theology manuals for training priests included these arguments, too. Unfortunately, though, after the Second Vatican Council, they became pretty much obsolete in seminaries. So not only were these apologetical arguments not known by laity—they fell into disuse among clergy, too.

But in the late 1980s, there was a new springtime of apologetics, especially within the domain of the Catholic-Protestant dialogue. The blockbuster book *Catholicism and Fundamentalism,* by Catholic Answers founder Karl Keating, helped spark a roaring revival of popular apologetics. Before you knew it, *everyone* serious about the Catholic faith was doing apologetics and becoming familiar with the biblical arguments. This didn't go unnoticed among Protestants, and many of them converted to Catholicism because of these sorts of arguments and became leading Catholic apologists themselves.

Others, however, weren't so convinced.

After hearing these arguments presented by Catholic apologists over and over, Protestant writers and scholars took up the mantle of the Reformers and built a formidable counter-response, justifying in their minds the truth of their anti/contra-Catholic beliefs. These second-wave Protestants inspired their own followers to take on the new Catholic apologetic movement. Now, it's not uncommon for Protestants to listen to a common Catholic argument, smile, and reply, "Yeah, we've heard that one before. And it doesn't work."

For example, a Catholic may confidently make an argument for the papacy from Matthew 16:18, where Jesus makes Peter the rock of the Church, only to have his confidence immediately deflated with the rebuttal: "Well, in the original Greek there are two different words used for 'Peter' and 'rock.' *Petros* is the Greek word translated as 'Peter' and *petra* is the word translated as 'rock.' Since there are two different words, they must refer to two different things."

The Catholic feels stung by the encounter; the Protestant comes away affirmed in his rejection of Catholic claims and continued belief in Protestant doctrines.

All this may explain why many of these same folks who express to me their joy in doing apologetics also often say things along the lines of, "Why don't Protestants get it? The evidence for the Catholic position is so clear!" In most cases, it's not that Protestants simply are closed-minded. They "don't get it" because they've been formed in the echo chambers of their own apologists who've been pushing back against these Catholic arguments and think they have effective counter-responses.

But *are* they effective? That's the question we're going to answer in this book.

The structure of the chapters is very simple. We begin with a Catholic argument in brief. Next, we articulate common ways in which Protestants counter the Catholic argument. Then we respond with a robust answer to that counter-response. Each chapter ends with a brief summary of why the Catholic argument *still stands* as a legitimate defense of the belief in question.

These Protestant comebacks provide Catholics an opportunity to get off the merry-go-round of prooftexting and dig deeper into the riches embedded in the sacred page. My hope is that this book will help you move beyond the approach of simply *citing* passages in defense of the Faith and get into the regular habit of showing *why* the text supports Catholic beliefs. Without this kind of careful exegesis (a word from Greek that means *to explain or interpret*), Protestants will just keep saying, "Yeah, I've heard that one before. Tell me something I don't already know."

After reading this book you'll be able tell them things they *don't* already know, planting seeds in our separated Christian friends that may grow into another springtime of embracing the fullness of truth in the Catholic Church.

I
Peter and the Papacy

CHAPTER 1

Rock of the Church
Matthew 16:18

In Matthew 16:18, Jesus tells Simon, "You are Peter, and on this rock I will build my Church." Catholics interpret the rock as a reference to Peter. From this, Catholics infer that Jesus intended Peter to be the visible foundation and head of his Church on earth. This makes Peter the source of unity for Christ's Church; for, wherever the foundation and head is, there is the true Church of Jesus.

Catholics appeal to this verse as biblical evidence for the papacy because the Catholic doctrine of the papacy is precisely that Christ appointed Peter and his successors to be the source of unity of and the identifying mark for Jesus' Church on earth.

Some Protestants reply by attempting to show that the rock must refer to something other than Peter, without trying to identify who or what the rock does refer to. Other comebacks try to identify what the rock refers to—for example, Jesus, Peter's confession, or Christian teaching. Other comebacks concede that Peter is the rock but challenge the idea that he is unique in being the foundation of the Church.

As we'll see, each counter-response fails in undermining the claim that Peter is the rock and all that this entails.

Let's start with responses that attempt to show that the rock in Matthew 16:18 must refer to something *other* than Peter, regardless of what that is.

"'Petros' and 'Petra' are two different words."

Some Protestants challenge the notion that Peter is the rock by appealing to the different words that the Greek text uses for Simon's new name (*Petros*) and the rock (*petra*). For example, Protestant apologist James McCarthy argues, "Why did not the Holy Spirit just repeat the word *petros* . . . ? Then Matthew 16:18 would read, 'You are Peter (*Petros*), and upon this rock (*petros*) I will build my church.'"[1]

The difference in words, it's asserted, *must* mean they refer to different things—*Petros* to Peter and *petra* to something other than Peter. McCarthy concludes, "When the Holy Spirit inspired the Greek text of the New Testament, He made a distinction between Peter (*Petros*) and the rock (*petra*)."[2]

Protestant apologist Ron Rhodes elaborates: "'Peter' (*petros*) is a masculine singular term, and 'rock' (*petra*) is a feminine singular term. *Hence, they do not have the same referent.* Jesus did not say to Peter, 'You are *Petros* and on this *Petros* I will build my church.' Jesus said, 'You are *Petros* (Peter), and upon this *petra*, I will build my church.'"[3]

ANSWERING THE COMEBACK

As Rhodes points out above, the two words differ in gender: *Petros* is masculine and *petra* is feminine. It would have been unthinkable to use a Greek feminine noun for the proper name of a man, as even Protestant scholars acknowledge. For example, Evangelical Scripture scholar D.A. Carson writes, "In Greek the feminine *petra* could not very well serve as a masculine name."[4] New Testament Protestant scholar R.T.

France concurs: "The reason for the different Greek form is simply that Peter, as a man, needs a masculine name, and so the form *Petros* has been coined."[5]

There are a few possible reasons why Matthew doesn't simply use the existing word *petros* in the second instance as well as the first. One is that, to Matthew's audience, *petra* would have been the more familiar term for "rock." France comments on this lack of familiarity with *petros* among Matthew's readers:

> The masculine noun *petros* occurs infrequently in classical poetic Greek to mean a stone (i.e., a broken piece of rock), though the distinction from *petra* is not consistently observed. But *petros* as a common noun is unlikely to have been familiar to Matthew's readers, as it is not found in the LXX [the Septuagint] (except twice in 2 Maccabees) or in the NT and related literature.[6]

Here's another possible explanation. By using *petra*, Matthew might have intended to make a connection with other teachings from Jesus.[7] In chapter seven of his Gospel, Matthew records Jesus' parable of the wise man who "built his house upon the rock [Greek, *petra*]" (v.24), and when the winds blew and the floods came, the house did not fall, "because it had been founded on the rock [Greek, *petra*]" (v.25). Perhaps Matthew intended to echo the parable: Jesus is the wise man building his house, the Church, on the rock (*petra*), which is Peter. As France notes, "[Peter] is to be a 'Rock.' And one important function of a rock, as [Matt.] 7:24–27 has reminded us, is to provide a firm foundation for a building. So, on this rock Jesus will build his church, and it will be forever secure."[8]

Still another possible reason for the use of different words is to preserve the distinction between a proper noun (*Petros* as a proper name) and a common noun (in this case, *petra* as a metaphor).[9] If Matthew had used *Petros* in the second instance, it would have read, "You are Peter, and upon this Peter I will build my church." It would have been a bit awkward to use a proper name this way. Using a common noun in the second instance is more natural.

Given that we can provide plausible reasons as to why there might be a difference in words without denying that the rock refers to Peter, the argument that Peter is not the rock, simply based on the use of *petros* and *petra* are different words, fails.

> Matthew's use of two different words no more means he's referring to two different things than my use of *rock* and *stone* means I'm referring to two different things other than the single rock I have in my hand.

"*Petros* and *Petra* mean different things."

The above comeback appeals to the *mere distinction* between *petros* and *petra*; another comeback, closely related, further argues that *petros* and *petra* have different meanings. And so, Jesus must be contrasting Peter with the rock rather than identifying them.

Protestant pastor Todd Baker makes this argument. In his book *Exodus from Rome (Volume I)*, he writes,

> The Greek text of Matthew 16:18 literally reads, "You are Peter" (*petros* or *Petros* as transliterated in English). *Petros* is

in the masculine gender and actually means a small rock, or "stone that might be thrown or easily moved." "And upon this rock I will build my church"—rock, here, in the second use, is *petra* (*Petra* as transliterated in English), which is feminine in gender and denotes a massive rock, like a foundation or bedrock (as distinct from *Petros*).[10]

Should we think that *petra* doesn't refer to Peter because it means something different from *petros*? Do *petros* and *petra* indeed even differ in meaning?

ANSWERING THE COMEBACK

Let's grant for argument's sake that there is a difference in meaning between the words and that Matthew chose them deliberately for that reason. This difference still wouldn't prove *petra* refers to something other than Peter.

This Protestant comeback assumes that Matthew is making an *antithetical* parallel, in which two different words or images are placed alongside each other in order to contrast what they refer to. So, in the case of *petros* and *petra*, the meaning would be, "You are a small stone, but on this *other* big rock . . ."

Another kind of parallel, though, is a *synthetic* parallel, in which the second image is meant to build upon and amplify the first. For example, I could say to my wife in reference to my seven-year-old daughter, Catherine, "Look at our little kitten. She's a wildcat!" The parallel between the two feline images is not by accident. The first image (kitten) expresses my daughter's playfulness and cuteness. The second image (wildcat) expresses the ferocious behavior that my daughter manifests in the moment, something that the first image doesn't capture.

Similarly—assuming for now that *petros* and *petra* have different meanings—*petra* in Matthew 16:18 could be building on *petros* to convey the idea that Jesus, by divine power, will make Peter, who as a fallible human is a small moveable rock (*petros*), into an immoveable rock (*petra*) that the Church can be set upon. If Jesus can make stones on the ground cry out, "Blessed is the king who comes in the name of the Lord" (Luke 19:38), then, surely, he can make a small rock into an immoveable foundation.

Therefore, even if there were a difference in meaning between *petros* and *petra*, we would still not be justified in concluding they refer to different things.

We don't, however, have to say that there is a difference in meaning between those words, at least within the Greek of the New Testament (called *Koine* Greek). Even Protestant scholars affirm this. D.A. Carson notes, "Although it is true that *petros* and *petra* can mean '[small] stone' and 'rock' respectively in earlier Greek, the distinction is largely confined to poetry."[11] New Testament scholar Craig Keener, another Protestant, agrees, stating that *petros* and *petra* "are cognate terms that were used interchangeably by this period."[12] We can add the late Lutheran theologian Oscar Cullman to the bunch. He writes that there is a "formal and material identity between *petra* and *petros*."[13]

So, this comeback does not work even when we grant for argument's sake that there's a difference in meaning between *petros* and *petra*. And there's a strong consensus even among respected Protestant scholars that there is no such difference.[14]

"The foundation is Jesus."

The comebacks so far have attempted merely to show that *petra* must refer to something other than Peter. But this raises the question of what they think *petra* does refer to. The two most common answers are (1) Jesus and (2) Peter's confession of faith. Let's start with the claim that *petra* refers to Jesus.

Ron Rhodes sums up the first argument when he writes, "We must not forget, 'No man can lay a foundation other than the one which is laid, which is Jesus Christ' (1 Cor. 3:11)."[15] For him, Peter can't be the rock in Matthew 16:18, because St. Paul tells us what the foundation of the Church is, and that's Jesus.

> Peter's role as the foundation of the Church is not apart from Jesus but only *in* and *through* Jesus. Peter's rockness doesn't rob Jesus of his glory. Peter is rock only as Christ grafts Peter into himself, delegating a role to Peter in his own image and likeness.

ANSWERING THE COMEBACK

This argument commits what philosophers call a *non-sequitur*, which is Latin for "it does not follow." Just because Jesus is called the foundation in one passage, it doesn't follow that Peter can't be called the foundation of Jesus' Church in other passages. There are three ways to show this.

In the Bible, metaphors and symbols are often used in more than one way. This can be seen even in these two passages under comparison. In Matthew 16:18, Jesus says he is the builder, yet in the Corinthians passage, Paul tells us that ministers are builders as well: "Like a skilled master builder I laid a foundation, and another man is building upon it. Let each man take care how he builds upon it" (1 Cor. 3:10).[16] Is Paul wrong for saying that he and other ministers build up the Church when elsewhere Jesus says that *he's* the one who will build his Church?

Rhodes and other Protestants who make this argument cherry-pick one aspect of 1 Corinthians 3 (Rock = Jesus) while ignoring the other aspect (builder = Paul). But they need to be consistent, either a) allowing each passage to be interpreted independently of the other (in which case they can't draw implications for Matthew 16:18, or b) shoving *all* of 1 Corinthians 3 into Matthew 16, in which case Jesus would be the rock but not the builder, or c) shoving all of Matthew 16 into 1 Corinthians 3, in which case the rock would be Peter and the builder would be Jesus. Since no Protestant would be satisfied with the last two, their only option is the first.

Other examples abound. We read that Jesus is the "living stone, rejected by men" (1 Pet. 2:4), but the next verse says that Christians are "living stones . . . built into a spiritual house" (1 Pet. 2:5). Jesus says that he is the "good shepherd" (John 10:11), yet he makes Peter the shepherd of his flock on earth by telling him to tend his sheep (John 21:15–17). Jesus calls himself the "light of the world" (John 9:5), but this doesn't stop him from teaching that Christians are the "light of the world" as well (Matt. 5:14).

If we were to apply the same strict logic of this counter in these instances, we would have to say that Peter is wrong for teaching that Christians are "stones" and that Jesus is confused about who is supposed to be shepherding and shining light in the world. But no Christian draws those conclusions. We recognize that metaphors can have layers of meaning and can be used in different ways according to their context.

Next, the Bible depicts the "foundation" of the Church in a variety of ways. In 1 Corinthians 3:11, Paul says that Christ is the one foundation, but in Ephesians 2:20 he also identifies *apostles* and *prophets* as the foundation of the Church: "You are fellow citizens with the saints and members of the household of God, built upon the foundation of the apostles and prophets, Christ Jesus himself being the cornerstone." (Paul's reference to the prophets likely refers to those of the New Testament age. This is made clear by Paul's other two references to such prophets in Ephesians 3:5 and 4:11.[17]) And so Paul sees no contradiction between Jesus being the foundation in one sense and the apostles and prophets being the foundation in another.

John likewise doesn't see a contradiction in Revelation 21:14 when he describes the foundation of the heavenly city of Jerusalem as having twelve stones with the apostles' names inscribed upon each of them. And as we saw above, Peter doesn't see a contradiction in Christ being the "living stone" and Christians being "living stones."

If neither Paul, Peter, nor John saw a contradiction between Jesus being the foundation of the Church and at the same time others being the foundation of the Church, why should we say there is a contradiction between Jesus and Peter both being the foundation of the Church, just in different respects? That the metaphor of being the foundation of the Church can be used in various ways should impress upon us the importance of considering carefully what Jesus says to Peter about being the "rock" of the Church.

"The foundation is Peter's confession of faith."

This next counter-argument attempts to show that *petra* refers to the *confession of faith* in Jesus that Peter had just uttered. Protestant apologists[18] note that Jesus begins with a personal address directed to Peter using the second-person pronoun *you*, "And I tell *you, you* are Peter," but then switches to the demonstrative adjective *this:* "and upon *this* rock." James White infers from this that Jesus makes "the differentiation between 'Peter' and 'this rock' complete," and that Jesus is "speaking to Peter, about the 'rock.'"[19]

If Jesus had intended "this rock" to refer to Peter, the argument continues, he would have continued to use the second-person pronoun and said, "You are Peter, and upon *you*, Peter, I will build my church." Instead, he's referring to the next-closest thing in the text: Peter's proclamation that Jesus is the Christ.

ANSWERING THE COMEBACK

Before we address this comeback, it's important that we note there's no reason why the metaphorical rock can't have a double meaning: one primary (Peter) and the other secondary (Peter's confession of faith). In fact, the *Catechism of the Catholic Church* (CCC) alludes to just this secondary meaning: "Moved by the grace of the Holy Spirit and drawn by the Father, we believe in Jesus and confess: 'You are the Christ, the Son of the living God.' On the rock of this faith confessed by St. Peter, Christ built his Church" (424).

However, given the context of the passage, as we'll see below, Peter's profession of faith can only be a secondary meaning, since Peter is the direct recipient of Jesus' address.

Just because Jesus switches from saying "you" to saying "this," it doesn't follow that he must be changing his object from Peter to something else. In Matthew 5:14, Jesus says of his disciples, "You are the light of the world." He could very well had added, "and this light will draw men to myself."

Upon hearing this solemn pronouncement, we wouldn't think that the word *this* refers to some separate thing besides the disciples whom Jesus is addressing. To suggest otherwise would undermine the force of the rhetorical device.

We see other examples in Scripture where *this* is used in reference to a person. In Acts 4:10–11, Peter says of Jesus, "Be it known to you all, and to all the people of Israel, that by the name of Jesus Christ of Nazareth, whom you crucified, whom God raised from the dead, by him this man is standing before you well. *This* is the stone which was rejected by you builders, but which has become the head of the corner."

Since the demonstrative "this" can be used to refer to the person who is spoken of in the preceding phrase, the argument that says Jesus can't be referring to Peter as the rock because he uses the demonstrative "this" fails.

A second response is that Peter's declaration of faith is two verses removed from the pronoun "this." So, when Jesus says "this rock," it's more reasonable to think he's referring to Simon, whom he just renamed Rock, because he is the nearest thing for the pronoun to refer to. There is nothing in the text to make us think that we need to dig back further to find the referent for "this rock."

In his commentary on the Gospel of Matthew, Reformed theologian J. Knox Chamblin argues along the same lines: "The demonstrative *this*, whether denoting what is physically close to Jesus or what is literally close in Matthew, more naturally refers to Peter (v.18) than to the more remote confession (v.16)."[20] We apply this principle of reading comprehension in Acts 4:10–11, which we just read above. There, "this stone" refers to the person spoken of immediately before: Jesus. And we do so here in Matthew 16:18.

There are many objections that Protestants give to the Catholic interpretation of Matthew 16:18. But we know that the switch from the personal pronoun to the demonstrative "this" is not one that proves Catholics wrong for interpreting Peter as the rock of Jesus' Church.

> That a single symbol in a single passage elsewhere in Scripture can refer to more than one thing is evidenced, for example, by the heads of the beast mentioned in Revelation 13. In Revelation 17:9–10, we're told the heads refer both to "seven mountains" and "seven kings."

"The central theme of the passage is the identity of Jesus."

Protestants also argue that the rock refers to Peter's confession of faith because the context of the passage is Jesus' identity, *not* Peter. James White states the argument this way:

> The confession that Peter gives of the messiahship of Jesus is the central thought of the entire passage. It is the reason for the trip to Caesarea Philippi. Jesus indicates that Peter has just been the recipient of *divine revelation.* God, in his grace, has given to Peter an insight that does not find its origin in the will of man, but in God the Father himself. The *content* of that confession is, in fact, *divine revelation,* immediately impressed upon the soul of Peter. *This is the immediate context* of verse 18, and to *divorce* verse 18 from what came before leads to the errant shift of attention from the identity of *Christ* to the identity of *Peter* that is found in Roman Catholic exegesis. Certainly we cannot accept the idea, presented in Roman theology, that immediately upon pronouncing the benediction upon Peter's confession of faith, the focus shifts *away from* that confession and what it reveals *to* Peter himself and some office with successors based upon him![21]

ANSWERING THE COMEBACK

It is true that Jesus' identity as Messiah and Son of God is a focal point of the text. But Protestants making this argument present it as if there were nothing in the text to suggest a shift in focus, in these verses, to Peter. And that's a problem, because Matthew explicitly tells us that Jesus begins to direct his comments to Peter, both before the statement under consideration ("upon this rock") and after.

> Unlike in English, Greek has a way of distinguishing the second-person pronoun singular from the second-person pronoun plural. Consider, for example, Matthew 16:15: "Who do you say that I am?" The Greek word for *you* is *humeis*, which is second-person plural. In verses 17–19, when Jesus directs his comments to Peter, the Greek word for *you* is *soi*, which is second-person singular.

Consider that in response to Peter's profession that Jesus is the Messiah and Son of God (v.16), the second-person singular "you" is used seven times in three verses, all of which are directed to Peter:

- "And Jesus answered him, "Blessed are *you*, Simon Bar-Jona!" (v.17a).

- "For flesh and blood has not revealed this to *you*, but my Father who is in heaven" (17b).

- "And I tell *you*, *you* are Peter, and on this rock I will build my Church" (v.18),

- "I will give *you* the keys of the kingdom of heaven" (v.19a).

- "And whatever *you* bind on earth shall be bound in heaven" (v.19b),

- "And whatever *you* loose on earth shall be loosed in heaven" (v.19c).

R.T. France comments: "The word-play, and the whole structure of the passage, demands that this verse is every bit as much Jesus' declaration about Peter as v.16 was Peter's declaration about Jesus."[22]

Catholic apologist Jimmy Akin[23] points out that if we look at the immediate context in which verse 18 is embedded, we notice a structure of three essential declarations that Jesus makes concerning Peter, each of which is followed by a longer explanation that unpacks the declaration made:

1. Blessed are you, Simon Bar-Jona! (v.17a).
   1a. For flesh and blood has not revealed this to you (v.17b),
   1b. but my Father who is in heaven (v.17c).

2. And I tell you, you are Peter (v.18a),
   2a. and on this rock I will build my church (v.18b),
   2b. and the gates of Hades shall not prevail against it (v.18c).

3. I will give you the keys of the kingdom of heaven (v.19a),
   3a. and whatever you bind on earth shall be bound in heaven (v.19b),
   3b. and whatever you loose on earth shall be loosed in heaven (v.19c).

Here Jesus calls Peter "blessed" and then elaborates on why. He gives Peter the keys of the kingdom of heaven and then explains what those keys signify. In between, he calls Peter "Rock" and says what will be built upon this rock. Given this structure, it becomes clear that "this rock" must refer to Peter. Why would every other statement that Jesus makes explain his main declarations to Peter except for that one? It doesn't fit the context.

"All the apostles are the foundation, not just Peter."

Another set of comebacks concede that Peter is the rock but reject the inference that Peter is therefore somehow unique in the role he plays as the foundation of the Church.

One argument appeals to Ephesians 2:19–20, where Paul teaches the "household of God" is "built upon the foundation of the apostles and prophets, Christ Jesus himself being the cornerstone." Well-known Protestant apologists Norman Geisler and Ralph MacKenzie write of this passage: "Two things are clear from this: all the apostles—not just Peter—are the foundation of the church."[24] Geisler and MacKenzie go on to add, "and the only one who was given a place of uniqueness or prominence was Christ, the capstone."[25]

Geisler and MacKenzie seem to be making two arguments here. First, since the apostles too are identified as the foundation of the Church, there's nothing unique about Peter being the rock of the Church in Matthew 16:18. The second argument is that if Peter were unique as the foundation of the Church, then he would have been distinguished from the other apostolic foundation stones, as Jesus is distinguished. But since he's not, Geisler and MacKenzie conclude that Peter is not unique.

ANSWERING THE COMEBACK

In response to the first argument, there's an assumed hidden premise that Geisler and MacKenzie never say out loud: *whenever something is said of two people, those two people must be equals with regard to what is said about them.* Only if this premise is true can Geisler and MacKenzie conclude that Peter has no unique status relative to the apostles based on the fact that the "foundation" metaphor is used for both Peter and the apostles.

The problem for Geisler and MacKenzie is that this hidden premise is demonstrably false. Consider, for example, how Jesus is called our shepherd in 1 Peter 2:25: "For you were straying like sheep, but have now returned to the shepherd [Greek, *poimena*] and Guardian [*episkopon*] of your souls." This Greek word for shepherd, *poimena*, is also used to describe pastors in the Church; for example, where Paul writes, "And his gifts were that some should be apostles, some prophets, some evangelists, some pastors [Greek, *poimenas*] and teachers" (Eph. 4:11). If we were to follow Geisler and MacKenzie's logic, we'd have to conclude that Jesus has no unique status as our pastor, since the Bible says there are other pastors in the Church, too!

Since this hidden premise is false, so too is the argument that Peter can't be a unique foundation of the Church because there are other "foundations."

Now, let's consider the second argument. Recall that Geisler and MacKenzie reason that if Peter were unique as the foundation of the Church, then Paul would have singled Peter out among the other apostles like he did for Jesus. Since Paul didn't do such a thing, Geisler and MacKenzie conclude that Peter has no special role as the foundation of the Church.

But why must we think that Paul would have singled Peter out among the apostles like he did for Jesus? It's only reasonable to think that if Paul's focus were Peter and his role as the rock of the Church in relation to the other apostles. But that is not Paul's focus.

Paul's focus is on the *Ephesians* and their relation to the apostles and Jesus as pieces that make up the edifice of the Church, which Paul calls a "holy temple" (v.21). The Ephesians are pieces built into the edifice. The apostles and prophets are the foundation. And Jesus is the cornerstone, "in whom the whole structure [of the Church] is joined together" (v.21).

Since Paul's concern is not the order among the apostles as the foundation of the Church, but simply the order that exists between the Ephesians, the apostles and prophets, and Jesus as pieces that make up the edifice of the Church, we shouldn't expect Paul to highlight Peter's unique status as the rock of the Church.

The "foundation" metaphor is being used in Ephesians 2:20 in a different context and for a different purpose. We must read it accordingly and not try to shoehorn its meaning into an entirely different context, such as that of Matthew 16:18. The reverse is true as well. We shouldn't take the Catholic interpretation of Peter as the rock in Matthew 16:18 and force its meaning onto Ephesians 2:20. We have to remember that metaphors can be used in more than one way in the Bible.

"Peter is only *a* pillar, not *the* pillar."

Another Protestant counter derives from Galatians 2:9, where Paul writes, "When they perceived the grace that was given to me, James and Cephas and John, who were reputed to be pillars, gave to me and Barnabas the right hand of fellowship." That Peter (called "*Cephas*," the Greek transliteration of the

Greicized Aramaic *Kephas*) is named second in this list of pillars is taken as proof that Peter is not unique in his role as the foundation of the Church. Protestant apologist Jason Engwer, makes the argument this way:

> It's doubtful that people would have been grouping Peter with other apostles as pillars of the church and naming him *second*, after James, if he was thought of as a pope. Remember, Catholics are the ones who place so much emphasis on the alleged significance of Peter's being a foundation of the church in Matthew 16, which is similar to the pillar concept in Galatians 2:9. It's highly unlikely that the early Christians believed that Peter was such a unique foundation of the church, the infallible ruler of all Christians, including the other apostles, yet perceived him as described in Galatians 2:9.[26]

We might summarize this argument as follows:

Premise 1: If Peter were unique as the foundation of the Church according to Matthew 16:18, then he would not have been listed second as a pillar of the Church in Galatians 2:9.

Premise 2: Peter is listed second as a pillar of the Church in Galatians 2:9.

Conclusion: Therefore, Peter is not unique as the foundation of the Church according to Matthew 16:18.

ANSWERING THE COMEBACK

The underlying assumption of premise one is that being listed second must reveal an inferior rank. But we can challenge this assumption, for there are additional plausible explanations for Peter being listed after James.

The order of the list, with James first, Peter second, and John third, may simply be a consequence of the order in which these men's names came into Paul's mind as he was dictating. When we list people or things when writing an email or telling a story, we typically do not intentionally list them in order of importance or greatness unless we have a reason to; and so, without any indication of such a reason *in this text,* there's no cause to think that Paul is doing so here.

Even if Paul *did* intend some significance to the ordering, it still does not require the conclusion that Peter did not have the special role that Catholics say he was given in Matthew 16:18.

First, because elsewhere in Galatians Peter seems to be ranked *above* James. Evidence suggests that this James became the leader of the Jerusalem church when Peter left after his imprisonment (Acts 12:17).[27] Recall Galatians 1:18–19, where Paul speaks of his first trip to Jerusalem shortly after his conversion and implies that Peter's in charge. He writes, "Then after three years I went up to Jerusalem to visit Cephas, and remained with him fifteen days. But I saw none of the other apostles except James the Lord's brother." So, it would be a mistake to portray Galatians as if it uniformly supported James holding rank over Peter. The first chapter of the letter does the reverse.

So what is happening in Galatians 2:9? This trip takes place fourteen years after Paul's initial visit with Peter (see Gal. 2:1), who had left Jerusalem and gone to Antioch after he escaped from prison (Acts 12:17). Peter's absence from Jerusalem would have given James the opportunity to take the reins to oversee the Jerusalem church (cf. Acts 21:17–24). Protestant New Testament scholar F.F. Bruce explains:

On Paul's earlier visit to Jerusalem, Cephas was the most important man in the church; Paul went up specifically to meet him, and adds that he also saw James. But all our evidence (scanty as it is) indicates that James became increasingly influential in the Jerusalem church. An opportunity to increase his influence at the expense of Cephas/Peter came with the latter's departure from Jerusalem after his escape from Herod Agrippa's prison (Acts 12:17).[28]

That James had become the bishop of the Jerusalem church at the time Paul visits Jerusalem in Galatians 2:9 provides a plausible explanation as to why Paul might have intentionally listed James first. It could have been a way of acknowledging his current headship in the local church. Peter was only there temporarily to attend the Council of Jerusalem.

There is yet another plausible explanation: Paul was undercutting the claims of the Judaizers.[29] These were a group of first-century Jewish Christians who argued that Gentiles needed to be circumcised if they wanted to be Christian. Paul called them the "circumcision party" in Galatians 2:12, and they held James in high esteem. In fact, in that same verse Paul tells us that the Judaizers, whom Peter feared offending, "came from James." So, if there were anyone that the Judaizers would have tried to pit against Paul concerning whether the Gentiles should be circumcised, it would have been James.

Paul counters this move by showing that James endorsed his view that circumcision was unnecessary for the Gentiles. And perhaps to drive home the point, Paul lists James first as a pillar: "When they perceived the grace that was given to me, James and Cephas and John, who were reputed to be pillars, gave to me and Barnabas the right hand of fellowship" (Gal. 2:9). Paul thereby undercut any attempt by the Judaizers to make their case by appealing to official backing from the Jerusalem church.

CHAPTER 2

Keeper of the Keys
Matthew 16:19

After Jesus reveals that he will make Simon the rock upon which he will build his Church, Jesus tells Simon in Matthew 16:19, "I will give you the keys of the kingdom of heaven, and whatever you bind on earth shall be bound in heaven, and whatever you loose on earth shall be loosed in heaven." The *key* (pun intended) to understand what's going on here is the "keys of the kingdom."

The image alludes to an institutional office in the Davidic kingdom known as the *royal steward* or *master of the palace* (Isa. 22:15–22). This official had authority over the king's household second to none except the king himself, receiving "the key of the house of David" (v.22) to symbolize such authority. He had authority to admit and exclude people from the royal house ("he shall open, and no one shall shut; and he shall shut, and none shall open"—v.22). He was "a father to the inhabitants of Jerusalem and to the house of Judah" (v.21).

Like the royal steward who received the key of David's kingdom, Peter is given the keys of Jesus' kingdom. The authority symbolized by the key of David's kingdom serves as the backdrop to understand the nature of Peter's authority symbolized by the keys given to him. Peter is the royal steward of Jesus' kingdom, which is the Church. As such, he is second to none except the king himself, Jesus.

This unique authority is also revealed by the fact that Jesus gives the keys of the kingdom only to Peter. Jesus gives the other apostles the authority to bind and loose (Matt. 18:18). But the absence of the keys is not mere formality. The keys of the kingdom don't merely represent the Rabbinic authority to bind and loose. Rather, it signifies that Peter is the chief steward who oversees the household of Christ. And there's only one *chief* steward.

There are several counter-responses to this argument that Protestants make. Some attempt to undermine the parallel with Isaiah 22. Others target the emphasis on the *uniqueness* of Peter receiving the keys. We'll look at the comebacks of each category in order.

"There's nothing important about the images of keys, gates, and doors. It's stock imagery."

One argument that challenges the parallel between Matthew 16:19 and Isaiah 22:15–22 is that since the relevant images of keys, gates, and doors are not restricted to Isaiah 22:15–22 but are found elsewhere in Scripture, there is no need to explain Matthew 16:19 in light of Isaiah 22:15–22. Protestant apologist Steve Hays states the argument this way:

> Catholic apologists typically allege that v.19 is an allusion to Isaiah 22:22, then imports the entire Isaian context into v. 19. However, the related metaphors of keys, gates, and doors are stock imagery (e.g. Matt. 23:13; 25:10; Luke 11:52; John 10:9; Acts 14:27; 1 Cor. 16:9; Col. 4:3; Rev.

1:18; 3:7–8,20; 9:1; 20:1), so it doesn't require any special explanation, in terms of literary dependence, to account for the imagery.[30]

Let's look at some different ways that we can respond.

ANSWERING THE COMEBACK

For Hays, the image of keys (along with doors and gates) shouldn't be taken as having a "literary dependence" on Isaiah 22:22, since such imagery is also used elsewhere in Scripture. Hays seems to be basing his argument on the idea that to the extent a given image is used in Scripture, the less likely it is that there is direct literary dependence.

This is generally true, although sometimes there are exceptions. For example, the phrase "in the beginning," occurs numerous times in Scripture.[31] Yet all competent scholars agree that John 1:1 ("in the beginning was the Word") involves a deliberate callback to Genesis 1:1. But the corollary to this principle is that the *fewer* times an image occurs, especially when it's found *prior to* its current use, the more likely it is that there's literary dependence. And that supports reading Matthew 16:19 in light of Isaiah 22:22. Far from being a "stock image," the metaphor of a key is found in only *one* place in the Old Testament: Isaiah 22:22.

Furthermore, in these two passages, the metaphor of the key is used in very similar circumstances. Consider, for example, the parallel imagery of the "kingdom." Isaiah 22:22 speaks of the "house of David," which is just another way of saying the "kingdom of David." Also, the parallel theme of having the authority to *admit* and *exclude* connects the two passages. This is signified by the "binding and loosing" language in Matthew 16:19 and the "opening and shutting" language in Isaiah 22:22: "He shall open, and none shall shut; and he shall shut, and none shall open."

Given that Isaiah 22:22 is the only text written before Matthew that has such a degree of similarity to Matthew 16:19, it is most likely meant to form part of the conceptual background that Matthew is drawing on. Even Protestant scholars affirm this interpretation. W.F. Albright and C.S. Mann write,

> Isaiah 22:15 ff. undoubtedly lies behind this saying [Matt. 16:19]. *The keys* are the symbol of authority, and Roland de Vaux (*Ancient Israel,* tr. By John McHugh [New York: McGraw-Hill, 1961], pp.129ff) rightly sees here the same authority as that vested in the vizier, the master of the house, the chamberlain, of the royal household in ancient Israel.[32]

Another response to Hays's objection is that none of the New Testament passages that he cites prove that Isaiah 22:22 *isn't* what Jesus has in mind. If anything, the question raised is, "How many of these other passages are *also* drawing on Isaiah 22?"

Clearly, at least one of them: Revelation 3:7–8, which reads, "And to the angel of the Church in Philadelphia write: 'The words of the holy one, the true one, who has the key of David, who opens and no one shall shut, who shuts and no one opens.'" This doesn't conflict with Matthew 16:18 because Jesus, the one who holds the keys of his kingdom in virtue of being the king, is free to entrust the keys of his kingdom to whomever he wishes.

The other New Testament passages cited by Hays are even more problematic. Some, for example, refer to what is clearly a different key than the key of David's kingdom:

- Luke 11:52 refers to the "key of knowledge."

- Revelation 1:18 refers to "the keys of death and Hades."

- Revelation 9:1 and 20:1 refer to the key to "the bottomless pit."

Remember, the question is not whether keys can refer to different concepts—of course they can. Rather, the question is whether the key imagery in Matthew 16:19 is drawing from Isaiah 22:22. And the mere fact that key imagery refers to different things elsewhere in the New Testament doesn't help us answer that question. The key imagery in Matthew 16:19 could very well be referring to the same underlying concept as that of Isaiah 22:22 even though other New Testament verses use different key metaphors.

We can use a similar line of reasoning in response to other passages that Hays cites, passages that involve doors rather than keys. None of these instances of door imagery come close to the door motif connected with the house/kingdom of David. They all refer to different things:

- Matthew 25:10—the door to the wedding feast in heaven

- Acts 14:27—a door of faith that God opened for the Gentiles

- Colossians 4:3—a door for the word of God to be spread

- Revelation 3:20—a door to enter into table fellowship with Jesus

Like we saw with key imagery, the question is not whether door imagery can refer to different things. The question is whether the door/gate imagery implied by the keys in Matthew 16:19 refers to the same underlying concept as that of Isaiah 22:22. The mere fact that door imagery is used for different concepts elsewhere in the New Testament does nothing for us to arrive at an answer.

One passage Hays cites does have some superficial conceptual similarity to the passages of interest: Matthew 23:13, where Jesus says, "But woe to you, scribes and Pharisees, hypocrites! because you shut the kingdom of heaven against men; for you neither enter yourselves, nor allow those who would enter to go in." Despite there being no mention of a key or a door, the theme of being excluded from the kingdom, along with a concept of inherited authority, provides some grounds for at least a loose connection with Matthew 16:19 and Isaiah 22:22.

However, in Matthew 23, the authority the scribes and Pharisees have inherited doesn't come from David. Rather, it comes from Moses. Thus, in 23:2, Jesus observes that they "sit on Moses' seat." This is a different source of authority, not related to the Davidic authority that Jesus possesses as the messianic Son of David, and which he shares with Peter.

> It's interesting to note that Matthew is the only Gospel writer to include this tidbit about the "keys of the kingdom" (cf. Mark 8:27–29). Perhaps this is so because his Jewish audience would be the only ones to pick up on the allusion to the "key of the house of David" and the office of the chief steward.

"If it's not an exact parallel, then there's no papal authority."

The next comeback charges the Catholic position with arbitrarily picking and choosing the relevant details from Isaiah

22:15–22 to justify a papal interpretation of Matthew 16:19. Jason Engwer puts it this way:

[A]ny Catholic appeal to Isaiah 22 would have to be a partial appeal, not a complete parallel, since a complete parallel wouldn't favor the claims of Roman Catholicism. God is the one who gives the key in Isaiah 22, so an exact parallel would put Jesus in the place of God, not in the place of the king. If Jesus is God and Peter is the prime minister, then who is the king? Some church official with more authority than Peter? What about Isaiah 22:25? Should we assume that popes can "break off and fall," and that the keys of Matthew 16 can eventually pass to God himself (Rev. 3:7) rather than to a human successor? If Catholics only want to make a general appeal to Isaiah 22, without drawing an exact parallel, then how can they claim that papal authority is implied by the parallel?[33]

Elsewhere, he gives a few other examples:

[H]ow do you allegedly know that . . . the prime minister role must be fulfilled only by Peter rather than by Peter along with the other apostles or some such thing? How do you know that the prime minister role in the New Testament era isn't better than its Old Testament counterpart by not requiring any successors (e.g., Peter's foundational work in building the church is sufficient and requires no succession, much as Jesus' work as high priest requires no succession)?[34]

ANSWERING THE COMEBACK

Engwer argues that for the parallel between Matthew 16:19 and Isaiah 22:22 to imply papal authority there must be an *exact* parallel between the relevant details. But this is an unreasonable demand because that's not how prophetic foreshadowing or *intertextuality* works. The New Testament authors themselves don't even honor Engwer's principle.

Consider, for example, Matthew 2:15's reference to Hosea 11. The first two verses of Hosea 11 read as follows:

> When Israel was a child, I loved him, and out of Egypt I called my son. The more I called them, the more they went from me; they kept sacrificing to the Baals, and burning incense to idols (vv.1–2).

Matthew takes the phrase "out of Egypt I called my son" in the first statement as a prefigurement of baby Jesus' return from the flight to Egypt (Matt. 2:15). Yet, Matthew did not intend the latter part of the passage to refer to Jesus, since Jesus did not go away from God, sacrifice to the Baals, and burn incense to their images.

There are numerous similar examples in the New Testament's use of the Old. Whenever prophetic foreshadowing is in play, some elements foreshadow and some don't. There are continuities and discontinuities. If the New Testament authors employ this type of hermeneutic when relating the Old Testament to the New, it's legitimate for Catholics to do the same.

How do we know what applies and what doesn't in these partial parallels? Sometimes the answer is found in other things Scripture teaches. For example, we know that the two figures of *God* and *king* both apply to Jesus because the New Testament reveals that Jesus is both, at the same time, God (by virtue of his divine nature) and heir to the throne of David (by virtue of his human nature—Luke 1:32).

Regarding the detail about the sure peg giving way (Isa. 22:25), Jesus says that the Church he builds on Peter, the rock, will withstand the onslaught of the forces of evil: "The gates of Hades shall not prevail against it" (Matt. 16:18). If the gates of Hades will not prevail against Jesus' Church, and the Church is built on Peter, then surely the image of the peg giving way *doesn't* apply to Peter (and by way of extension to his successors). Unlike the foundation of the house of David that will give way, the foundation of Christ's house, or kingdom, will not.

We know that the royal steward role belongs to Peter alone because Jesus gives only Peter the keys of the kingdom. And only after promising to give Peter the keys does Jesus reveal that the other apostles can *corporately* participate in the authority of the keys by "binding and loosing" (Matt. 18:18). And in response to Engwer's last question, we know that Peter would not be the *only* royal steward because his job was not to build the Church—Jesus had that job: "I will build my church" (Matt. 16:18)—but rather to govern it. And since the Church is promised to exist until the end of time, there's going to be a need for other royal stewards to govern it beyond Peter.

"The key is not the keys."

The next Protestant comeback attempts to undermine the parallel between Matthew 16:19 and Isaiah 22:22 by highlighting the difference between the *key* (singular) in Isaiah 22:22 and the *keys* (plural) in Matthew 16:19. James White makes this argument in his book *The Roman Catholic Controversy*:

> [U]pon what basis do we identify the *keys* (plural, Greek: κλειδας [*kleidas*]) of the kingdom of heaven, which are associated plainly with the preaching of the gospel of Jesus Christ, with the *key* (singular, Greek: κλειν [*klein*]

as cited in Rev. 3:7 . . .) of the house of David, which is messianic in nature? And should we not instead accept the interpretation given by the Lord Jesus himself, when he cites Isaiah 22:22 of himself in Revelation 3:7, "And to the angel of the church of Philadelphia write: He who is holy, who is true, who has the key of David, who opens and no one will shut, and who shuts and no one opens, says this." Jesus has, present tense (Greek: ὁ ἔχων [ho echōn]), the key of David. He does not say that he gives this key to anyone else.[35]

ANSWERING THE COMEBACK

White's issue about Jesus possessing the "key of David" (Rev. 3:7) poses no threat to a papal argument from the "keys of the kingdom," since Catholics affirm that Jesus is the Davidic king and that the key belongs to him by right. This being the case, he can bestow it upon whomever he chooses.[36]

The real question is whether the key of David in Isaiah 22:22, and its relevant context concerning the office of the royal steward, serves as an interpretative context for the *keys* of the kingdom in Matthew 16:19. White says no, in part because one is singular and the other is plural.

We already gave reasons to think that Isaiah 22:22 and its context serve as an interpretive context for Matthew 16:19. Beyond those, there are a few ways that we can show why this argument fails.

First, it should be noted that White's difficulty with the singular and plural distinction is a minority view among Protestant scholars.[37] For example, the late Evangelical Protestant biblical scholar F.F. Bruce writes,

And what about the "keys of the kingdom"? The keys of a royal or noble establishment were entrusted to the chief steward or major domo; he carried them on his shoulder in earlier times, and there they served as a badge of the authority entrusted to him. About 700 B.C. an oracle from God announced that this authority in the royal palace in Jerusalem was to be conferred on a man called Eliakim: "I will place on his shoulder the key to the house of David; what he opens no one can shut, and what he shuts no one can open" (Isa. 22:22). So in the new community that Jesus was about to build, Peter would be, so to speak, chief steward.[38]

As we saw in the Hosea example above, there are other examples in which New Testament authors interpret an event in light of an Old Testament text without an exact one-to-one match of every detail. That one passage says "key" and the other "keys" does not mean Matthew couldn't have been doing likewise in this case.

Indeed, an interpretative principle that would demand an exact one-to-one match of every detail would lead to absurdities, even for a Protestant. Consider how Revelation 3:7 says that Jesus has the "key of David." As White argues above, this is a clear reference to Isaiah 22:22. Must we conclude that Jesus is *not* the Davidic king but merely the royal steward, since it was the royal steward who was given the "key of the house of David" (Isa. 22:22)?

If White is able to interpret Revelation 3:7 in light of Isaiah 22:22 without an exact match of details, then so can Catholics when it comes to interpreting Matthew 16:19.

"Uniqueness doesn't entail papal authority."

The next group of comebacks targets a Catholic's appeal to the fact that Jesus gives the keys only to Peter. The first concedes for argument's sake that the keys are unique to

Peter but challenges the inference that his unique posses-
sion of them supports papal authority.

Jason Engwer argues,

> Even if the keys of Matthew 16:19 had been unique to
> Peter, would that prove that he was pope? Obviously
> not, since uniqueness doesn't prove papal authority. Peter
> could have uniquely used the keys of Matthew 16:19 in
> the book of Acts, when he "opened a door of faith" (Acts
> 14:27) with those keys by preaching to the Jews and Gen-
> tiles at Pentecost (Acts 15:7).[39]

ANSWERING THE COMEBACK

Engwer suggests that the "keys of the kingdom" could have
referred not to an ongoing authority but only to Peter's
"opening the kingdom" through preaching. This is a common interpretation among some Protestant apologists,[40] but
it ignores the interpretive context of Isaiah 22:15–22.

If the "key of the house of David" and the office of the
royal steward described in Isaiah 22:15–22 are the analogy for
understanding Peter's role in Christ's kingdom, as we argue,
then the "keys of the kingdom" could not refer merely to
opening the kingdom through preaching, even if it may be
one aspect of their exercise. Per Isaiah 22, having the keys
means that Peter also would be able to "shut"— but Jesus did
not authorize Peter to refuse to preach the gospel to any group
of people and so exclude them from the kingdom (which
would contradict his command for the apostles to preach to all
nations (Matt. 28:20; Acts 1:8). Therefore, the power of opening and shutting, conferred by the keys, cannot be understood
solely in terms of preaching or withholding the gospel.

Also, scholars widely agree that the keys are connected with
the command to "bind and loose." (This will become clear

below when we respond to the counter that appeals to the apostles having the power to bind and loose in order to show that the keys are not unique to Peter.) But the authority to "bind and loose" didn't refer to preaching. Rather, in Jewish tradition, this language denotes judicial authority—deciding what was forbidden or allowed according to the law.[41] The rabbis were also said to bind and loose when they would "pronounce and revoke an anathema upon a person," thus excluding or restoring a person from or to membership in the faith community.[42]

Engwer also argues that other apostles had unique characteristics, yet no one thinks that this gave them papal authority, so why do we say this of Peter?

> Even if we assume that the keys were unique to Peter, uniqueness obviously doesn't prove papal authority. John was uniquely called "the beloved disciple" (John 21:20), was uniquely referred to as living until Christ's return (John 21:22), and uniquely called himself "the elder" (2 John 1). Paul was uniquely called a "chosen vessel" who would bear Christ's name before the world (Acts 9:15), uniquely asserted his authority over all the churches (1 Cor. 7:17), and was uniquely the only apostle to publicly rebuke and correct another apostle (Gal. 2:11–14).[43]

The first thing to note in response is that it's not uniqueness by itself that suggests Peter's papal authority. Rather, it's the uniqueness of the *keys* and what they signify. Appealing to unique statements made to other people distracts from the real issue at hand: what it means for Peter to possess the keys. Unless those statements about other apostles involve the keys of the kingdom or have some bearing on what sort of role Peter plays in Christ's kingdom, they don't argue against Peter's unique authority.

Consider John uniquely being called "the disciple whom Jesus loved" (John 21:20). Since papal authority has nothing to do with Christ having special affection for a particular disciple, we don't have to infer papal authority from Jesus' unique love for John. Likewise the claim that John was "uniquely referred to as living until Christ's return" (John 21:22). In fact, John explicitly *debunks* this rumor in the very next verse. Yet even if John had been promised to be the only one living at Christ's return, this special privilege wouldn't tell us anything about the level of John's authority in the Church—unlike the uniqueness of the keys being given to Peter in Matthew 16:18–19.

What about the passages involving Paul? In Acts 9:15, the Lord uniquely calls Paul "a chosen instrument." Yet there is nothing in being chosen for a special mission that requires us to infer papal authority. Paul can have a special mission to a particular group of people, the Gentiles, and still not be the leader of the Church.

What about the appeal to 1 Corinthians 7:17, where Paul says in reference to the instruction he gave (whether spouses should remain or leave the unbelieving spouse—vv. 12–16) that everyone should lead the life the Lord has assigned to them, "This is my rule in all the churches." Engwer thinks we must conclude that Paul has papal authority because he alone asserts authority over these churches.

But it's not clear whether Paul means *all* the churches throughout the entire Christian world or only the local churches that he founded and oversees.

If he means only the churches that he founded, then the Catholic view of papal authority wouldn't exclude Paul from exercising legitimate authority over these churches. An apostle can have authority over local churches and still not be the apostle that has *supreme* authority over *all* the churches, just as a bishop today can have authority over his local church and not thereby be the pope.

Even if we interpret Paul to mean "all the churches" in the sense of the universal Christian church, it still wouldn't imply that he has papal authority. Paul can give wise counsel, or even a unique command, for *all* Christians to heed and still not thereby be the pope. Simply being an apostle gives him an authority to do so. We only need recognize that such authority is subordinate to Peter's unique authority *as the rock* of the Church and the *keeper of the keys*.

In Acts 15, we're told that Paul takes his controversial message that the Gentiles didn't need to be circumcised to be saved and submits it to the judgment of Peter (Acts 15:1-2, 7-11). In 2 Peter 3:15-16, Peter confirms the authority of Paul's letters as Scripture, giving them universal binding force (2 Pet. 3:15-16).

To say that Paul wouldn't give a universal rule to the Church unless he were the pope is to imply that the pope must dictate everything. But that's not true. Even the pope today delegates authority to various officials and congregations to make judgments and give norms for things with universal scope, such as doctrine and worship. Yet their authority remains subordinate *to* that of the pope.

Finally, there is the appeal to Paul being the *only* apostle that publicly rebukes and corrects another apostle—that other apostle being Peter (Gal. 2:11-14). But nothing in

Catholic teaching says that Peter's papal authority excludes him from receiving fraternal correction from a fellow apostle. Catholics believe fellow bishops can offer correction to the pope, especially when it comes to matters of living the Christian life.

"Jesus uniquely rebukes Peter."

There's another comeback that some Protestants make to undermine a Catholic's appeal to Jesus giving only Peter the keys. Geisler and MacKenzie articulate it this way:

> No Catholic commentator gives Peter primacy in evil simply because he was singled out in Jesus' rebuke a few verses later: "Get behind me, Satan! You are an obstacle to me. You are thinking not as God does, but as human beings do" (v.23). Why then should Peter be given primacy in authority because of Jesus' affirmation?[44]

ANSWERING THE COMEBACK

Peter is revealed to have a unique role in Christ's kingdom analogous to the chief steward in David's kingdom. *That* gives Peter primacy in authority.

With regard to Jesus' rebuke: Peter was the only one present who made remarks questioning Jesus' mission to redeem the world. Since he was the only one, Jesus rebukes him alone. Had the other apostles said similar things, surely Jesus would have corrected them, too. There is no "primacy in evil" that Jesus' rebuke confers by necessity.

Conversely, had the other apostles replied *with* Peter, "You are the Christ" (v.16), Jesus would not have given them all the keys. Why? Because by definition there only can be one chief steward of the household. The interpretative context of Isaiah 22:15–22 excludes the idea of Jesus giving the other apostles the keys of his kingdom in the way that he gave them to Peter. Other apostles could have said something requiring a rebuke from Jesus, but only one person can wield the keys.

"The other apostles have the same authority to bind and loose."

Some Protestants collapse the meaning of the "keys of the kingdom" into the meaning of "binding and loosing" and argue that since Jesus gives this latter authority to the other apostles in Matthew 18:18, "Peter is not unique."[45] Geisler and MacKenzie concur: "The same authority Jesus gave to Peter (Matt. 16:18) is given later to all the apostles (Matt. 18:18)."[46]

ANSWERING THE COMEBACK

This counter-argument assumes that the "keys of the kingdom" and the power of "binding and loosing" are synonymous—as it must, if it wants to prove that Peter is "not unique" despite his unique reception of the keys. But the structure of Matthew 16:15–19,[47] consisting of three essential declarations that Jesus makes concerning Peter, each of which is followed by a longer explanation that unpacks the declaration, suggests otherwise.

1. Blessed are you, Simon Bar-Jona! (v.17a).
   1a. For flesh and blood has not revealed this to you (v.17b),
   1b. But my Father who is in heaven (v.17c).

2. And I tell you, you are Peter (v.18a),
   2a. And on this rock I will build my Church (v.18b),
   2b. And the gates of Hades shall not prevail against it (v.18c).

3. I will give you the keys of the kingdom of heaven (v.19a).
    3a. And whatever you bind on earth shall be bound in heaven (v.19b).
    3b. And whatever you loose on earth shall be loosed in heaven (v.19c).

The logic of this Protestant comeback would have us likewise collapse major clauses 1 and 2 into their supporting a and b clauses. But although it's true that "Upon this rock I will build my Church" is related to "I say to you, you are Peter," these statements are not merely two ways of saying the same thing. Nor does "Upon this rock I will build my Church" contain the whole meaning of "I say to you, you are Peter." If we're not going to make the meaning of these related statements strictly synonymous (and no one does), then we shouldn't do so for the statement "I will give you the keys of the kingdom of heaven" and Peter's authority to "bind and loose."

The interpretive context of Isaiah 22:15–22 also helps answer this comeback. The office of the chief steward involved institutional authority that was unique to him. Since Peter's role in Christ's kingdom is to be interpreted in light the chief steward's role, it follows that Peter has institutional authority that is unique to him.

Although *part* of what it means for Peter to have the "keys of the kingdom" is the power to bind and loose, the keys also signify that Peter is the chief steward of Christ's kingdom. For this reason, the "keys of the kingdom" should not be equated with or collapsed into the meaning of "binding and loosing." A Protestant, therefore, cannot appeal to the apostles all having the authority to bind and loose as proof that the keys are not unique to Peter.

Remember, the Catholic argument here is not that the apostles *don't* have the power to bind and loose and only

Peter does, but rather that Peter also received from Jesus a unique, individual power. This is the reason why we emphasize the interpretive context of the chief steward in Isaiah 22:15–22.

Leader of the Church
Luke 22:31–32

Catholics don't just appeal to Matthew 16:18–19 to argue for Peter as the first pope. They also make an argument from Luke 22:31–32. There, Jesus says, "Simon, Simon, behold, Satan demanded to have you, that he might sift you like wheat, but I have prayed for you that your faith may not fail; and when you have turned again, strengthen your brethren."

Here we find two clues that, when taken together, reveal Peter's unique role as leader of the Church. The first is Jesus' prayer of protection. Jesus informs the apostles that Satan desires to sift *all* of them, which we know from the use of the Greek second person plural pronoun, *humas*. When Jesus speaks of his protection prayer in the next verse, however, the Greek text switches to second person singular, *sou*. Jesus thus singles out Peter when he makes the promise, "I have prayed for *you* [Greek, *sou*] that your faith may not fail." Jesus then commands Peter, and only Peter to strengthen the brethren.

If Jesus intended all the apostles to be equal in their mission of leading his Church, with no kind of priority or prominence whatsoever, it's hard to see why Jesus would have promised only Peter a special protection that's connected to his unique command for Peter to strengthen the brethren. In fact, such words would be outright misleading. The Catholic view, therefore, comports best with this passage. Peter receives a special prayer of protection from Jesus because he's the preeminent apostle who must strengthen the others.

Imagine that you were there when Jesus announced Satan's desire and his exclusive prayer for Peter. Wouldn't you think, "Hey Jesus, why don't you throw some prayers my way!" To benefit from that prayer and be protected from the sifting of Satan, we all have to stick with Peter (and his successors).

Some Protestant comebacks to this argument attack the inference from the unique promise to protect Peter in faith; others attack the inferred significance of the unique command to strengthen the brethren. Let's first take the counter-responses that aim at the promise of protection.

"The prayer is to ensure that Peter will repent and not lose his faith completely."

The claim here is that Jesus' prayer has nothing to do with Peter being the chief leader of the Church. Rather, the prayer is merely to ensure that Peter would repent of his future betrayal and not completely lose faith like Judas. Here's how Steve Hays puts the argument:

Peter is singled out, not because he outranks the other disciples, but because he will betray Jesus. The prayer anticipates his denial. Jesus prays for Peter's restoration in advance of his betrayal. As a matter of faith, Peter's faith did fail. He lost his nerve and publicly renounced Jesus. That's a paradigmatic act of infidelity. In context, the meaning of the statement is not that his faith will be unwavering, but that his failure won't be permanent. Jesus prays that Peter won't abandon the cause. Having betrayed Jesus, he will repent of his betrayal and renew his commitment.[48]

ANSWERING THE COMEBACK

Hays's denial of papal primacy in this text doesn't engage with the intentional singling-out of Peter and his faith within the context of Satan's desire to "sift" *all* the apostles. Now, the Greek conjunction *de* ("but") is present in the Greek text, and this word is "used to connect one clause to another, either to express contrast or simple continuation."[49] To determine which, we have to look at the context.

We have seen that Jesus is telling the apostles that Satan desires to sift *all* of them, and that the promise to protect Peter is addressed to him alone, in the singular. This signifies a shift in focus and thus *contrast*. This is why most Bibles translate the phrase in Luke 22:32 as "*but* I have prayed for you." All the apostles are being tested, but Peter and his faith are singled out in contrast to the others'.

There's another problem with Hays's interpretation: *all* the apostles betrayed Christ to some extent.[50] Jesus had told them explicitly, "You will all fall away because of me this night" (Matt. 26:31), and his prophecy comes to fruition when the apostles desert him and flee (Matt. 26:56). If Peter wasn't special and Jesus' prayer was simply meant for restoration after betrayal, then it should have been directed to all the apostles, who were all to be sifted and who all abandoned Jesus at the beginning of his passion. Why promise restoration only for Peter when the others would need it as well?

From a Catholic perspective, there's an intelligible answer: the promise was not made to the other apostles because Jesus is intending more than restoration—namely, a role for Peter as chief leader in the Church. And the next thing Jesus says—the command for Peter to strengthen his fellow apostles—confirms this.

Another response turns the tables and shows that the attention Jesus gives to Peter's impending fall also implies his unique role as leader.

Luke records Peter's stated haste to be a martyr for Jesus. First, he records the bold claim: "Lord, I am ready to go with you to prison and to death" (Luke 22:33). Luke then tells us how Jesus disabuses Peter of his rash pledge: "I tell you, Peter, the cock will not crow this day, until you three times deny that you know me" (22:34).

But Matthew tells us that it wasn't just Peter who had bold illusions about themselves: *all* the apostles did. After telling us that Peter promised not to deny Jesus, he adds, "And *so said all the disciples*" (Matt. 26:35). Matthew then records, in verse 56, "Then [after his arrest] all the disciples deserted him and fled."

It's interesting that Luke records neither the apostles' false confidence nor their abandonment of Christ like Matthew does. He only records the foretelling and the actual event of Peter's denial. Why is that? Bible scholar Joseph Fitzmyer gives an interesting answer:

> For a test of fidelity can come even to one who will prove to be the "greatest" among them, the one most ready to

protest of his readiness to go with Jesus to prison or to death. The Lucan Jesus is making it clear to the reader of the Gospel that no disciple, not even the one for whom Jesus has prayed, will be safe from a test to his/her loyalty and fidelity.[51]

This line of reasoning makes sense. If you want to convey to your readers not to be presumptuous about witnessing to Christ in the face of persecution (as all the apostles were), there's no better way to do that than by showing that even the leader of the Christian community can falter. That Luke emphasizes *only* Peter as the one who fails the test of loyalty and fidelity to Christ indicates that Luke considered Peter the leader of the Church.

This is similar to Paul's rebuke of Peter in Galatians 2:11. Far from proving that Peter didn't have any higher-ranking authority than he had, as some Protestants argue,[52] Paul's rebuke suggests the opposite. If Peter didn't have a special authority, there would be no need for Luke to record the rebuke. It would be no big thing, not worth the ink and the space on the scroll. Protestant scholars Albright and Mann, in their commentary on Matthew in the Anchor Bible Commentary, concur:

> To deny the preeminent position of Peter among the disciples or in the early Christian community is a denial of the evidence. . . . The interest in Peter's failures and vacillations does not detract from the pre-eminence; rather, it emphasizes it. Had Peter been a lesser figure his behavior would have been of far less consequence.[53]

Similarly, Luke's interest in Peter's failure doesn't detract from Peter's pre-eminence; rather, it underscores it.

"Jesus prays for others as well."

Another comeback that aims to undercut the significance of the prayer for Peter appeals to Jesus' general role as intercessor. Protestant apologist Ron Rhodes argues, "Jesus' prayer for Peter is in keeping with his general intercessory ministry for all believers."[54] He then goes on to cite Romans 8:34, Hebrews 7:25 and John 17:15, which affirm that Christ intercedes for us. So Jesus was not signaling a special role for Peter but merely doing what he does for all his flock—interceding before the Father.

ANSWERING THE COMEBACK

It's true that Jesus has a general ministry of intercession for all believers. But this argument ignores the context of Jesus' prayer for Peter, which intentionally follows his telling the apostles that Satan desired to sift *all* of them. Jesus is not exercising his general intercessory ministry for all believers in this passage because Luke explicitly tells us the prayer is for Peter *alone*, even though Satan was going to test them all. That Jesus has a general intercessory role as our high priest in heaven doesn't take away from the fact that, here, Jesus prays for Peter in a unique way. And that unique prayer reveals Peter's unique role as chief leader in the Church.

"Peter only strengthens by helping others not to make the same mistake that he did."

The next couple of Protestant comebacks aim to under-cut the significance of Peter's instruction to strengthen the brethren. One attempts to limit the *nature* of the instruction to helping fellow Christians repent when they have fallen. Todd Baker takes this approach:

As an apostolic minister of the gospel, Peter was to learn from this past mistake, and in turning back to faith in Christ, which he previously fell from when he denied his Master three times, the apostle was to "strengthen" fellow Christians who had also fallen in a moment of weakness. He was to further safeguard other believers from making the same mistake he made, particularly in times of severe trial and persecution. Peter did this very thing so eloquently in both of the canonical epistles in the New Testament bearing his name (see 1 Pet. 1:5–9; 5:6–10; 2 Pet. 1:5–12; 2:9; 3:17–18).[55]

ANSWERING THE COMEBACK

This interpretation is basically speculation without evidence. There is nothing in the context of these verses to suggest that Peter must "strengthen the brethren" only by keeping them from denying Christ like he did. Could this be involved? Sure! But there's nothing in the text to suggest it, and definitely nothing to suggest this restrictive view.

There are, however, details in the context that support the idea that Jesus intends Peter to strengthen the brethren (the apostles) *as their leader,* and this is what Luke is highlighting. The instruction to strengthen the brethren caps off a discourse about leadership and authority within the kingdom of God.[56]

Luke begins by telling us that a dispute broke out among the disciples concerning "which of them was to be regarded as the greatest" (Luke 22:24). In response, Jesus contrasts worldly leadership with the leadership the apostles are to exercise: "The kings of the Gentiles exercise lordship over them; and those in authority over them are called benefactors. But not so with you; rather let the greatest among you become as the youngest, and the leader as one who serves" (Luke 22:25–26).

Jesus' contrast with the royal authority of Gentile kings suggests that he intended the apostles to exercise authority as well—but differently than what the apostles were accustomed to. Catholic apologist Joe Heschmeyer points out,[57] the word *leader* here is translated from the Greek *hēgeomai,* which is the same word Matthew uses for the "ruler [Greek, *hēgoumenos*] who will govern my people Israel" (Matt. 2:6). Luke also uses the word to describe Joseph as "governor [Greek, *hēgoumenon*] over Egypt" (Acts 7:10).

In Luke 22:29–30, Jesus makes explicit his intention that the apostles were to exercise royal authority: "As my Father appointed a kingdom for me, so do I appoint for you that you may eat and drink at my table in my kingdom, and sit on thrones judging the twelve tribes of Israel." That the apostles are to judge reveals that their role is administrative and judicial.[58]

So, up to this point we have the apostles arguing about who is the greatest. Jesus explains the general principle of servant leadership (Luke 22:25–26). He then assures the apostles that they all have a prominent place of authority in his kingdom (Luke 22:29–30). Immediately after this, Jesus makes the exclusive promise to pray for Peter as a response to Satan's attempt to sift all the apostles like wheat and gives Peter the exclusive instruction to strengthen the brethren.

Notice how Jesus progressively moves from the general to the specific.[59] When seen in this light, it becomes clear that Jesus intends Peter to be the leader among the apostles. But Peter is to be a *servant* leader and "strengthen the brethren" (v.32), not "exercise lordship over them" (v.25).

Peter's service, therefore, is not *merely* preserving others from denying Christ like he did or helping them repent if they have fallen. Rather, his service is one of leadership among those who exercise administrative and judicial authority within Christ's kingdom.

Luke's record of this promise and the instruction given to Peter anticipates Peter's missionary role in the rest of the Lucan narrative, which provides further support for our interpretation concerning Peter's leadership and Luke's intention to highlight it. Consider, for example, how Luke focuses on Peter as a witness to the resurrection (Luke 24:34). Luke also records Peter taking the initiative for two key events at the beginnings of the Church's life: the reconstitution of the Twelve with Matthias (Acts 1:15–26) and the preaching of the gospel on the day of Pentecost (Acts 2:14–41).

Luke continues to highlight Peter's role of servant leadership in chapters three through five: Peter heals a lame beggar (Acts 3:1–10), he addresses the people in Solomon's Portico (Acts 3:11–26), he speaks on behalf of himself and John before the council (Acts 4:5–22), he pronounces judgment on Ananias and Sapphira (Acts 5:1–11), and he speaks on behalf of the apostles before the council after they were arrested (Acts 5:29–32).

Luke rounds off his elucidation of Peter's leadership role by recording his visits to converts in Samaria, Lydda, and Joppa (Acts 8–9), his involvement in the conversion of the Roman centurion Cornelius (Acts 10–11), his targeting by Herod Agrippa as a key Christian leader to be executed (Acts 12), and his judgment—at the Jerusalem council—that the Gentiles did not have to be circumcised to be saved (Acts 15:7–11).

For Luke, Peter's command to strengthen the brethren is not merely one of keeping Christians from losing faith and helping them repent when they do. Peter is to strengthen the brethren by leading the Church.

"The Bible says that other people 'strengthen' as leaders in the Church."

Some Protestants also deny the significance of Peter's instruction to strengthen the brethren because the terminology of "strengthening" is used elsewhere in the New Testament. James White is one example:

> [W]e find no basis for reading papal prerogatives into the passage, for such terminology is common in the New Testament. For example, the term used here [*stērizein*] (14:22; 15:32; 15:41; 18:23) is used of Paul's confirming the churches of Syria and Cilicia, of Judas and Silas's confirming the brethren at Antioch, and of Timothy's confirming the Thessalonian Church. Amazingly, Paul uses the same Greek term in writing to the Church of Rome: "For I long to see you so that I may impart some spiritual gift to you, that you may be established" (Rom. 1:11). And in Romans 16:25 Paul praises God, who is able to strengthen them according to his [Paul's] gospel! No mention is made of Peter at all![60]

ANSWERING THE COMEBACK

There's an underlying assumption of White's argument that we need to discuss. Notice that he rejects a Catholic reading of the text based on the idea that the biblical motif of "strengthening" applies to others as well. The assumption seems to be that if a word or motif is used for two people, it must mean the same thing for both of them. But this is not the case in Scripture.

Consider, for example, that the *foundation* motif is used for both Jesus and the apostles. Jesus is the "one foundation" in 1 Corinthians 3:11 and the apostles are the "foundation" of the Church in Ephesians 2:20. Must we conclude that Jesus and the apostles are *equal* with regard to being the foundation of the Church? White's logic would have us answer yes, but that's surely not a conclusion that he or any Christian would accept.

Similarly, Jesus says he's the "light of the world" (John 8:12) and yet he calls all Christians the "light of the world" (Matt. 5:14). Surely, we're not the light of the world *in the same way* that Jesus is the light of the world.

So, the apparent underlying premise is false. A motif being used for multiple people doesn't mean they are equal with regard to what that motif expresses. In our case, Scripture tells us that God strengthens, and Paul strengthens, and Peter strengthens, but we are not forced to conclude that each means the same thing. Other details must be taken into consideration to determine how the motif applies to each individual.

Are there details indicating that Peter must strengthen the brethren in a way that's unique to his role as leader? There are: all the evidence we gave in our response to the previous objection. Peter receives the command to strengthen the brethren, which the context reveals to be the apostles, immediately after Jesus told them that Satan was going to sift them all and promised to pray exclusively for Peter. This indicates that Peter had a special task of "strengthening" that the other apostles did not.

Also, both the promised prayer and the command to strengthen come after Jesus told all the apostles that he's assigning to them the kingdom (v.29) but affirming that among them one is the greatest and the leader.

CHAPTER 4

Chief Shepherd of the Flock
John 21:15–17

Another Catholic argument that Peter was the first pope comes from John 21:15–17:

> When they had finished breakfast, Jesus said to Simon Peter, "Simon, son of John, do you love me more than these?" He said to him, "Yes, Lord; you know that I love you." He said to him, "Feed my lambs." A second time he said to him, "Simon, son of John, do you love me?" He said to him, "Yes, Lord; you know that I love you." He said to him, "Tend my sheep." He said to him the third time, "Simon, son of John, do you love me?" Peter was grieved because he said to him the third time, "Do you love me?" And he said to him, "Lord, you know everything; you know that I love you." Jesus said to him, "Feed my sheep."

For Catholics, the exclusive command to feed Jesus' sheep clearly signals Peter's unique role as leader of Jesus' Church. As in Matthew 16:18–19, where Jesus singles out Peter and makes him the visible foundation of his Church, here Jesus singles out Peter again and makes him the shepherd of his flock—a universal charge that extends to both the young "lambs" (Greek, *arnion*) and the old "sheep" (Greek, *probaton*).

As with other arguments for Peter's papal role, Protestants have comebacks to John 21:15–17 that challenge the Catholic claim.

"The exchange is merely to give Peter the opportunity to make up for the three times he denied Christ."

Perhaps the most common counter-response given to John 21:15–17 is that Jesus was simply giving Peter an opportunity to repent for his three denials.[61] Geisler and MacKenzie put it succinctly:

> The overall import of the passage in John speaks more to Peter's weakness and need for restoration than to his unique authority. The reason Peter is singled out for restoration, being asked three times by Jesus . . . was that *only Peter denied the Lord three times and so only Peter needed to be restored*. Thus, Jesus was not exalting Peter above the other apostles here but bringing him back up to their level.[62]

ANSWERING THE COMEBACK

Catholics have no problem with identifying the connection between Peter's threefold denial and his threefold restoration. It's highly doubtful that any New Testament scholar would dispute that. The problem is restricting the exchange *merely* to Peter's restoration.

One reason is that Peter, as we mentioned above, wasn't the only apostle to abandon Christ. At the Last Supper, Jesus warned *all* the apostles that they would desert him, and Matthew 26:56 tells us that they did.

Given that all the apostles abandoned Christ in some way, there must be something more to the exchange between Jesus and Peter in John 21:15–17. That something more is what Peter is being restored *to*: a unique role of leadership to feed Jesus' lambs and shepherd his sheep, including the other apostles. The Gospels reveal that Jesus had already given Peter a unique position among the apostles, and now, following his lapse, Peter is being reconfirmed in that position—not merely being brought "back up to their level." As the scholar Bradford Blaine Jr. writes,

> Although the three professions of love do allow him to mitigate some of the damage of the three denials, they function primarily as warrants for the three pastoral responsibilities he receives: feeding lambs, tending sheep, and feeding sheep. I concur with [the Protestant biblical scholar Herman Ridderbos] that "Jesus has sought not so much Peter's triple retraction of his denial . . . it is rather what awaits Peter in the future that prompts Jesus to reinforce his ties with him as never before."[63]

The presence of the other core disciples when Jesus gives this command underscores the uniqueness of Peter's role as shepherd. It means that they are included among Jesus' sheep whom Peter is to pastor.

Another reason why this comeback's restrictive view is problematic is simply that restoration isn't really connected with shepherding. Peter's threefold expression of love for Jesus would have effected his restoration without his being then invested with shepherding duties. These duties involve governance and leadership, which the motif of restoration does not require.

The Greek word here for "tend" (*poimainō*—v.16) suggests the ruling dimension of Peter's shepherding. *Poimainō* is used three times in the book of Revelation to refer to Christ ruling with an iron rod as the messianic king (Rev. 2:27, 12:5, 19:15). The Orthodox theologian Veselin Kesich has this to say about *poimainō*:

> The verb *poimainein* conveys more than *boskein*. In a figurative sense, *poimainein* points to the duties and responsibilities of church leaders—protecting, governing, leading, and caring for the people under their charge. *Boskein*, on the other hand, points to the shepherd's activities of feeding or tending.[64]

Other passages where the verb *poimainō* is used to suggest governance and rule.

- Matt. 2:6—"a ruler who will govern [Gk. *poimainō*] my people Israel"

- 1 Peter 5:2—"Tend [Gk. *poimainō*] the flock of God that is your charge."

"There are other shepherds."

Similar to one of the above comebacks to Luke 22:31–32, some Protestants[65] try to undermine a papal interpretation of John 21:15–17 by saying that others have the role of shepherding, too—both apostles and those of lower rank, such as the presbyters in Acts 20:28. If Christ wants others to be shepherds, then Peter's commission to shepherd Christ's flock doesn't make him a unique leader. He's just one shepherd like the others.

ANSWERING THE COMEBACK

As with the earlier objection based on the use of "strengthen" in the New Testament, this objection rests on the assumption that if an idea is used for multiple people, then they must be equal with regard to that idea. But, as we showed above, this assumption is false. We must consider other relevant details to see if the common idea, in this case the idea of shepherding, applies equally to Peter and the other apostles.

> All Catholic bishops are shepherds, and that's why they carry *crosiers*—shepherd staffs—as a symbol of that office. So, Catholicism acknowledges that others are shepherds, too, but clearly there can be shepherds of greater or lesser authority and jurisdiction, as with any other kind of rule.

One detail that favors Peter's unique shepherding role is the fact that Jesus singles him out in the presence of the others. Protestant New Testament scholar David A. DeSilva drives home the point nicely:

Peter is the one commissioned to tend the sheep and feed them; the Beloved Disciple [who the text presents as the author of John's Gospel] is not given any specific commission or responsibility for the church in that scene or any other.[66]

Another detail is that Peter is the only person that Jesus *directly* and *explicitly* commissions as shepherd of his sheep.

Jesus does commission the other apostles to administer the sacraments and teach, each of which is a shepherding role, but it's to Peter alone that Jesus gives the *explicit* role to shepherd his flock. This reveals that among all the shepherds in Jesus' Church, Peter is unique.

Finally, as we noted earlier, Jesus pointedly entrusts *all* his sheep, both old (sheep) and young (lambs), into Peter's care, making Peter the universal shepherd of *all* Jesus' flock. As Lutheran Bible scholar Joachim Jeremias puts it, "Only in John 21:15–17, which describes Peter's appointment as a shepherd by the Risen Lord does the whole church appear to have been in view as the sphere of activity."[67] Jeremias contrasts Peter's universal shepherding role with that of presbyters and bishops overseeing local churches, citing 1 Peter 5:7 and Acts 20:28 as evidence.[68]

CHAPTER 5

Decider at the Council
Acts 15:7–11

The previous Catholics arguments given in defense of the papacy deal with Christ appointing Peter as the first pope. But there's a passage in Acts that Catholics often point to as evidence that Peter *exercised* his papal authority—Acts 15:7–11.

> And after there had been much debate, Peter rose and said to them, "Brethren, you know that in the early days God made choice among you, that by my mouth the Gentiles should hear the word of the gospel and believe. And God who knows the heart bore witness to them, giving them the Holy Spirit just as he did to us; and he made no distinction between us and them, but cleansed their hearts by faith. Now therefore why do you make trial of God by putting a yoke upon the neck of the disciples which neither our fathers nor we have been able to bear? But we believe that we shall be saved through the grace of the Lord Jesus, just as they will."

Peter underscores his unique role by calling to mind that God chose him from "among" them to be the *first* one through whom the Gentiles would hear the gospel and believe (see the story of Cornelius in Acts 10:17–48). It was Peter to whom Christ *first* gave the revelation that Gentiles were to be accepted into the Christian community (Acts 10:9–16). And it's upon this unique privilege that Peter bases his declaration that the Gentiles do not have to be circumcised to be saved.

The significance of the declaration is highlighted by Luke's statement, "And after there had been much debate, Peter rose and said to them" (Acts 15:7). That Peter takes the initiative, in the midst of this debate, to pronounce on this issue suggests he recognized that he had authority to do so. It's also significant that no one challenged his exercise of such authority to pronounce judgment on such an important doctrinal belief in the life of the Church; nor did the assembly continue to consider the issue open for debate, but rather it moved on to other matters (vv.13–30).

The comebacks that Protestants make to the Catholic argument from Acts 15 all attempt to show that Peter was not, in fact, acting as a leader. But each does so in a different way.

"Peter doesn't speak on behalf of the council. His view had to be judged by the council."

Steve Hays argues that Peter exercises no more or less authority than Paul or James, both of whom also speak at the gathering. Moreover, he argues that Peter's view concerning the Gentiles stands to be judged by the council. He writes,

> [Peter is] one of three delegates to the "council." He speaks with no more or less authority at the "council" than Paul and Barnabas. And Peter isn't speaking *for* the council. He is speaking *to* the council. Speaking *before* the council. Not speaking on *behalf* of the council. Indeed, he's a defendant.

He must explain and justify his actions before the assembly of apostles and elders. They sit in judgment of his actions. It's more like a heresy trial than a council.[69]

ANSWERING THE COMEBACK

The first thing we can say in response is that we agree with Hays that Peter, in verses 7–11, is not speaking "for the council" but rather "to the council." But that's beside the point. What matters is the context of Peter's speech, its content and the manner in which he gives it, and how his audience responds.

The *context* is a central dispute as to whether circumcision is necessary for salvation, a dispute that Paul and Barnabas could not settle. "And when Paul and Barnabas had no small dissension and debate with them, Paul and Barnabas and some of the others were appointed to go up to Jerusalem to the apostles and the elders about this question" (Acts 15:2). The *content* is that circumcision is *not* necessary for salvation.

> According to Acts 15:2, this question of whether Gentiles needed to be circumcised was no small issue. Not even Paul and Barnabas could settle it. By taking it to the council of apostles and elders, the early Church followed the instruction that Jesus gave in Matthew 18:17: whenever there is unsettled debate, "take it to the Church."

The *manner* of Peter's speech is authoritative, since it is he who takes the initiative. James doesn't get up and give a speech until after Peter (v.13). And before James lays out his proposed plan, he first acknowledges and affirms what Peter said: "Simeon has related how God first visited the Gentiles, to take out of them a people for his name" (v.14).

Moreover, Peter doesn't preface his judgment as his *own* opinion in the way that James does: "Therefore *my* judgment is that we should not trouble those of the Gentiles who turn to God" (v.19). Peter simply declares, "we believe" (v.11), and thus speaks *on behalf* of the Christian community.

His *audience*, which consisted of "apostles and elders" (v.6), doesn't challenge his doctrinal judgment. In fact, Luke's narrative seems to suggest that Peter's declaration was what settled the debate among the apostles and elders concerning the question of circumcision and salvation. Luke tells us about the debating in verse 6, verses 7–11 record the speech, and then in verse 12 Luke says, "And all the assembly kept silence." The narrative flow suggests that Luke intends the silence to be contrasted with the debate mentioned in verse 6.

Some might say that the silence in verse 12 is meant to set the stage for what Luke records in verse 13: the assembly "listened to Barnabas and Paul as they related what signs and wonders God had done through them among the Gentiles." But Luke doesn't use any connectors; he doesn't say that "they kept silence *in order to* listen" or "they kept silence *to* listen." Rather, Luke uses the conjunction "and" in a rapid-fire manner: "*And* all the assembly they kept silence; *and* they listened to Barnabas and Paul" (v.12). These two statements beginning with the conjunction "and" seem to be meant to be read along with verse 7, which reads, "*And* after there had been much debate, Peter rose and said to them." Luke's use of the conjunction *and* suggests that he's summarizing the series of events.

Since there's nothing to connect the keeping silence to the assembly listening to Paul and Barnabas, but there is the narrative flow that connects the assembly's silence to the prior debating in verse 6, we can conclude that the apostles and elders gathered heeded Peter's teaching. And if that's the case, then Peter is not standing to be judged by the council.

"Peter didn't convene the council. It was a voluntary inquiry into the issue."

Some Protestants think that if Peter had been the first pope, he would have convened the assembly in Jerusalem. Since he doesn't, or at least there is no evidence that he did, he must not have been the first pope. Geisler and MacKenzie seem to make this argument when, attempting to undermine Peter's authority here in Acts 15, they write, "The inquiry into the issue was a voluntary one, coming from the church in Antioch (Acts 15:2–3)."[70] Hays concurs: "Peter didn't convene the 'council.'"[71]

ANSWERING THE COMEBACK

The problem with this argument is the assumption that if Peter were the first pope, he would have *had* to convene the Jerusalem council. For Catholics don't believe a pope must be the one to convene a council. A pope can still be a pope and not convene a council. Some ecumenical councils in history were not called by popes, though they had to be confirmed by popes in order to have ecumenical authority. Therefore, Peter can still be pope and not have convened the Jerusalem council.

The pope's role at a council is to approve whatever teachings come from it. Peter definitely approves of the council's teaching concerning circumcision and salvation because he's the one who gave it, declaring on behalf of the whole Christian community that Gentiles do not have to be circumcised in order to be saved.

"The Jerusalem council just confirmed revelation already given to Paul."

Geisler and MacKenzie offer another comeback:

> The Jerusalem conference was only confirmatory of the revelation Paul had previously received directly from God. There was no new infallible declaration from God . . . the conference recognized the supernatural confirmation of God on the message of Paul (Acts 15:12), which was the divinely appointed sign that he spoke by revelation from God (2 Cor. 12:12; Heb. 2:3–4).

ANSWERING THE COMEBACK

This comeback claims no papal significance to Peter's actions because the council confirmed a revelation that had already been given to Paul, and thus gave "no new infallible declaration from God." Since Peter gives *no new revelation*, his speech has no authoritative significance.

There are two problems here. First, it was *Peter* who received the revelation to receive the Gentiles into the Church before anybody else, even before Paul. Peter was the first! He indicates this in his speech: "In the early days God made choice among you, that by my mouth the Gentiles should hear the word of the gospel and believe" (v.7). This is relevant to his special position in the Church.

Second, the Catholic argument for Peter's authority in Acts 15 doesn't base itself on the claim that Peter gives new revelation. The claim is that Peter authoritatively confirms *for the Church* the revelation that the Gentiles can be saved. Even though the revelation had already been given to Peter and Paul, the Church needed to know the truth of the matter. That was the whole point of the gathering: "And when Paul and Barnabas *had no small dissension and debate with them,* Paul and Barnabas and some of the others were appointed to go up to Jerusalem to the apostles and the elders about this question" (Acts 15:2).

Though the answer had been revealed, not everyone agreed on this issue. This disagreement among the brethren gave rise to the need for a council. The issue had to be settled. There needed to be an authoritative interpretation of the revelation given. And it was *Peter* who provided it.

> The revelation that was given Peter is something that goes beyond the papal ministry. The pope does not give new revelation. The papal nature of Peter's speech at the council was the definitive *proclamation* of the revelation and the settling of the dispute concerning that revelation.

"James was the leader of the council, not Peter."

James White champions this counter-argument in his book *The Roman Catholic Controversy.* He appeals to two things in the text.[72] First, Luke uses the imperative mood—the mood of command—for "listen" when James says, "Brethren, listen [Greek, *akousate*] to me" (v.13). The second is James's statement, "Therefore my judgment is that we should not trouble those of the Gentiles who turn to God" (v.19). For White, since James is commanding those present to listen to him and deciding the results of the council, he must have been at the helm for the council.

ANSWERING THE COMEBACK

First, the imperative mood in Greek doesn't necessarily connote authority over the group—any more than it does in English.

Imagine that everyone is throwing around ideas in a business meeting, and you say, "Listen!" (in the imperative) and then go on to share your ideas. This doesn't necessarily mean that you are in charge of the meeting. You may be simply trying to get the others there to pay attention to what you have to say. Or, similarly, if a bishop got up to speak in an ecumenical council and exhorted everyone to "listen," this wouldn't imply that he considers himself in authority over the pope.

This is clear elsewhere in Scripture. In Acts 22:1, Paul says to his Jewish brethren, "Brethren and fathers, hear [Greek, *akousate*] the defense which I now make before you." Paul wasn't thereby asserting authority over the group; he merely was asking for their undivided attention. The following verse bears this out: "And when they heard that he addressed them in the Hebrew language, they were the more quiet" (v.2).

Given that the imperative mood doesn't necessarily connote authority, its use in Acts 15 doesn't establish that James had authority over the council proceedings. In any given instance, context must be taken into consideration in order to determine the force of the imperative.[73]

So what does the context tell us? First, as we mentioned above, Peter takes the initiative to settle the dispute. James doesn't get up and give a speech until *after* Peter, and he acknowledges and affirms what Peter said before he makes his proposal ("Simeon has related"—v.14). If James had just as much authority over the group as Peter (or more), he would have been the one to take the initiative and settle the substance of the debate, not Peter.[74]

Second, James's speech stands in stark contrast to Peter's. The content of Peter's speech was a matter of divine revelation. It was God who chose to reveal that the Gentiles could be saved, for he had given them the Holy Spirit just as he did the apostles, cleansing their hearts by faith and making no distinction between the circumcised and the uncircumcised (Acts 15:8–9). Based on that revelation, Peter makes a doctrinal statement that is more than mere opinion: "We *believe* that we shall be saved through the grace of the Lord Jesus, just as they [the Gentiles] will" (v.11). Peter doesn't offer this view as what he thinks *should* be believed. He offers it as what *is* believed.

James's speech, on the other hand, has a pastoral orientation,[75] intended to address the problem of how to unify Jewish and Gentile Christians (Acts 15:1–5). It's for the most part a practical problem that only arises because of the truth that Gentiles can be saved and enter into the Christian family, a truth that Peter already authoritatively declared.

At that time, Gentile converts were coming into a community of Jewish Christians who were still holding fast to many of the Old Testament precepts (Acts 21:15–26). And in order to keep the Gentiles from offending Jewish sensibilities, James proposes that the Gentile converts adhere to certain precepts that Jewish converts would have considered scandalous to violate: abstinence from "the pollutions of idols and from unchastity and from what is strangled and from blood" (Acts 15:20). Of these four precepts, only one is of a strictly moral nature, namely "unchastity" (Greek, *porneia*), which may refer to marriages that would be considered invalid under Jewish law.

James's speech also stands in contrast to Peter's because, unlike Peter, who stated *what is the case*, James offers his ideas for consideration: "Therefore *my* judgment is that we *should* not trouble those of the Gentiles who turn to God, but *should* write to them" (Acts 15:19–20). The Greek word translated as "judgment" in verse 19 (*krinō*) has a range of meanings, including "selection," "preference," "opinion," "think," and "consider."[76] Thus James is just saying this is his *opinion*. He's not issuing a formal ruling on behalf of the council.

In fact, what James proposes, unlike Peter's declaration, required a collaborative decision. Luke tells us that after James's proposal the apostles and elders gathered collectively and agreed on these proposals: "For it has seemed good to the Holy Spirit and to us to lay upon you no greater burden than these necessary things: that you abstain from what has been sacrificed to idols and from blood and from what is strangled and from unchastity" (vv.28–29). Notice that the collaboration didn't include the question of whether the Gentiles must be circumcised to be saved. That had already been taken care of by Peter. This suffices to refute the comeback that appeals to James's use of "judgment" as support for him being the leader of the council.

II
The Sacraments

CHAPTER 6

Born of Water and the Spirit
John 3:3–5

The vast majority of Christians believe that baptism is a means of salvation—Catholics, Eastern Orthodox, Oriental Orthodox, Lutherans, Anglicans, Methodists, and even some Calvinists. Only Baptists and those springing from the radical side of the Reformation reject this. On the part of Catholics, the *Catechism of the Catholic Church* teaches that baptism is "necessary for salvation" because "God has bound salvation to the sacrament" and that the Church "does not know of any means other than baptism that assures entry into eternal beatitude" (1257). To support this claim, Catholics, as well as other Christians who agree with us on baptism, appeal to John 3:3–5, where Jesus says to Nicodemus:

> "Truly, truly, I say to you, unless one is born anew, he cannot see the kingdom of God." Nicodemus said to him, "How can a man be born when he is old? Can he enter a second time into his mother's womb and be born?" Jesus answered, "Truly, truly, I say to you, unless one is born of *water and the Spirit*, he cannot enter the kingdom of God.

Since the second birth consists of water *and* Spirit, so it's argued, and baptism consists of water and Spirit, the new birth must be baptism. And since this new birth, which is baptism, is necessary for entrance into the kingdom of God, it follows that baptism is necessary for salvation.

Some Protestants read John 3:3–5 and arrive at different conclusions about what it means to be "born of water."

> Protestants like to ask people, "Are you born again?" If you're ever asked that question, your answer should be, "Yes, I was born again when I was baptized!"

"Jesus' reference to 'birth by water' refers to our biological birth. The 'birth by Spirit' refers to the new birth."

One explanation sees the "water" as referring to our biological birth. The second birth, so it's argued, is being born *only* of the Spirit—when you confess Jesus as Lord. Ron Rhodes explains:

Notice how Jesus went about his explanation to Nicodemus. He first speaks about being "born of water and the Spirit" in John 3:5, and then explains what he means by this in verse 6. It would seem that "born of water" in verse 5 is parallel to "born of the flesh" in verse 6, just as "born of the spirit" in verse 5 is parallel to "born of the Spirit" in verse 6. Jesus' message, then, is that just as each person has had a physical birth to live on earth, so he or she must also have a spiritual birth in order to enter the spiritual kingdom of God. A person must be "born from above." Seen in this light, this verse has nothing whatsoever to do with water baptism."[77]

ANSWERING THE COMEBACK

There are some problems with this interpretation. First, the context reveals that Jesus includes *both* Spirit *and* water in the one act of the second birth. He doesn't say, "You must be born of water, and *then* born of the spirit."[78]

This interpretation is further confirmed by the preceding and subsequent context of the passage in question. Consider, for example, that the images of Spirit and water *together* constitute the one event of Jesus' baptism, which John hints at in John 1:29–34. In John 3:23, John the evangelist records how John the Baptist was *baptizing* at Aenon near Salim. We're also told in John 4:1–2 that the apostles went about *baptizing.*

Since the instruction to be born again of water and Spirit comes in the midst of strongly baptism-centered imagery, then it's reasonable to conclude that baptism is what Jesus has in mind when he speaks of the necessity to be born of water and Spirit for entrance into heaven.

A second problem with this counter-argument is that it fails to consider an Old Testament prophecy that Jesus alludes to in his conversation with Nicodemus, and the Jewish understanding that an eschatological baptism was expected.

Note that when Nicodemus expresses astonishment at Jesus' instruction, Jesus replies, "Are you a teacher of Israel, and yet you do not understand this?" (John 3:10). The implication here is that Jesus' teaching about water, spirit, and new birth is rooted in Jewish tradition. And since Nicodemus is a teacher of that tradition, he should know about it.

But where in Jewish tradition? The answer is Ezekiel 36:25–27:

I will sprinkle clean water upon you, and you shall be clean from all your uncleannesses, and from all your idols I will cleanse you. A new heart I will give you, and a new spirit I will put within you; and I will take out of your flesh the heart of stone and give you a heart of flesh. And I will put my spirit within you, and cause you to walk in my statutes and be careful to observe my ordinances.

Notice how this passage contains the same themes present in Jesus' conversation with Nicodemus: water, God's spirit, and renewal. Given the conjunction of these themes, we have good reason to think this is what Jesus expects Nicodemus to think of when Jesus speaks of a *new* birth by *water* and *Spirit*. Jesus is teaching Nicodemus that the rebirth by water and Spirit *is* the eschatological event that Ezekiel prophesied.

But what is this rebirth by water and Spirit precisely? First-century Jews associated the eschatological hope of water and Spirit found in Ezekiel's prophecy with an eschatological baptismal ministry. The late New Testament scholar George Beasley-Murray explains,

The conjunction of water and Spirit in eschatological hope is deeply rooted in the Jewish consciousness, as is attested by Ezek. 36:25–27 and various apocalyptic writings . . . but above all the literature and practices of the Qumran sectaries, who sought to unite cleansing and the hope of the Spirit *with actual immersions* and repentance in a community beginning to "see" the kingdom of God.[79]

If the event of Ezekiel's prophecy was seen by Jews as an eschatological baptism, and Jesus intends Nicodemus to understand rebirth by water and Spirit in terms of that eschatological event, then it follows that Jesus intends baptism to be the new birth by water and Spirit—the *fulfillment* of the Jewish hope for an eschatological baptism.

Therefore, there is good reason to think the water and Spirit *together* constitute the second birth Jesus speaks of in the "born again" discourse.

A third problem is that "born of water" is not the language John uses for biological birth. Take his record of Jesus' teaching, for example, in John 3:6. In response to Nicodemus's query about entering again into his mother's womb (natural birth), John records Jesus saying, "That which is *born of the flesh* is flesh, and that which is born of the Spirit is spirit." John reports Jesus using the phrase "born of flesh," not "born of water," for natural birth.

John has his own way of referring to biological birth, and it also doesn't involve water:

> But to all who received him, who believed in his name, he gave power to become children of God; who were born, *not of blood* nor of the will of the flesh nor of the will of man, but of God (John 1:12–13).

Like Jesus, John draws a distinction between the new birth of God and biological birth. But he doesn't describe the latter with "water." He speaks of it as "born of blood."

Since we have contextual details that give us good reason to think the birth by water is referring to baptism, and the immediate context of the passage in question already provides language for biological birth that doesn't involve water, it's unreasonable to interpret the birth by water in John 3:3–5 as referring to our biological birth. This comeback, therefore, fails to undermine an appeal to John 3:3–5 as support for baptism being necessary for salvation.

"The 'water' that Jesus speaks of refers to the word of God."

Proponents of this interpretation, like Todd Baker, use 1 Peter 1:23 for support: "You have been born anew, not of perishable seed but of imperishable, through the living and abiding word of God."[80] Notice how Peter associates the second birth with the "word of God."

Baker also attempts to support this claim with Ephesians 5:25–26, where Paul speaks of Christ cleansing the church "by the washing of water with the word." He then couples this with John 15:3, where Jesus says, "You are already made clean by the word which I have spoken to you."

When you take into consideration that the second birth elsewhere in Scripture is associated with the word of God, and that the word of God is that which washes us clean, then it seems plausible for a Protestant to conclude that the water in the born again discourse refers to the word of God and *not* the waters of baptism.

ANSWERING THE COMEBACK

The problem with this argument is that the conclusion, "the water in the born again discourse *doesn't* refer to baptism" does not follow from the premise, "we are born anew by the word of God." To be born again by the word of God is not mutually exclusive of being born anew through the waters of baptism. It's possible that one can be born again by *both*.

For example, the "word of God" that Peter speaks of in 1 Peter 1:23 is the "good news preached"—the oral preaching that Paul calls the "word of God" in 1 Thessalonians 2:13. It's unreasonable to think Peter would think our second birth is made actual by the apostolic preaching alone and *not* the waters of baptism, since he was the one who commands those listening on the day of Pentecost to "repent and be baptized" in order that they may receive the forgiveness of sins and the gift of the Holy Spirit (Acts 2:38). This was in response to the people requesting to be saved after hearing the word of God proclaimed to them. So being born anew can come by *both* the word of God and baptism because it's the hearing of the preaching of "the good news" *that leads people to baptism.*

Therefore, Peter is not excluding baptism when he speaks of being born anew through "the living and abiding word of God." In fact, later in the same epistle (3:21), he directly says, "baptism now saves you." (See the discussion for this passage below.) For Peter, it's not either "the good news" or baptism; it's both-and.

CHAPTER 7

Baptized for the Forgiveness of Sins
Acts 2:38

In baptism, we're "freed from sin" (CCC 1213). So baptism is believed to be *more* than a symbol. Often, Acts 2:38 is a go-to passage for those who want to give biblical support for this belief. The verse reads:

> And Peter said to them, "Repent, and be baptized every one of you in the name of Jesus Christ for the forgiveness of your sins; and you shall receive the gift of the Holy Spirit.

Many argue that this verse proves the spiritual efficacy of baptism: it *brings about* the forgiveness of sins and the reception of the Holy Spirit. And if that's the case, then baptism isn't *just* a symbol. It's a perceptible sign that effects that which it signifies—namely, salvation.

There aren't many comebacks made to this argument by those Protestants who deny the spiritual efficacy of baptism. However, there are a couple, and they need to be answered.

> Right after saying that we're forgiven of our sins
> and receive the Holy Spirit through baptism, Peter
> says in verse 39, "For the promise is to you and
> to your children." What promise is he speaking
> about? The promise of the forgiveness of sins
> and the Holy Spirit that's given through baptism.
> Therefore, Peter views baptism as something for
> children as well as adults.

"Baptism is not the cause of salvation but rather follows it."

Ron Rhodes bases this argument[81] on a particular reading of the Greek preposition *eis*, translated as "for." Rhodes rightly points out that *eis* "can indicate causality ('in order to attain') or a result ('because of')." An example of the causal sense is, "I'm going to the office for (in order to get) my paycheck." An example of the resultant sense is, "I'm taking an aspirin for (because of) my headache."

Rhodes asserts that in Acts 2:38 *eis* is used in the resultant sense: Peter is *not* saying, "Repent, and be baptized *in order to attain* the forgiveness of sins" but rather, "Repent, and be baptized *because* you've been forgiven." Rather than baptism being a cause of salvation, it's something we do once we're saved.

ANSWERING THE COMEBACK

Our first response is that there's no argument here from the verse itself or the immediate context as to why *eis* should be interpreted in the resultant sense in this passage. It's simply asserted. Therefore, anyone who interprets it in the causal sense would likewise be entitled simply to assert his own position without argumentation.

As a backdrop to Acts 2:38, a Protestant can appeal to Acts 10:47 (and Ron Rhodes does), where Peter instructs Cornelius and a group of Gentiles to be baptized *after* they receive the Holy Spirit. But someone can reasonably interpret this reception of the Holy Spirit not as an instance of salvation, but simply as a visible confirmation that membership in God's family is extended to the Gentiles.[82]

We're told that when the Holy Spirit fell upon Cornelius and the other Gentiles present, the "believers from among the circumcised who came with Peter were amazed because the gift of the Holy Spirit had been poured out even on the Gentiles" (v. 45). They knew that this had happened because "they heard them speaking in tongues and extolling God." It seems that God gave his Spirit to convince the circumcised what Peter had said at the outset of his speech in verse 34 that "God shows no partiality" and that "in every nation anyone who fears him and does what is right is acceptable to him."

On the interpretation that this event is an instance of salvation, which is the more probable one, receiving the Holy Spirit *before* baptism was fitting in *this* case, an *exceptional* case, given the need for a public demonstration of God's approval of the admission of Gentiles into the Church without the conditions of submitting to the Jewish ceremonial laws. Peter (Acts 10:9–16) and Cornelius (Acts 10:3–7) had both received private visions, but this occasion provided public evidence.[83]

The necessity of baptism is not *absolute*. Catholic teaching allows for the belief that God can administer the graces of baptism without the sacrament. As the *Catechism* states, "God has bound salvation to the sacrament of baptism, but he himself is not bound by his sacraments" (1257). The event involving Cornelius and his Gentile friends could have been one of these cases where God acts without the sacrament.

A second response to the "baptism follows salvation" counter-argument is that Acts 2:38 is not the only information we have concerning the relationship between baptism and the forgiveness of sins. In the same book of Acts, baptism precedes the removal of sins. Consider Acts 22:16, where Ananias tells Paul, "Rise and be baptized, and wash away your sins, calling on his name." Notice what Ananias *doesn't* say: "Rise and be baptized, *because* you've been forgiven your sins." Moreover, and more importantly, the verb in the above passage, "wash away," clearly connects baptism with sins. This reveals that baptism *is* a washing. The statement "be baptized and wash away your sins" depicts the *washing* of baptism as what *removes* the sins.

The early Christians also viewed baptism as *bringing about* the forgiveness of sins. For example, the *Letter of Barnabas*, not written by the apostle Barnabas although it does date to around A.D. 75, reads, "We descend into the water full of sins and defilement, but come up bearing fruit in our heart, having the fear of God and trust in Jesus in our spirit" (11).

The *Shepherd of Hermas*, also known as *The Shepherd*, which dates to around A.D. 80, says it's "sound doctrine" to say a person receives the remission of his former sins in baptism. It then alludes to Paul's teaching in Romans 6:3–4, writing, "they go down into the water dead, and they come up alive."[84]

If baptism is seen as an instrumental cause of the forgiveness of sins elsewhere in the Bible, as well as in early Christian testimony, then we have good reason to interpret "for" in Acts 2:38 in the causal sense.

Here's a third response: the data in the verse itself, along with its immediate context, gives credence to a causal interpretation of "for." In the subsequent verses, you'll notice that nowhere does it say those listening to Peter were forgiven their sins before they received baptism. That's only an *assumption*.

Verse 37 merely tells us the crowd mourns Peter's indictment of their sin of crucifying their Messiah and asks what must be done. Peter responds by instructing the people to repent and be baptized for the forgiveness of their sins, speaks of the promise to them and their children, and further exhorts them to save themselves from their crooked generation. Verse 41 then tells us 3,000 people received Peter's word and were baptized. Nowhere does it say they were forgiven for their sins before they were baptized.

Since there's no evidence that their sins were forgiven before they received baptism, and we know that Peter links baptism with the forgiveness of sins (1 Pet. 3:21), the natural reading of the text is that the forgiveness of sins *occurs with* the reception of baptism.

Also, consider that Peter links the reception of the Holy Spirit with baptism as an effect to a cause. He says, "Repent, and be baptized . . . and *you shall receive* [Greek, *lēmpsesthe*— future tense] the gift of the Holy Spirit" (Acts 2:38). For Peter, the reception of the Holy Spirit is an *effect* of baptism.

Our final response is that the "resultant" interpretation entails unnecessary mental gymnastics when reading the flow of Peter's instructions.[85] We would need to envision repentance, then move forward in time to baptism, then conceptually move back in time to repentance again when we come to the forgiveness of sins, and then move forward again to the future with regard to the reception of the Holy Spirit. That's a strained reading to say the least. The more natural reading of the text is simply to take all the parts as referring to the future: repentance, baptism, and with it the forgiveness of sins and the reception of the Holy Spirit.

"The order of salvation in the New Testament is repentance, faith, and then baptism. Salvation comes first, then baptism."

"The New Testament order for salvation," argues Todd Baker, "is repentance, faith, and then water baptism. The rite of baptism does not precede the forgiveness of sins."[86]

To make this argument, Baker appeals to the common practice found in the New Testament. He cites several New Testament passages for support, including Acts 2:41, 8:12–13 and 36-38, and 9:18.[87] For Baker, these passages show that salvation is granted in response to faith. Therefore, he reasons, as soon as a person has faith, he's saved. He doesn't need to wait for baptism.

ANSWERING THE COMEBACK

In all these passages, the faith that precedes baptism can be explained by what theologians call *imperfect* faith.[88] The assumption here is that the faith exercised before baptism in the passages cited is *perfect* faith, a faith animated by charity (Gal. 5:6) and that which justifies (Rom. 5:1). But that's not necessarily true. There is such a thing as *imperfect* faith that God gives in order to lead a person to and prepare him for the faith that justifies, which is given in baptism.

As St. Thomas Aquinas explains, faith, insofar as we distinguish it from hope and charity (1 Cor. 13:13), is an act of the intellect assenting to God's revelation by command of the will (*Summa Theologiae* II–II:2:1). There is nothing in this understanding of faith that tells us whether charity informs it or not. There is nothing that tells us whether it's a faith that justifies or not, since charity is necessary for faith to justify.

God, nevertheless, gives this gift of faith to heal the person from unbelief. Belief in God's revelation, like repentance, is a necessary starting point for conversion (Mark 1:15).

Since there is a type of faith that exists without charity, you can't automatically conclude that the people who believed in the passages cited above were saved before baptism. Their belief that preceded their baptism could have been, and most likely was, that gift of faith not informed by charity, but which is necessary to cease in unbelief and then believe. Such faith would become perfect, or saving faith, upon receiving the virtue of charity that God grants in baptism. Therefore, the order found in the New Testament of repentance, belief, and baptism doesn't undermine the Catholic argument for the salvific value of baptism from Acts 2:38.

CHAPTER 8

Baptism Now Saves You
1 Peter 3:21

Another argument for the belief that baptism saves comes from 1 Peter 3:20–21:

> God's patience waited in the days of Noah, during the building of the ark, in which a few, that is, eight persons, were saved through water. Baptism, which corresponds to this, now saves you, not as a removal of dirt from the body but as an appeal to God for a clear conscience, through the resurrection of Jesus Christ.

Peter can't be any clearer, Catholics (and the majority of other Christians) argue. He says plain as day, "Baptism . . . now saves you." And Peter expounds the meaning of that salvation by telling us baptism brings about an interior cleansing inasmuch as it brings about a clear conscience. That implies that sins are forgiven, and the individual is saved.

But not all Christians accept this argument. Each comeback that we're going to consider here attempts to counter the argument from 1 Peter 3:21 by offering an alternative explanation as to what saves us.

> Don't be shy to use 1 Peter 3:21. It works. I remember from a 2001 talk at the Fullness of Truth Conference in Houston, Texas, the late deacon Alex Jones, a former Pentecostal pastor turned Catholic, stated that for all the years he was a Pentecostal pastor this passage never caught his attention until someone pointed it out to him.

"What saves us is our pledge to God to follow Jesus."

Some Protestants who deny the salvific efficacy of baptism argue that Peter isn't saying baptism actually saves us. Rather, it's the "appeal to God for a clear conscience," which is interpreted as a pledge to God to follow Jesus, that saves us, and baptism is merely an appropriate symbol for that confession of faith. Again, we look to Todd Baker for his articulation of the argument:

> Peter states in verse twenty-one the real purpose of baptism is the "appeal" or "answer" of a good conscience toward God. The believer makes the pledge that he will now follow Jesus Christ as his obedient disciple united with the Lord in his death, burial, and resurrection. Baptism is an appropriate symbol of this reality for a public confession and act upon the one baptized openly declaring he or she now trusts in Jesus Christ for the forgiveness of sins with a pledge or an appeal to have a clear conscience now, cleansed from all guilt, condemnation, and accusation, that provides a good answer before God.[89]

ANSWERING THE COMEBACK

The first thing to note is the interpretation of the phrase "an appeal to God for a clear conscience" as a *pledge* that we make to follow Jesus. This is important because if we translate it as an "appeal to God for a clear conscience," then Peter would be teaching us that we need to ask God to cleanse our conscience through baptism, which would support the idea that baptism saves. But if we're instructed to *pledge* a clear conscience to God, then the matter isn't as clear.

What should we make of this?

Well, there are a variety of opinions on how to read Peter's statement, "an *appeal* to God for a clear conscience." Some see this appeal as a "pledge" or "answer" with a good conscience to follow Jesus. The Protestant *New International Version* translation of the Bible renders the word as "pledge" rather than "appeal." This is not unreasonable because the Greek word for "appeal," which is *eperotēma*, can mean "a pledge."[90] Others translate *eperotēma* as an "appeal," as the *Revised Standard Version* does, the implication being that in baptism, Peter is saying we make a *request* of God to give us a clear, or good (1 Pet. 3:16), conscience. This is the primary meaning that many Greek dictionaries give for the word.[91]

Regardless of which translation we use for *eperotēma*, both correspond with the salvific efficacy of baptism. Take the view we're disputing right now, for example. The pledge to God to follow Christ with a good conscience doesn't preclude a sacramental understanding of baptism.

Christians who believe in the salvific efficacy of baptism profess that such a pledge to Christ is a necessary condition to receive baptism (in the case of an infant, the parents and the Church make such a pledge on behalf of the child). The pledge is part of the baptismal rite. And this pledge is made "with a good conscience," either because it's a sincere commitment or the person making the pledge in the baptismal rite is doing so having repented of sin, which is necessary to be baptized.

The view that translates *eperotēma* as "appeal" fits with the sacramental view of baptism as well. If we believe that God interiorly cleanses our souls by giving us a good conscience through the waters of baptism, then submitting ourselves to the baptismal waters is a request that God effect within our souls a clear, or good, conscience.

We can go further in our response to Baker. Consider that Peter's statement, "an appeal to God for a clear conscience," is one of two statements that Peter intends to explain what he means when he says, "Baptism now saves you." The other explanatory statement, which comes first and is set in opposition with the other, is "not as a removal of dirt from the body."

This creates a few problems for the interpretation that baptism *doesn't* save us and is *merely* a symbol of our pledge to follow Jesus. First, it's unreasonable to think Peter would make such an explicit statement about the salvific efficacy of baptism—"baptism now saves you"—and then immediately afterward deny such efficacy in his explanatory remarks.

Second, we end up having to think the language "as an appeal to God for a clear conscience" is meant to oppose the statement "baptism now saves us." But that's not what Peter says. Peter contrasts "as an appeal to God for a clear conscience" with the idea that baptism saves us "as a removal of dirt from the body."

This leads us to a third problem. It's true that Peter's denial of an external cleansing implies the affirmation of an internal cleansing: a "cleansing of guilt," as he puts it. But the argument runs off the rails by divorcing this internal cleansing from baptism, saying baptism is merely a symbol of the internal cleansing and is *not at all* an external cleansing. On the contrary, it's obvious that baptism *does* remove dirt from the body, so what

Peter is denying is that baptism is *merely* "a removal of dirt from the body." It thus is *also* an internal cleansing.

"It's Jesus' resurrection that saves, not baptism."

Todd Baker puts it this way: "Peter tells his audience in verse 21 that it is the resurrection of Jesus Christ, symbolized by the waters of baptism, which actually saves the Christian."[92]

ANSWERING THE COMEBACK

The main problem here is a false dichotomy: our salvation is brought about *either* by Jesus' resurrection *or* by baptism. But, if we consider Paul's teaching on baptism in Romans 6, we see that baptism is that which allows for us to *participate in* Jesus' resurrection, by which we are saved. Paul introduces baptism in this chapter as the experience of death *and* resurrection in Christ:

> Do you not know that all of us who have been baptized into Christ Jesus were baptized into his death? We were buried therefore with him by baptism into death, so that as Christ was raised from the dead by the glory of the Father, we too might walk in newness of life (vv. 3–4).
>
> Paul goes on to articulate the effects of this baptismal death and resurrection:
>
> We know that our old self was crucified with him so that the sinful body might be destroyed, and we might no longer be enslaved to sin. For he who has died is freed from sin (vv.6–7).

What's interesting about this passage, as pointed out in Catholic circles by apologist Jimmy Akin, is that the Greek doesn't say "freed from sin." The Greek word translated "freed" is *dikaioō*, which means "to put into a right relationship (with God); acquit, declare and treat as righteous."[93] This is the same word Paul uses when he speaks of our justification by faith: "Since we are justified [Greek, *dikaiōthentes*] by faith, we have peace with God through our Lord Jesus Christ" (Rom. 5:1). So the phrase "freed from sin" in Romans 6:7 can literally be translated "justified from sin."

Modern translations render it as "freed from sin" because the context is clearly about sanctification. For example, in the verse before Paul speaks of baptismal death, he speaks of those in Christ as having "died to sin." As quoted above, Paul speaks of those who have died the death of baptism as "no longer enslaved to sin."

In verses 17–18, Paul actually uses a form of the Greek word for "free" (*eleutheroō*) in relation to the freedom from sin that we receive in Christ:

> But thanks be to God, that you who were once slaves of sin have become obedient from the heart to the standard of teaching to which you were committed, and, having been set free [Greek, *eleutherōthentes*] from sin, have become slaves of righteousness.

This tells us that, for Paul, justification can include sanctification, which is the interior renewal of the soul whereby the objective guilt of sin is removed. And that justification, or salvation, takes place in baptism.

A third problem with the "Resurrection" counter-argument is that it contradicts the plain sense of the text: "baptism now saves you." Peter doesn't say, "The Resurrection saves you." It would have been unnatural for Peter to use the language "baptism now saves you" in order to convey the message "baptism *doesn't* save you; Christ's resurrection does."

CHAPTER 9

The Bread of Life Discourse
John 6:48–67

The Catholic Church teaches that when we partake of the Eucharist in Holy Communion, we are literally consuming the body and blood of Jesus Christ. Paragraph 1244 of the *Catechism* says we "receive the food of the new life, the body and blood of Christ." In 1275, it states that the Eucharist nourishes us with "Christ's body and blood" in order for us to be transformed in Christ. According to paragraph 1335, the faithful "drink the new wine that has become the blood of Christ."

A key passage from Scripture that Catholics, and other believers in the Real Presence, have looked to throughout the centuries as biblical support for this teaching is John 6:48–67. Jesus' words of institution at the Last Supper ("this is my body . . . this is my blood") are important as well, as we'll see in our next chapter. But Jesus' Bread of Life Discourse sheds light on the words of institution and gives us strong reasons to believe he meant the words of institution to be taken literally and not metaphorically. Here's the passage from John 6:

> I am the bread of life. Your fathers ate the manna in the wilderness, and they died. This is the bread which comes

down from heaven, that a man may eat of it and not die. I am the living bread which came down from heaven; if any one eats of this bread, he will live forever; and the bread which I shall give for the life of the world is my flesh." The Jews then disputed among themselves, saying, "How can this man give us his flesh to eat?"

So Jesus said to them, "Truly, truly, I say to you, unless you eat the flesh of the Son of Man and drink his blood, you have no life in you; he who eats my flesh and drinks my blood has eternal life, and I will raise him up at the Last Day. For my flesh is food indeed, and my blood is drink indeed. He who eats my flesh and drinks my blood abides in me, and I in him. As the living Father sent me, and I live because of the Father, so he who eats me will live because of me.

This is the bread which came down from heaven, not such as the fathers ate and died; he who eats this bread will live forever." This he said in the synagogue, as he taught at Capernaum. Many of his disciples, when they heard it, said, "This is a hard saying; who can listen to it?" But Jesus, knowing in himself that his disciples murmured at it, said to them, "Do you take offense at this? Then what if you were to see the Son of Man ascending where he was before? It is the Spirit that gives life, the flesh is of no avail; the words that I have spoken to you are Spirit and life. But there are some of you that do not believe."

For Jesus knew from the first who those were that did not believe, and who it was that would betray him. And he said, "This is why I told you that no one can come to me unless it is granted him by the Father." After this many of his disciples drew back and no longer walked with him. Jesus said to the Twelve, "Will you also go away?" (vv. 48–67).

There are many reasons Catholics, and other believers in the Real Presence, give as to why we should take Jesus' words, "eat my flesh, drink my blood," literally. But perhaps the most persuasive is that both the Jews and his disciples understand him literally, and Jesus doesn't correct them. In verse 52, the Jews respond, "How can this man give us his flesh to eat?" In verse 60, his disciples respond, "This is a hard saying; who can listen to it?" You would think that if his audience were mistaken, and given the gravity of this teaching, Jesus would have corrected their literal understanding. To the contrary, he affirms them. In response to the Jews, Jesus reiterates the need to eat his flesh and drink his blood no fewer than six times in six verses. He affirms his disciples' literal understanding by letting them walk away.

Since the figurative interpretation doesn't make sense of Jesus' response to the difficulty the Jews and his disciples were having with the teaching, a believer in the Real Presence is on solid ground taking Jesus' words literally and seeing in them evidence for the belief that the Eucharist is Jesus' real and substantial body and blood.

The number of Protestant comebacks to this one passage would suffice for an entire book. Given that the Eucharist is not the central topic of this book, we must limit ourselves to those counter-arguments that are prevalent among Protestant apologists who reject the doctrine of the Real Presence.

The arguments we'll consider in this chapter can be divided into three categories. The first category targets specifically the appeal to Jesus' lack of clarification. The second consists of arguments that give reasons why the language should *not* be interpreted literally, but rather should be interpreted metaphorically, while not dealing with the actual meaning of the words. The third offers an alternative meaning of Jesus' words "eat flesh" and "drink blood," arguing that such language should be taken to convey the idea that we must *believe* in Jesus.

"Jesus left his audience in ignorance all the time. Nothing special here."

Some Protestants try to undercut the appeal to Jesus' lack of clarification by basically saying, "It's no big deal. He does it all the time." Protestant apologist Robert Zins, founder of the ministry A Christian Witness to Roman Catholicism, makes this argument and appeals to John 2:15–21 for support.[94]

There, Jesus drives the corrupt moneychangers out from the Temple and then is challenged by the religious authorities to provide a sign to authenticate his messianic authority. Jesus responds, "Destroy this temple, and in three days I will raise it up." His critics respond, "It has taken forty-six years to build this temple, and will you raise it up in three days?"

Notice they understood Jesus to be speaking of the physical temple. But John tells us that Jesus "spoke of the temple of his body." And there's no indication that Jesus corrected their misunderstanding.

For Zins, since Jesus didn't correct their misplaced literal thoughts here, there's no reason to expect that Jesus would have done so in John 6, as Catholics claim he would have if his audience were mistaken.

ANSWERING THE COMEBACK

It's interesting that just a few verses later, at the beginning of the next chapter (John 3:3–5), John records Jesus' conversation with Nicodemus about being born again in order to enter the kingdom of heaven. Like Jesus' critics in the previous chapter, Nicodemus takes Jesus' words in a literalistic way, asking, "How can a man be born when he is old? Can he enter a second time into his mother's womb and be born?"

Now, unlike with Jesus' critics in the previous chapter, Jesus clarifies Nicodemus's crass literalism, saying, "Unless one is born of water and Spirit, he cannot enter the kingdom of God." So why does Jesus clarify the literalism of Nicodemus and not the literalism of his critics?

One possible explanation is that the critics were hard-hearted, and so merited to be left in the dark concerning the true meaning of Jesus' statement. Having foreknowledge of what was to come at his trial, Jesus knew they would seek "false testimony" (Matt. 26:59) and twist his claims to provide grounds for sentencing him to death. Notice that John records Jesus saying, "Destroy *this* temple" (John 2:19), yet Matthew reports that those charging Jesus at his trial accused Jesus of saying that *he* would destroy the temple *of God*: "This fellow said, '*I* am able to destroy the temple *of God*'" (v. 61). Jesus' critics present in John 2 were closed off to embracing the truth that he would rise from the dead, and so Jesus, on this reading, leaves the ambiguity.

Nicodemus, on the other hand, was not hard-hearted and thus did not merit being left in ambiguity. So Jesus clarifies his misunderstanding.

Another possible explanation is that Jesus simply doesn't clarify his critics' thoughts because they weren't his followers. It was common for Jesus to clarify things for his disciples but not for others. For example, Mark tells us in 4:33–34, "With many such parables [Jesus] spoke the word to them, as they were able to hear it; he did not speak to them without a parable, but privately to his own disciples he explained everything."[95] Matthew records a conversation that Jesus had with his disciples concerning this very issue: "Then the disciples came and said to him, 'Why do you speak to them in parables?' And [Jesus] answered them, 'To you it has been given to know the secrets of the kingdom of heaven, but to them it has not been given" (13:10–11).

Now, a Protestant might object, "This line of reasoning doesn't help the Catholic interpretation of John 6 because if Jesus left his critics in the darkness of ambiguity due to their hard-heartedness, then perhaps that's what Jesus did in John 6. John tells us it was 'the Jews' (John's label for those who didn't follow Jesus) who said, 'How can this man give us his flesh to eat?'"

The problem here is that it's not just those who don't follow Jesus who have a hard time with Jesus' teaching. His "disciples" (John's label for those who believe in and have been following Jesus) have difficulties as well. In response to Jesus' sixfold affirmation that we must eat his flesh and drink his blood, his disciples say to him, "This is a hard saying; who can listen to it?" (John 6:60).

Jesus doesn't give any sort of explanation to his disciples that eases the difficulty they're having with his teaching. Rather, his response underscores it: "Do you take offense at this? Then what if you were to see the Son of Man ascending where he was before?" (John 6:61–62). In other words, Jesus is saying, "If you think *this* saying is hard, wait til you see what's coming! It's going to be even *more* difficult to believe!" Why would Jesus appeal to his ascension, something even more difficult to believe, given its observably miraculous nature, if he were trying to ease the difficulty by clarifying the literal thoughts of his disciples concerning his teaching to eat his flesh and drink his blood? Such a response suggests that Jesus is *not* clarifying his disciples' literal thoughts. Rather, he's affirming them.

"Jesus does correct his disciples' literal thinking. He says, 'The flesh is of no avail; the words that I have spoken to you are Spirit and life' (John 6:63)."

In contrast to the above comeback, which recognizes that Jesus offers no clarification of his remarks in John 6, this comeback argues that Jesus did. Some Protestants[96] appeal to Jesus' words in John 6:63: "It is the spirit that gives life, the flesh is of no avail; the words that I have spoken to you are spirit and life."

Apologist Matt Slick, founder of Christian Apologetics and Research Ministry, interprets this text as Jesus "stating that the words he was speaking were *spiritual* words when talking about eating his flesh and drinking his blood."[97] Slick concludes, "[Jesus] did not say they were literal words; that is, he did not say that they were his actual body and blood."

ANSWERING THE COMEBACK

One problem with this comeback is that it doesn't explain why Jesus' disciples still leave him. The disciples leave Jesus immediately *after* he gives the "spirit and life" teaching. If people recognized the word *spirit* as meaning *symbolic*, why would the disciples leave Jesus?

The whole point of interpreting his words as having *merely* a symbolic meaning is to suggest that his command to eat his flesh and drink his blood should not be that difficult of a teaching. The difficulty, therefore, should have disappeared for the disciples after this supposed clarification, and they would have thereby stayed with Jesus. But that's not what happened.

Moreover, the word *spirit* does not mean *symbolic*; nor does "being spiritual." For example, the Bible says that "God is spirit" (John 4:24) and that angels are "ministering spirits" (Heb. 1:14). Does that mean God and angels are mere symbols? Of course not.

Paul says in Romans 15:27 that Gentiles have come to share in the "spiritual blessings" of the Christians in Jerusalem. Should we interpret these blessings to be mere symbols? If we were to follow the logic of Slick's counter-argument, we'd have to say yes. But that's absurd.

Now, a Protestant might counter further with an objection made by James White. In his online video entitled "John 6 for Roman Catholics," White argues that the reason why the disciples left was not because of his teaching to eat his flesh and drink his blood but rather because Jesus said in the previous verse, "No one can come to me unless it is granted him by the Father."[98] White states his argument this way:

> What is the antecedent of *ek toutou* [the first two Greek words] in verse 66? *Ek toutou* means "because of this": "Because of this many of his disciples withdrew and were not walking with him anymore" (v.66). Because of what? Because of what? And the answer is verse 65: Jesus' repeated assertion of what? The Father's kingly freedom and man's inability.

There are a few ways we can respond to this. First, although it is true that *ek toutou* can be translated as "because of this," it can also be translated as "after this."[99] In fact, many Bible translations use "after this" to introduce verse 66. So what's said in verse 65 *could* be the cause of the disciples leaving in verse 66. But it's *also* possible that John simply records what happened in its temporal sequence without intending to convey a causal connection with Jesus' specific statement at the end of verse 65. And this fits with the entire context: Jesus said things that understandably would cause someone to leave him—"unless you eat the flesh of the Son of Man and drink his blood, you have no life in you." So simply appealing to the Greek phrase *ek toutou* doesn't prove the Protestant's point. We have to see which of the two translations—the causal or temporal—makes more sense.

Let's take the causal translation first. One reason why this doesn't make sense is because the "disciples" were already following Jesus, so they would have simply concluded that the Father had granted them the grace to believe, in keeping with the predestinarian views of many Jews. For such disciples, Jesus' teaching about the Father wouldn't have given them cause for rebellion. It would have given them cause for gratitude and celebration—"thank God I'm among those the Father has drawn to Jesus!"

Another reason the causal translation doesn't make sense is because it doesn't account for Jesus' previously made statement about the Father in verse 44: "No one can come to me unless the Father who sent me draws him." There's no indication in the surrounding context that Jesus' disciples took offense at the statement here. The only negative response Jesus receives shortly after this statement is the non-believers disputing among themselves about Jesus giving us his *flesh* to eat. If Jesus' disciples didn't take offense at his teaching about the Father and coming to him in verse 44, it's unreasonable to think they would take offense at it in verse 66. And if they never take offense at Jesus' teaching about the Father, then the disciples' offense at his statements about eating his flesh and drinking his blood serves as the more reasonable basis for their leaving Jesus.

A third reason to reject the causal translation is that Jesus needs to repeatedly defend his statement about his body and blood but not his statement about the Father. Jesus finds himself responding multiple times to both the Jews and the disciples. But concerning his teaching about the Father, there's no negative response and thus no defense on the part of Jesus. Again, that the disciples are offended by Jesus' teaching about eating his flesh and drinking his blood is the more reasonable explanation for why they leave.

For these reasons we should reject the causal translation ("because of this") and go with the temporal one ("after this").

But even if for argument's sake we go with the causal translation—translating *ek toutou* as "because of this"—the objection still doesn't succeed. The reason is that John just as easily may have used "this" to refer to the *entirety* of the previous discussion, which included Jesus' hard sayings about his flesh and blood. And this would make sense if John were seeing the disciples leaving as the climax to Jesus' hard sayings recorded in the previous verses.

So an appeal to *ek toutou* doesn't undermine our argument, because the disciples leave after the so-called clarifying statement in verse 63.

The argument that Jesus actually did correct the crowd's literalistic thinking also fails because it doesn't consider Jesus' statement about "the flesh," which Jesus contrasts with "the spirit": "It is the spirit that gives life, the flesh is of no avail." Understanding the idiom of "the flesh" sheds light on what Jesus means by his statement, "my words are spirit and life."

The flesh is a New Testament expression that often describes human nature apart from God's grace (Rom. 8:1–14), as well as those who see reality only from such an unaided perspective. John uses the expression this way in John 8:15, where Jesus says to the Pharisees, "You judge according to the flesh."

So when we come back to John 6:63, and Jesus says, "The flesh is of no avail," Jesus means that his teaching can't be analyzed from a purely human perspective. The eyes of faith are needed, since eating his flesh and drinking his blood are going to involve the miraculous, like his ascension into heaven, which Jesus appeals to in response to the disciples' difficulty.

The need for faith is the reason why Jesus bookends his teaching with these commands: "No one can come to me unless the Father who sent me draws him," and "no one can come to me unless it is granted him by the Father." It's not that his exhortation to "eat" and "drink" has a symbolic meaning, but rather that it is possible to accept the reality of what he is saying only by divine grace. And accepting the reality of what he's saying can be done only if the Father grants faith through the Holy Spirit; hence Jesus' words, "It is the spirit that gives life."

"Jesus moves away from a physical mentality in John 6:27."

Some comebacks give specific reasons why Jesus is *not* speaking literally, without any attempt to explain *what* Jesus meant. One appeals to John 6:27 and argues that Jesus has moved away from a physical mentality and takes things in a spiritual direction.[100] John records Jesus saying, "Do not labor for the food which perishes, but for the food which endures to eternal life, which the Son of Man will give to you."

Todd Baker sees this distinction of foods as forming "the basis for taking Jesus' words about eating his flesh and drinking his blood figuratively instead of literally." Baker argues that if we were to interpret Jesus' words in John 6 as referring to his actual body and blood, as believers in the Real Presence do, then we'd be contradicting our Lord's explicit words about perishable food, since his body and blood are of the material world and would be *in* the material bread of the Eucharist, which Baker says is "potentially perishable."[101]

ANSWERING THE COMEBACK

The first thing we can say in response is that there's a faulty assumption here: that Jesus' body and blood would be confined within the boundaries of material reality, thus making his body and blood *perishable* food. We only need look to Jesus' glorified and resurrected body to see that this need not be so. Jesus gave his body and blood qualities that break the restrictions of physical reality (e.g., appearing and disappearing—Luke 24:31; passing through locked doors—John 20:19). If Jesus gives his body such supernatural qualities in the Eucharist, as Catholics say he does, then the "imperishable food" label *would* apply to Jesus' body and blood since Jesus gives his flesh in the Eucharist—both at the Last Supper and today—the quality of being imperishable. Therefore, an appeal to the distinction between perishable and imperishable to undermine the Catholic argument doesn't work.

A Protestant might counter and say the material bread of the Eucharist is still material food that perishes. But, according to Catholic teaching, it is only the *accidental* features of bread that will pass away after consecration. The *reality* or the *substance* is Jesus' body and blood—our spiritual food that does not perish.

A second response is that there's evidence contrary to the claim. Did Jesus really move *away* from the physical toward the spiritual? Well, the Greek text in verses 54 through 58, the key section for Jesus' command to eat his flesh and drink his blood, suggests something *very* physical.

John records in verse 53 the Jews' struggle with Jesus' claim that the bread he will give for the life of the world is his flesh. Then, in verse 54, John begins to recount Jesus' response to such difficulty. Prior to Jesus' response that begins in verse 54, the Greek word that John uses for "eat" is *phagēte*, which is a generic term for eating.

After John tells us the Jews have a difficult time accepting Jesus' claim, and within the verses where Jesus affirms the Jews' literal thoughts, the language for eating intensifies. The Greek word changes to *trōgō*, which literally means "to gnaw," "to bite," "(audibly) to chew."[102]

Such a word is used in only two other places in the New Testament: Matthew 24:38 and John 13:18. In reference to the days before the Flood, Matthew 24:38 reads, "For as in those days before the Flood they were eating [Greek, *trōgōntes*] and drinking, marrying and giving in marriage, until the day when Noah entered the ark." In John 13:18, Jesus quotes Psalm 41:9 in reference to Judas: "He who ate [Greek, *trōgōn*] my bread has lifted his heel against me."

So should we suppose that John switches to more graphic terminology for eating to convey a less than real meaning of eating? That doesn't make sense. The Catholic argument, however, does make sense. The switch to the more graphic terminology is meant to support the claim that Jesus meant his words to be taken literally, and *not* in a figurative sense.

It is true that such language merely *suggests* a literal reading and doesn't prove it, since physical terms can be used as symbols for spiritual realities. But when we take other things into consideration, the literal reading (contra the symbolic reading) is strengthened. For example, it's not merely *that* the more graphic terminology is used. Rather, it's the *escalation* of its intensity, or the *switch* from the less graphic to the more graphic, *within* the midst of Jesus responding to the difficulty. Moreover, the exaggeration of the intensity continues. Jesus doesn't give any clarifying remarks to ease the difficulty for his disciples. He's even willing to let the Twelve leave. *All* these things *taken together* support the view that the words are meant literally rather than symbolically.

"Jesus can't intend us to literally drink his blood because the Bible prohibits the partaking of blood in Leviticus 17:10–12."

Here's the Mosaic prohibition of consuming blood:

> If any man of the house of Israel or of the strangers that sojourn among them eats any blood, I will set my face against that person who eats blood, and will cut him off from among his people.

The late American theologian Loraine Boettner appealed to this verse in his book *Roman Catholicism* and argued that the Catholic understanding of John 6 violates this prohibition of drinking blood.[103] Protestant apologist Matt Slick follows suit, concluding, "It would certainly appear that the Roman Catholic view is in contradiction to the Old Testament Scripture since it advocates the eating of the blood of Christ."[104]

ANSWERING THE COMEBACK

Our first answer to this counter-argument is that the dietary laws of the Old Law, to which the prohibition of drinking blood belonged, passed away with the advent of Christ. The prohibition of consuming blood was not a precept rooted in the natural moral law, which is forever binding (Rom. 2:14–15). Rather, it was one of many dietary regulations that involved the ritual purity of Jews—disciplinary in nature, not moral, and thus subject to change.

From a Christian's perspective, we know that this precept was not rooted in the moral law of human nature because Jesus gives the explicit command to drink his blood. If it were otherwise, then Jesus would have been commanding us to do something immoral. Even if we were to interpret his words figuratively, he would have been telling us to perform some action that symbolizes immoral behavior.

But this can't be. Jesus is the Word made flesh and therefore can't do anything that's immoral. Therefore, a Christian must believe that the prohibition spelled out in Leviticus 17:12 is not rooted in the natural moral law, but is a precept subject to change.

That the precept did change is proven by the New Testament's affirmation that the dietary laws of the old law are no longer binding for Christians. Consider, for example, what Jesus says in Mark 7:15: "There is nothing outside a man which by going into him can defile him; but the things which come out of a man are what defile him." Mark tells us that by saying this, Jesus "declared all foods clean."

This is made even clearer in God's revelation to Peter in Acts 10:9–16. We're told that Peter "fell into a trance" and saw a "great sheet" in which were "all kinds of animals and reptiles and birds of the air." Peter heard a voice command him to "kill and eat." But Peter refused, saying, "No, Lord; for I have never eaten anything that is common or unclean." The voice responded, "What God has cleansed, you must not call common." Luke tells us that this happened three times.

We find this new revelation in Paul's writings as well. For example, he instructs the Colossians,

> Having canceled the bond which stood against us with its legal demands; this [Jesus] set aside, nailing it to the cross. . . . Therefore let no one pass judgment on you in questions of food and drink or with regard to a festival or a new moon or a Sabbath. These are only a shadow of what is to come; but the substance belongs to Christ (2:14–17).

Similarly, Paul writes to the Corinthians: "Food will not commend us to God. We are no worse off if we do not eat, and no better off if we do" (1 Cor. 8:8).

If the dietary laws of the Old Law are no longer binding for Christians, and the prohibition of consuming blood was a part of those dietary laws, it follows that the prohibition of consuming blood is no longer binding for Christians. This challenge from Leviticus 17:10, therefore, doesn't undermine the argument that Jesus meant for us to literally eat his flesh and drink his blood.

> The Council of Jerusalem's decree for the Gentiles to abstain from blood was a temporary peacekeeping measure to stop newly converted Gentiles from offending Jewish sensibilities. That it was disciplinary in nature, and thus temporary and subject to change, is confirmed by God's revelation to Peter in Acts 10:9–16 and Paul's teaching in 1 Corinthians 8:8.

"Jesus meant his words figuratively, as he did in John 10:9, when he spoke of himself as a 'door,' and in John 15:5, when he spoke of himself as 'the vine.'"

If Catholics interpret Jesus' command to eat his flesh and drink his blood literally in John 6, then they have to take him literally in other passages when he says he's a door (John 10:9) and a vine (John 15:5). As Geisler and MacKenzie write, Jesus "said, 'I am the door' . . . and 'I am the vine' . . . and Roman Catholic scholars do not take these statements literally, even though they come from the same book that records 'This is my body'!"[105]

Todd Baker bolsters this argument by highlighting the fact that Jesus' words in John 6 are part of a series of "I Am" statements in John's Gospel.[106] In John 10:9, Jesus says, "I am the door." He says, "I am the vine" in John 15:5. In John 6:48, the beginning of Jesus' Bread of Life Discourse, he says, "I am the bread of life."

Baker argues that this "I Am" statement clues us in to how we're to understand his words concerning the bread he will give, which he identifies as his "flesh," and that we must eat it. Like in John 10:9 and John 15:5, we should interpret him figuratively.

ANSWERING THE COMEBACK

This comeback fails because the door and vine passages are disanalogous to the bread of life passage. The people in the audience in the door and vine passages don't interpret Jesus literally, as they do in John 6. No one listening to the door and vine teachings said, "How can this man be a door made out of wood?" or "How can this man claim to be a plant?" Jesus' audience recognized he was speaking metaphorically. So no further inquiry is needed.

This stands in stark contrast to the audience in John 6. Both the Jews and Jesus' disciples understand Jesus to be speaking literally. This gives us reason to think something different is going on in John 6 from what's happening in the door and vine passages. And the contextual evidence confirms this initial hunch.

As we mentioned above, Jesus affirms the literal thoughts of both the Jews and his disciples. He even lets the latter walk away in verse 66, and then turns to the apostles and says, "Do you also wish to go away?" This stands out as remarkably different from how Jesus handles teachings with hidden meanings elsewhere. For example, in Mark 4:33–34, we're told, "With many such parables he spoke the word to them, as they were able to hear it; he did not speak to them without a parable, but privately to his own disciples he explained everything."

Given the presence of the literal thoughts among Jesus' audience in John 6 compared to the lack of such thoughts in the door and vine passages, and Jesus' engagement with those literal thoughts by way of affirming them, we can conclude that the door and vine passages are meant to be read differently from how we should read Jesus' teaching about eating his flesh and drinking his blood.

"The context reveals that 'eat' and 'drink' mean belief."

The next category of comebacks doesn't merely attempt to undermine the literal interpretation of Jesus' words to eat his flesh and drink his blood. Rather, these counter-arguments attempt to give an actual explanation as to what the language refers to: belief in Jesus.

The first comeback appeals to the context that precedes Jesus' command to eat his flesh and drink his blood. Consider that Jesus says in verse 35, "I am the bread of life; he who comes to me shall not hunger, and he who believes in me shall never thirst.'" Robert Zins identifies this verse as "the controlling verse of John 6."[107]

In explaining this verse, Protestant apologist Eric Svendsen notes, "There can be no doubt that what Jesus meant by 'eating' and 'drinking' him was *to come* to him and *to believe* in him."[108] For Svendsen, since Jesus speaks of hunger and thirst symbolically here, he must be speaking symbolically of eating his flesh and drinking his blood later in verse 54. James White concurs:

"Coming" and "believing" will become "eating" and "drinking" in verse 54 . . . the definitions assigned to these terms by the Lord (being spiritual and symbolic, not literal and earthly) must be carried through the rest of the text.[109]

Both White and Svendsen further cite verse 47, where Jesus says, "Truly, truly, I say to you, he who believes has eternal life," and infer from this that eating equals believing.[110] For example, when White gets to the "eating" of the bread of life mentioned in verse 54, he comments,

The "eating" here is paralleled with the "believing" of verse 47—*any attempt to make this a physical action misses the entire point the Lord is making.* He who believes has eternal life—he who eats of the true bread from heaven will never die. Eating = believing. This is clearly the *literal* meaning of the text.[111]

ANSWERING THE COMEBACK

It's true that in verses 27–48, Jesus speaks about the necessity to believe in him. But in verse 51, Jesus introduces his flesh and identifies it as the bread from heaven that he will give for the life of the world. It's this detail that adds something new to the conversation.

Initially, the Jews murmured about Jesus saying he came down from heaven. But in verse 52, they quarrel *specifically* over Jesus identifying his flesh as the bread from heaven and saying whoever eats it will live forever, for they say, "How can this man give us his flesh to eat?" Belief in Jesus is not the issue here. It's eating his flesh. So, at least within the thinking of the Jews, there is something new added to the mix of Jesus' teaching about believing in him—something that causes them distress.

Is there something new that *Jesus* intends to add as well? There is! If Jesus intended his statement about eating his flesh to be understood as *mere* belief, and not something that a believer will do in order to have his spiritual hunger and thirst satiated, then he could have easily retracted his language about *eating* his flesh and gone back to the metaphorical language of coming to him and never hungering and believing in him and never thirsting, as he did in verse 35. This would have gone a long way in calming the Jews' fear that he was suggesting they *actually* eat his flesh.

But he doesn't do that. As we mentioned above, he develops even more emphatically what the Jews understood to be a direct command to eat his flesh by speaking of eating his flesh and drinking his blood six times in six verses. Moreover, as we said above, the language for eating in the Greek intensifies in those verses.

The same line of reasoning applies to his disciples. Remember, his disciples struggle just as much as the Jews. If Jesus intended his words "eat my flesh" and "drink my blood" to be taken metaphorically, as *only* to convey the idea that they must come to and believe in him, then Jesus could easily go back to the metaphorical language in verse 35. This would easily quell the disciples' fear since they already believe in Jesus. They are his *disciples*!

But Jesus doesn't do that. In fact, he underscores the difficulty by saying how it will be even more difficult to believe his ascension, and then teaches his disciples that an earthly perspective will not suffice to believe his words. The difficulty of the teaching to eat his flesh and drink his blood explains why Jesus spends some time priming his disciples with a teaching about coming to him and believing in him in verse 35. Belief in Christ *must* precede belief in the Eucharist, since one can believe the Eucharist only on account of belief in Christ.

There are a few other things to consider in response. Note how Jesus says, "The bread which I *shall* give [Greek, *dōsō*, future tense of *didōmi*]." He doesn't say, "The bread which I give now in the present." The future tense doesn't jibe with taking Jesus' words to mean belief. Why would his disciples need to wait to believe in him in the future? Shouldn't they believe in Jesus at that moment? Furthermore, Jesus identifies the bread that he will give as his flesh. He's clearly referring to the giving of his flesh on the cross and at the institution of the Eucharist at the Last Supper. If the one is a literal giving, so is the other.

"The words *eat* and *drink* are used in the Bible as metaphors to refer to our relationship with God."

Like the comeback above, this counter-argument asserts that Jesus meant belief when he spoke of eating his flesh and drinking his blood. But the path to this conclusion is different.

It argues that the language of "eating" and "drinking" were symbols frequently used in the Old Testament to signify, in the words of Todd Baker, "personally experiencing and appropriating the words and blessings Yahweh has lavishly and freely given to his prophets and people."[112] Baker, as well as other Protestant apologists,[113] appeals to several passages in the Old Testament, one of which is Jeremiah 15:16: "Your words were found, and I ate them, and your words became to me a joy and the delight of my heart."[114]

Baker infers from this biblical use of the Hebrew idioms of eating and drinking that Jesus must be "following his Old Testament predecessors" and making "the same practical use of these Hebrew eating idioms throughout John chapter six to convey the indispensable truth that one must fully receive his life-giving death . . . to receive eternal life."[115]

ANSWERING THE COMEBACK

The reason why this inference is false is that the appeal to Old Testament passages shows only that "eating" and "drinking" *could* be used as metaphors in John 6:53–58. It does not prove that *Jesus* uses these images in a metaphorical way. Other contextual evidence would be required for such a conclusion. And given what we've said above, the contextual evidence favors a literal interpretation.

CHAPTER 10

This Is My Body
Matthew 26:26–28

When it comes to defending the Real Presence of Christ in the Eucharist, a believer in the Real Presence naturally turns to Jesus' words at the Last Supper:

> Now as they were eating, Jesus took bread, and blessed, and broke it, and gave it to the disciples and said, "Take, eat; this is my body." And he took a cup, and when he had given thanks he gave it to them, saying, "Drink of it, all of you; for this is my blood of the covenant, which is poured out for many for the forgiveness of sins (Matt. 26:26–28).

The argument based on this passage is quite simple. If Jesus meant for the bread and the wine to merely represent his body and blood, he would have said so—he would have said, "this *represents* my body . . . this *represents* my blood." Since Jesus doesn't use the word *represents,* but rather says, "this *is* my body . . . this *is* my blood," we can conclude that Jesus meant the perceived bread and wine to *be* his body and blood.

There are several counter-arguments that Protestants make to the argument for the Real Presence from Jesus' words at the Last Supper. Unlike comebacks in previous chapters, each of these is distinct.

"Jesus identifies the contents of the chalice as the 'fruit of the vine' after the words of consecration."

James White argues that Jesus couldn't have meant for the substance in the chalice to be Jesus' real blood because *after* Jesus pronounces what Catholics call "the words of consecration" ("this is my body . . . this is my blood"), Jesus says, "I tell you I shall not drink again of *this fruit of the vine* until that day when I drink it new with you in my Father's kingdom" (Matt. 26:29; Mark 14:25).

White drives home his point, writing, "One can picture the Lord Jesus, still holding the cup, and referring to it as he speaks. But what does he say? Does he say it is literally blood? No, he says it is the fruit of the vine."[116] For White, this provides a "basis for the symbolic interpretation of the words of the Lord."

ANSWERING THE COMEBACK

The first thing to note is that this objection fails to consider that Luke puts the disputed words *before* the consecration:

> And he took a cup, and when he had given thanks he said, "Take this, and divide it among yourselves; for I tell you that from now on I shall not drink of the fruit of the vine until the kingdom of God comes. . . . And likewise the cup *after supper*, saying, "This cup which is poured out for you is the New Covenant in my blood" (22:17–18, 20).

Given the ambiguity as to where the words *actually* were placed, White can't appeal to these words to show that the

127

contents of the chalice post-consecration were merely wine since it just as well could have referred to the contents of the chalice *before* the words of consecration.

An appeal to chronological ambiguity is not our only response, however. Notice that it's "*a* cup" that contains "the fruit of the vine," which is a distinct cup from "the cup *after* supper" that Jesus says contains his blood. So, at least according to Luke, the cup that Jesus says contains the "fruit of the vine" is *not* the cup of consecration. You can't appeal to "the fruit of the vine" saying of Jesus to undermine belief in the Real Presence when the cup that contains the "fruit of the vine" might not even be the cup that is believed to contain Jesus' blood.

We can go even further in our response: Luke's version was probably the more accurate one.

There is evidence that Luke may have placed the "fruit of the vine" phrase before the words of consecration to clarify the sequence in Mark's and Matthew's account.

It was known in the first century that Mark did not write things in chronological order. A second-century Christian bishop named Papias records John the presbyter, an eyewitness of Jesus' ministry, as saying, "Mark, having become an interpreter of Peter, wrote down accurately, *though not in order*, whatsoever he remembered of the things said or done by Christ."[117]

Luke tells us explicitly in the prologue to his Gospel that he set out "to write an *orderly* account" of the things accomplished among them, even though many before him, such as Mark, had already compiled such a narrative (Luke 1:1–3).

Therefore, it's reasonable to conclude that Luke diverts from Mark's order because he is clarifying Mark's placement of Jesus' statement. If so, the Protestant challenge loses its force. But even if not, in Luke the order is reversed, weakening any argument based strictly on the order in Mark and Matthew.

For our second response, we can concede for argument's sake that Jesus uses the "fruit of the vine" phrase after he says, "This is my blood." Even on this supposition, it wouldn't necessarily follow that he intended to attest that the substance was merely wine. That's because biblical authors often described things according to their appearance. Scholars call this *phenomenological language.*

We use it even today. For example, the weatherman says the sun will "rise" at six A.M. and "set" at seven P.M. Should we conclude that the weatherman is an advocate of geocentrism, who believes that the sun moves up and down over the Earth? Of course not! He's simply describing something according to the way we see it.

In the Bible, angels and even God are described according to how they are revealed to the senses. The book of Genesis describes the Lord and his angels as men since that is the form they took when they conversed with Abraham (Gen. 18:2; cf. 18:10, 19:1). Tobit does the same thing with reference to an angel in Tobit 5:2–4.

These authors were not trying to say God and angels are actually men. They simply described phenomena in a common way as they were observed according to the senses.

Similarly, the Bible often refers to death as "sleep." Take Job 3:11–13, for example: "Why did I not die at birth, come forth from the womb and expire? . . . For then I should have lain down and been quiet; I should have slept; then I should have been at rest." Or John 11:11, where Jesus says, "Our friend Lazarus has fallen asleep, but I go to awake him out of sleep." Or Paul in 1 Thessalonians 4:15, contrasting those "who are alive, [and] who are left until the coming of the Lord" with those "who have fallen asleep."

A similar line of exegesis can be applied to Mark's and Matthew's record of Jesus' words at the Last Supper. It's perfectly reasonable for Jesus to employ the phenomenological language of "wine" even when referring to his precious blood, since that is how it appears to the senses. The mere reference to "the fruit of the vine," therefore, doesn't prove that the substance in the chalice is wine.

A third response is that it's common for a biblical author to describe something according to its prior state. For example, Eve is called Adam's bone (Gen. 2:23), and Aaron's rod is said to have devoured the "rods" of the magicians even though they had become serpents (Exod. 7:12). This idiom of describing something according to its prior state could explain why Jesus describes his blood as wine. He could simply be referring to it according to what it once was. Paul does the same thing when he refers to the Eucharist as "bread" (1 Cor. 11:26), even though we know he believed it to be participation in the literal body of Christ (10:16).

Finally, we can acknowledge there is a mystery. But that mystery doesn't disprove the Real Presence. Jesus doesn't point to the chalice and say, "The substance in here is *not* my blood." The gist of his statement seems to be about not identifying the contents of the chalice, but to prophesy that he would not drink of the "fruit of the vine" until the coming of the kingdom.

What this means is something of a mystery—especially since his death was less than a day away.

Was he referring to the heavenly banquet (Isa. 25:6–8; Rev. 19:9)? It's possible, given that Jesus describes heaven as a banquet: "I tell you, many will come from east and west and sit at table with Abraham, Isaac, and Jacob in the kingdom of heaven" (Matt. 8:11).

Was he referring to the sour wine he would partake of while hanging on the cross (John 19:30)? That's also possible, since it's the first time he drinks wine since his cryptic statement in the upper room.

Or it could refer to what St. John Chrysostom (c. 347–407) thought it referred to—Jesus' drinking wine with his disciples after his Resurrection. For Chrysostom, Jesus' talk about the kingdom refers to his resurrection. And Jesus' talk about drinking wine "new" refers to drinking wine "after a new manner . . . no longer having a passible body, or needing food."[118] In any case, despite the mystery, the words "fruit of the vine" don't disprove the Real Presence.

"The 'blood of the covenant' can't be of a living person."

Notice that when Jesus speaks of the contents of the chalice, he says, "this is my *blood of the covenant*." This is a direct allusion to the "blood of the covenant" that Moses sprinkled on the people to ratify the Mosaic covenant on Mount Sinai (Exod. 24:8).

James White directs our attention to the fact that "the blood of the covenant was blood from a sacrificial victim, *not a living person*."[119] Had the blood not been shed, it wouldn't have been the blood of the covenant.

In light of this, White argues that because Christ's blood had not been shed yet on Calvary when he spoke of the substance in the cup as his "blood of the covenant," the contents of the cup couldn't have been the blood of the New Covenant, for the blood of the New Covenant is Christ's blood shed on the cross. Given this premise, White concludes that the contents of the cup "have to be symbols," symbols of Jesus' blood that would be shed the next day.

ANSWERING THE COMEBACK

One response is that the issue of whether real blood is present is different from the issue of whether that blood presently has the *status* of being "blood of the covenant." Consider the victims on Sinai, for example. Before they were slain, their blood didn't have the status of being the "blood of the covenant." But that doesn't mean the blood present in the victims wasn't real blood.

Christ's blood at the Last Supper could still be present in the chalice even if it didn't yet have the status of being the "blood of the covenant," since he hadn't been slain yet. And that's all the doctrine of transubstantiation requires: the belief that Christ's real and substantial blood was made present in the cup at the Last Supper. Whether his real blood is technically the "blood of the covenant" at that moment doesn't bear on whether the wine became Jesus' blood. We could suppose, for the sake of argument, Jesus was simply speaking about the substance in the cup as his real blood that *would soon become* "blood of the covenant," but it would still be real blood.

> The allusion to the ratifying ceremony for the Sinaitic covenant gives credence to a literal interpretation of Jesus' words at the Last Supper. If real blood was used to ratify the Old Covenant at its ratifying ceremony, and the Last Supper is the ratifying ceremony for the New Covenant, then why would our Lord use something less sacred than blood—mere wine—to ratify something more sacred than the Old Covenant, namely, the New Covenant?

Another way we can respond is to challenge the assumption that Christ's blood at the Last Supper cannot be described—even at this stage—as the "blood of the covenant." There are two ways that we can do this.

First, if it is true that Jesus' blood is truly present in the cup at the Last Supper, then his blood *is* the blood that will be used to solemnize the New Covenant on the cross. It thus can be described as "blood of the covenant," whether or not the covenant has been solemnized yet, because it *is* the blood of the covenant. The same would be true of the blood of the offerings Moses used for the original covenant the day before they were slain and their blood was used to solemnize it.

Second, the objection wrongly assumes that Christ's blood can't be the "blood of the covenant" *because* Christ's sacrifice hadn't been offered yet on the cross. Why should we believe that Christ's redemptive sacrifice is restricted to just the moment of his *death*? If we consider what the Bible teaches about sacrifices, there is good reason to think that Jesus' redemptive sacrifice was *not* restricted to his death.

For example, death was a key moment in Old Testament sacrifices, but they didn't begin at the moment of death. The sacrificial rituals consisted of many things that preceded death: bringing the animal into the sacred precincts (Exod. 29:42; Lev. 1:2–3), examining the animals for any blemish, placing hands on its head (Lev. 1:4; 4:15), the confession of sins by both the priest (Lev. 16:21) and the penitent (Lev. 5:5), etc. All of these things made up the one sacrifice.

Moreover, the New Testament teaches us that there's such a thing as a *living* sacrifice. Paul tells the Romans, "Present your bodies as *a living sacrifice*, holy and acceptable to God, which is your spiritual worship" (Rom. 12:1). Elsewhere, he considers *the Gentiles* as his "offering" in his "priestly service of the gospel of God" (Rom. 15:16).

This wide range of what's possible for sacrifices in God's plan of salvation shows that Christ's redemptive sacrifice may not have been restricted to his death but may have begun while he was alive.

So did it?

The *Catechism of the Catholic Church* answers in the affirmative: "Redemption comes to us *above all* through the blood of his cross, but this mystery is at work throughout Christ's *entire life*" (517; emphasis added). Even if an individual doesn't accept such an expansive understanding of Christ's sacrifice, Protestant theologians also identify Jesus' sacrifice with his Passion as a whole.

On this we can agree: his redemptive sacrifice may reasonably include the sufferings that immediately led up to it and were intentionally directed toward the Crucifixion. The obvious example is his agony in the Garden, where he requests three times that the Father remove the cup of suffering from him (Matt. 26:39–46).

Was Jesus already suffering at the time of the Last Supper (the relevant time frame for our purposes)?

Consider that Jesus would have been in distress over Judas' betrayal, which he predicts at the Last Supper (Matt. 26:24–25; Mark 14:18–21; Luke 22:21–23; John 13:21–30). In John's account, we even get a hint at Jesus' inner suffering when he tells Judas, "What you are going to do, do quickly" (John 13:27). This suggests that Jesus isn't looking forward to what is to come and—like most of us—wants to complete his Passion as quickly as possible without prolonging it.

Now, because this suffering at the Last Supper is directed to the cross we can reasonably say it's a part of his redemptive sacrifice. And since Christ's redemptive sacrifice is the New Covenant institution sacrifice, we can conclude that the New Covenant redemptive sacrifice has already begun at the Last Supper.

Thus, at the time of the Last Supper Christ's blood already had the status of "blood of the covenant": the real and substantial blood of the New Covenant sacrificial victim present in the cup and the New Covenant redemptive sacrifice. Yes, the sacrifice will culminate in his death the next day. But his blood is still blood of the New Covenant sacrifice, and thus reasonably can have the status of "blood of the covenant."

"In 1 Corinthians 10:4, Paul says Christ is the rock in the wilderness, yet we don't take that literally."

This sort of counter was often made by older Protestant authors, and it's been reproduced online on modern websites for biblical commentary.[120]

Basically, it goes like this: "Wait a minute. If we take the bread and wine to be really Jesus' body and blood because he says, 'This *is* my body . . . This *is* my blood,' then we're gonna have to say Paul meant the rock that followed the Israelites in the wilderness to be really Jesus, since he says, 'the rock *was* Christ' (1 Cor. 10:4). But most Christians don't believe that the rock *really* was Jesus, as believers in the Real Presence believe that the consecrated host really is Jesus' body. Therefore, we shouldn't take Jesus to mean that the bread and wine really became his body and blood because he says, 'This *is* my body . . . This *is* my blood.'"

ANSWERING THE COMEBACK

First, the appeal to 1 Corinthians 10:4 doesn't show that Jesus' use of "is" *must* be taken figuratively. It shows only that the verb "is" *can* be taken figuratively. So this argument gets only as far as saying a figurative interpretation, like in 1 Corinthians 10:4, is possible.

But this is a moot point, because a believer in the Real Presence could agree that Jesus' words "this is my body . . . this is my blood" *taken by themselves*, can be interpreted literally or figuratively. There's nothing in the words themselves that determines one interpretation over the other. So believers in the Real Presence need not have any qualms about saying that these words *could* be taken figuratively when they're considered in isolation from other evidence.

Second, the objection demands that a Catholic interpret Jesus' use of the verb *to be* at the Last Supper in the same way it's used in 1 Corinthians 10:4—figuratively, the reason being that it's supposedly obvious that bread and wine can't be Jesus' body and blood. However, such a demand makes sense only on the supposition that Jesus is not performing a miracle.

For example, I might hold up a picture of my father and say, "This is my father," and you know that the picture is not literally my father, but a figure of him. But—and here's the key—your conclusion would be based on the assumption, and a true one at that, that I'm not performing the miracle of making my father substantially present under the form of ink and paper.

Similarly, to interpret Jesus' use of "is" at the Last Supper figuratively would be natural *if* we already knew he's not performing a miracle. But if there is evidence that what Jesus is doing at the Last Supper is miraculous, then a literal interpretation becomes a viable option, and even a more probable one.

And there is an abundance of such evidence. Due to the limited space here, however, we're going to consider only some of it.

When Jesus first makes the promise to give his flesh to eat in John 6:49–50, he does so against the backdrop of the manna of old: "Your fathers ate the manna in the wilderness, and they died. This is the bread which comes down from heaven, that a man may eat of it and not die . . . the bread which I shall give for the life of the world is my flesh."

This bread that God gave in the wilderness was not ordinary bread. It was *miraculous* bread:

- It appeared every day when the morning "dew" would burn off (Exod. 16:13).

- It never lasted more than a day, except on the Sabbath. When the Israelites didn't obey the instruction to leave none until the next day, it "bred worms and became foul" (Exod. 16:19–20).

- But when the Israelites held it over in accordance with the Lord's command—that is, to assure that they did no work on the Sabbath—it did not breed worms and become foul (Exod. 16:22–26).

- It appeared every day for forty years, and stopped only upon the Israelites entering the promised land (Exod. 16:35; Josh. 5:10–12).

- A jar with an omer's worth was kept in the Israelites' sanctuary "throughout the generations" (Exod. 16:31–34).

As Bible scholar Brant Pitre argues in his book *Jesus and the Jewish Roots of the Eucharist*, to say the Eucharist at the Last Supper, the new manna, is *merely* a symbol, we'd have to conclude that the old manna in the wilderness was superior to the new, since miraculous bread is clearly greater than ordinary bread.[121] But that's a no-go in biblical theology.

The New Testament fulfillment is always greater than the Old Testament type.

That the Eucharist is supernatural is further confirmed by Jesus' teaching that faith is required to accept his command to eat his flesh and drink his blood. Jesus prefaces his revelation that his flesh is the bread of life by saying, "No one can come to me unless the Father who sent me draws him." Then, after giving his discourse about eating his flesh and drinking his blood, he says, "There are some of you that do not believe. . . . This is why I told you that no one can come to me unless it is granted him by my Father." If Jesus begins and concludes his remarks about eating his flesh and drinking his blood with faith, a gift that only the Father can give, then Jesus is revealing that faith is required to accept his teaching.

There's something else Jesus says that reveals the requirement of faith—something we looked at in our last chapter: "It is the spirit that gives life, the flesh is of no avail; the words that I have spoken to you are spirit and life."

Recall, "the flesh" is a New Testament phrase often used to describe human nature apart from God's grace (Mark 14:38, Rom. 8:1–14, 1 Cor. 2:14–3:1). What Jesus means is that without God's grace, and in particular the grace of faith, acceptance of Jesus' command to eat his flesh and drink his blood is impossible. If his disciples are to believe his teaching, they must avail themselves of that grace.

Jesus' statement about his words being "spirit and life" means that his teaching is *of* the Spirit and therefore can be accepted only *by* the power of the Spirit. This makes sense of why Jesus' command to eat his flesh and drink his blood is bookended by his teachings about faith (v. 44, v. 65).

Since what Jesus says in John 6 is a promise of what will be fulfilled at the Last Supper, and he teaches that faith is required to accept what he says, it follows that faith would also be required when confronted with the words at the Last Supper: "This is my body . . . this is my blood."

Now, what need would there be for faith if the bread and wine at the Last Supper were intended by Jesus to merely represent or signify his body and blood? Faith would not be needed to believe that bread and wine serve as a symbol of Jesus' body and blood any more than we would need God-given faith to believe that a photograph is a picture of my father. Faith isn't required for one thing to be a symbol of another—but faith would be needed to believe that Jesus changed bread and wine into his body and blood, which, of course, would be miraculous.

Since Jesus teaches that faith is required to accept what he says about the bread and wine being his body and blood, it follows that there is a supernatural dimension to the Eucharist. And if the Eucharist is supernatural, then we have good reason not to automatically take Jesus' words to be metaphorical. The supernatural nature of the Eucharist makes the literal interpretation a plausible option.

St. Irenaeus, a bishop in the second century, believed that divine power was needed for Jesus to say what he did at the Last Supper: "If the Lord were from other than the Father, how could he rightly take bread, which is of the same creation as our own, and confess it to be his body and affirm that the mixture in the cup is his blood?"[122] Why would Jesus need divine power simply to state that bread and wine were mere symbols of his body and blood?

A Protestant may object here, "All the above arguments assume that Jesus' teaching in John 6 is connected to Jesus' words at the Last Supper. But that's an assumption that we don't have to accept. In fact, two different Greek words are used: *sarx* for flesh in John 6 and *sōma* or "body" at the Last Supper."[123]

One problem with this argument is that *sarx* and *sōma* are used interchangeably in the New Testament. Consider Paul's teaching in 1 Corinthians 6:16, for example:

> Do you not know that he who joins himself to a prostitute becomes one body [Greek, *sōma*] with her? For, as it is written, "The two shall become one [flesh] [Greek, *sarka*—dictionary form *sarx*]."

Notice that Paul uses *sarx* for the Bible's talk of union of flesh and identifies it with the one body (*sōma*) that results from a man joining himself to a prostitute.

Another example is 2 Corinthians 4:10–11. Paul writes:

> Always carrying in the body [Greek, *sōmati*] the death of Jesus, so that the life of Jesus may also be manifested in our bodies [Greek, *sōmati*]. For while we live we are always being given up to death for Jesus' sake, so that the life of Jesus may be manifested in our mortal flesh [Greek, *sarki*]. So death is at work in us, but life in you.

If we were to follow the logic of the objection, we'd conclude that Paul here is saying the life of Jesus is manifested in two different things. But clearly, that's not the case. Whether Paul speaks of bodies (*sōma*) or flesh (*sarx*), he's referring to the same thing—"the earthen vessel." Paul is teaching the Corinthians how Christians view their physical sufferings for the Faith.

THIS IS MY BODY

Other examples where Paul uses *sarx* and *sōma* inter-changeably are Romans 7:24–25 and 8:13; Ephesians 5:28–30; and Colossians 2:23.

This makes sense because bodies are made of flesh. So, if there is no indication that *body* is being used in some sense as *not* to include flesh, we're justified in reading *body* as entail-ing *flesh*. Since Jesus doesn't say anything at the Last Sup-per to preclude our understanding of *body* as *flesh*, we can take *body* to mean *flesh*, and thereby affirm the connection between John 6 and the Last Supper.

Second, the image of drinking Jesus' *blood* is used in *both* narratives. And both narratives are the *only* places in the New Testament where Jesus speaks of drinking his blood. The fewer times an image or cluster of words is used, espe-cially when it's found *prior to* its current use, the more likely it is that there is literary dependence.

Given that the Last Supper is the *only* place in the New Tes-tament where Jesus speaks of drinking his blood other than in John 6, and Jesus' command to drink his blood in John 6 occurs prior in Jesus' ministry to the command given at the Last Sup-per, we're justified in reading the words of institution at the Last Supper in light of what Jesus says in John 6. To say there's no connection between the words of institution at the Last Supper and Jesus' command to eat his flesh and drink his blood in John 6 would be akin to saying John doesn't have the creation story in mind when he writes in John 1:1, "In the beginning."

Moreover, in John 6, Jesus doesn't give us any indica-tion that he intends his audience to eat his flesh and drink his blood right then and there. Rather, he speaks as if it's something to be done at some later time, which fits with our interpretation that the Last Supper is that moment.

For example, he speaks in the future tense in John 6:51: "the bread which I *shall* give for the life of the world is my flesh." The other times when he gives instructions about eating his flesh and drinking his blood, it's hypothetical and general in nature:

- *"if* anyone eats this bread, he will live forever" (v. 51a)

- *"unless* you eat the flesh of the Son of Man and drink his blood" (v. 53)

- *"he who* eats my flesh and drinks my blood abides in me" (v. 56)

- *"he who* eats me will live because of me" (v. 57)

- *"he who* eats this bread [his flesh] will live forever" (v. 58)

Contrast this with the Last Supper, where Jesus says, "Take, eat; this is my body" (Matt. 26:26). Jesus *promised* in John 6 to give the disciples his flesh and blood to eat and drink, but at the Last Supper, he commands it to be done. Given what we said above about these being the only two instances where Jesus speaks of drinking his blood, we're justified in saying the promise in John 6 is fulfilled at the Last Supper.

Third, biblical scholars recognize that it's John's intent to supplement with his Gospel what's found in the synoptics by adding depth. For example, Mark and Matthew record Jesus' instruction concerning baptism. Matthew's record reads: "Go therefore and make disciples of all nations, baptizing them in the name of the Father and of the Son and of the Holy Spirit" (Matt. 28:19). Mark's report reads: "He who believes and is baptized will be saved" (Mark 16:16).

John doesn't record the great commission, which includes the instruction for the apostles to baptize, but he does add depth to our understanding of what baptism is: the rebirth by water and spirit (John 3:3–5). Where the others simply give the command *that* the apostles baptize, John gives the theology behind what they are to do.

As he did for the sacrament of baptism, John adds depth to our understanding of the sacrament of the Eucharist. He's revealing to us that the Eucharist at the Last Supper is the new bread from heaven, and thus the new manna. He's teaching us that the Eucharist not only forgives our sins, but gives us eternal life. He's providing us confirmation that Jesus *did* intend for us to take his words at the Last Supper literally—hence his record of Jesus' use of *flesh*, which underscores the literalness of the language Jesus used. Therefore, John intends to inform his readers that just as Jesus' instruction to eat his flesh and drink his blood in John 6 was literal, so too are his words at the Last Supper.

Given the supernatural nature of the Eucharist, there's no need to give up the literal interpretation of Jesus' use of the verb *is* in favor of a figurative interpretation as we see in 1 Corinthians 10:4. The two cases are disanalogous, and thus cannot be read in light of each other. Believers in the Real Presence, therefore, don't have to settle for the claim that Jesus became a rock in the wilderness in order to keep our literal interpretation of the words of institution: "this is my body . . . this is my blood."

"In John 16:25, Jesus confirms that his words at the Last Supper were figurative."

The comebacks so far have appealed to evidence from which a Protestant *infers* that Jesus was not speaking literally when he said, "This is my body . . . this is my blood." Todd Baker, however, makes an argument that Jesus, in John 16:25, explicitly tells his disciples that his words are to be understood figuratively.

Indeed, right after the Last Supper was celebrated, Jesus told the disciples that his teachings and the words he spoke to them up to that point in time were given in figurative language. "These things I have spoken to you in figurative language" (John 16:25).[124]

Baker argues that since Jesus says this after the Passover meal, which included the words of institution, we must conclude that "the words Jesus spoke about the bread and wine being his body and blood were figurative expressions for the New Covenant and of the Messiah's imminent death on the cross for the salvation of man."[125]

ANSWERING THE COMEBACK

The fundamental problem with this argument is that it takes a verse in John (16:25) and applies it to the words of institution . . . but John's account of the Last Supper doesn't include the words of institution. This is exegetically implausible and violates the standard rules of hermeneutics. Even numerous Protestant scholars do not endorse this proposal in their commentaries on John. Instead, they identify "these things" as the things John has just reported Jesus speaking about.[126]

Furthermore, if we were to entertain this proposal, how would we know *which* statements from the other evangelists' accounts of the Last Supper should be taken figuratively? Unless we were to say that *everything* the other evangelists reported Jesus saying at the Last Supper was figurative (which is certainly untrue—see below), we would have no basis for applying a figurative interpretation to their accounts of the words of institution *unless John quoted those*, which he does not. Since John does not quote the words of institution, Baker's comeback is an arbitrary and exegetically fallacious move to try to apply John 16:25 to words that John does not even quote rather than understanding it in the obvious sense of applying to words John has quoted Jesus saying.

This comeback suffers from yet another problem: the assumption that just because Jesus used figurative language for one thing at the Last Supper, he must have intended to use figurative language for *everything* he said at the Last Supper.

It's true that Jesus said *some* things that included metaphors. For example, in John 15:5, he said, "I am the vine." In 16:21–22, Jesus says, "When a woman is in labor, she has pain, because her hour has come; but when she is delivered of the child, she no longer remembers the anguish, for joy that a child is born into the world. So you have sorrow now, but I will see you again, and your hearts will rejoice."

But surely not *everything* Jesus said at the Last Supper was meant to be taken figuratively. Presumably, a Protestant wouldn't want to say Jesus' comment about his disciples being persecuted as he was persecuted was figurative: "If they persecuted me, they will persecute you" (John 15:20). Nor would he think Jesus speaks figuratively when he says, "they will put you out of the synagogues; indeed, the hour is coming when whoever kills you will think he is offering service to God" (16:2). Since Jesus spoke both figuratively and literally, more work would have to be done to discern whether Jesus' words about eating his flesh and drinking his blood fall into the figurative category that he spoke of in 16:25.

Finally, this comeback is problematic because it fails to consider the immediate context in which we find two plausible referents for Jesus' words. Consider that just four verses earlier, Jesus uses the metaphor of a woman in labor, which we quoted above. With this immediate referent, there's no need to suggest that Jesus is referring to the words of institution that he said earlier in the evening.

Another possible referent, which even Protestant scholars recognize,[127] is Jesus' various statements about the Father. Notice that Jesus contrasts the things of which he spoke in "figures" with speaking "plainly of the Father" (John 16:25). This suggests that what he spoke in figures had to do with what he said about the Father.

Within the immediate context, there are several things he says of the Father that are a bit cryptic:

- "he who hates me hates my Father also" (15:23).

- "the Spirit of truth, who proceeds from the Father" (15:26).

- "now I am going to him who sent me" (16:5).

- "because I go to the Father, and you will see me no more" (16:10).

- "all that the Father has is mine; therefore I said that he will take what is mine and declare it to you" (16:15).

John even explicitly records that the apostles didn't understand what Jesus meant when he spoke of going to the Father (v. 18).

So a believer in the Real Presence doesn't have to conclude that Jesus was speaking figuratively when he said, "This is my body . . . this is my blood."

"The apostles were already thinking symbolically in light of the symbolism of Passover."

James White argues against a literal interpretation of Jesus' words based on how he thinks the apostles interpreted them, since, as White says, "the words of Christ must be that which *the disciples themselves would have understood at the time*." For White, the apostles surely would have been thinking symbolically because they had just celebrated the Passover, which "itself [is] incredibly rich in symbolism." Since they were already thinking symbolically, White concludes, "clearly, then Christ is using the wine as a symbol of the blood of the New Covenant and the bread as a symbol of his broken body."[128]

ANSWERING THE COMEBACK

Our first target here is the premise that "the words of Christ must be that which the disciples themselves would have understood at the time." But why must what the apostles think determine what *Jesus* meant? Surely, we wouldn't apply this principle elsewhere in Jesus' ministry.

Consider, for example, that when Jesus spoke of his "food to eat" in John 4:32, the apostles thought he was talking about real food. If we were to follow the logic of the Protestant argument, we'd have to say Jesus was speaking of real food, since that's what the apostles thought he was talking about. But clearly that's not the case, since Jesus says, "My food is to do the will of him who sent me, and to accomplish his work."

Similarly, in Matthew 16:6, Jesus warns, "beware of the leaven of the Pharisees and Sadducees," which causes the apostles to think he is commanding them not to eat the bread from the local Pharisaic and Sadducean sandwich shop. Must we say that's what Jesus meant, since that's what the apostles understood *at that time*? The answer is no, because John tells us that Jesus was referring to the *teaching* of the Pharisees and Sadducees (v. 12).

There's more: the apostles could have *later* embraced the realistic understanding of Jesus' words. We know, for example, that the apostles didn't immediately grasp the full significance of Jesus' quote from Zechariah 9:9 about the messianic king coming and sitting on a donkey's colt (John 12:14). Only later, when "Jesus was glorified" (v. 16b), did they fully understand it.

Since the apostles at times only later came to grasp the full significance of things Jesus said, it's possible the apostles only later came to grasp the literal meaning of Jesus' words at the Last Supper, assuming for argument's sake that they didn't understand his words literally at that time.

But it's possible, even likely, that the apostles *did* understand Jesus literally. By revealing the Eucharist to be the new manna (see the previous chapter), and by affirming, instead of clarifying, the literal thoughts of his audience concerning the Eucharist, Jesus creates a supernatural, miraculous context in which he tells the apostles to eat his body and drink his blood. Add to this the fact that the apostles came from a pro-miracle culture, they attributed great miraculous powers to Jesus, and they had even received such powers from him, it's likely that the apostles *did* take Jesus literally even during the Last Supper.

CHAPTER 11

If You Forgive the Sins of Any
John 20:23

When it comes to providing biblical evidence for the sacrament of confession, no Bible passage seems to be clearer than John 20:23: "If you forgive the sins of any, they are forgiven; if you retain the sins of any, they are retained." The power to forgive and retain implies the confession of sins, since in order for the apostles to judge whether to forgive or retain, they would have to know which sins were committed and whether the penitent was sorry for them.

The Council of Trent gave its full backing of this passage as support for the sacrament:

> The Lord then especially instituted the sacrament of penance when, after being risen from the dead, he breathed upon his disciples, and said: *Receive ye the Holy Ghost, whose sins you shall forgive, they are forgiven them, and whose sins you shall retain, they are retained.* The consensus of all the Fathers has always acknowledged that by this action so sublime and words so clear the power of forgiving and retaining sins was given to the apostles and their lawful successors for reconciling the faithful who have fallen after baptism. . . . Therefore, this holy council, approving

and receiving that perfectly true meaning of the above words of the Lord, condemns the grotesque interpretations of those who, contrary to the institution of this sacrament, wrongly contort those words to refer to the power of preaching the word of God and of making known the gospel of Christ (Session 14, *The Most Holy Sacraments of Penance and Extreme Unction*, Chapter 1).

For a Catholic, therefore, the sacrament of confession is instituted by Christ.

Really, there's only one major objection that Protestants make to the Catholic argument from John 20:23: Jesus' instruction is a command for the apostles to *preach* the forgiveness of sins, and God is the one who will forgive or retain based on how the hearer of the gospel message responds. However, there are several ways Protestants try to justify this alternative interpretation, each of which requires a distinct response.

"Jesus means for the apostles to preach the forgiveness of sins, and the hearer's sins will be forgiven or retained by God based on how he responds."

The general counter-argument challenges the assumption that the command to "forgive and retain" refers to the *apostles* forgiving and retaining sins. For Protestants who give this counter, it's God who forgives or retains depending on how a person responds to the gospel message. If the hearer receives the gospel message, then his sins will be forgiven. If the hearer rejects the gospel message, on the other hand, his sins will be retained, or held bound.

Concerning the preaching aspect, Protestant apologist Robert Zins writes, "It is apparent that the commission to evangelize is tightly woven into the commission to proclaim forgiveness of sin through faith in Jesus Christ."[129] Ron Rhodes maps out the parallel between sins being forgiven or retained and a person accepting or rejecting the gospel:

> Only God can judicially forgive sins committed against him (Mark 2:7). All John 20:23 is saying is that when people respond positively to the gospel and accept it, we have the right to declare to them, "Your sins are forgiven," based on the promise of Jesus. Likewise, when people respond negatively to the gospel and reject it, we have the right to declare to them, "Your sins are not forgiven," based on the promise of Jesus. We are simply declaring or announcing heaven's verdict regarding what will happen if people respond one way or the other in regard to Christ.[130]

ANSWERING THE COMEBACK

There are several reasons why this alternative explanation is problematic. First, nowhere in the immediate context of John 20 does Jesus talk about the apostles going out to preach the gospel. It's just not there!

Second, the wording itself doesn't suggest an instruction to preach. The actions that Jesus' ministers are to perform are forgiving and retaining: "if you *forgive* . . . if you *retain*." Telling someone to forgive is not the same thing as telling someone to preach. When I tell my eight-year-old daughter to forgive her eleven-year-old brother for pushing her, I don't mean, "Tell him that what he did was wrong and that he needs to repent in order for God to forgive him."

To suggest that forgiving sins (and retaining sins) means the same as preaching the gospel is to force the text to be taken in an unnatural sense. And since there is no evidence in the context to suggest otherwise, we're justified in taking the language in its natural sense.

Third, if Jesus meant what the objection suggests (tell people their sins will be forgiven or retained *by God* depending on whether they accept or reject the gospel), then why does Jesus say the disciples are the ones that will be forgiving and retaining ("if *you* forgive . . . if *you* retain")? Of course, God is ultimately the one who forgives and retains sins. But the apostles are the ones Jesus highlights as performing the action.

Fourth, the command to forgive and retain is something new, unlike the instruction to *preach* the gospel. Consider that Jesus sent out the apostles to preach the gospel years before when he first called them. Mark records:

> And [Jesus] called to him the Twelve, and began to send them out two by two, and gave them authority over the unclean spirits. . . . So they went out and preached that men should repent (6:7,12).

According to Rhodes's and Zins's interpretation above, the apostles would have been "forgiving and retaining" sins (people having their sins forgiven or retained depending on their response to the call to repentance) way before Jesus ever commissioned the apostles to forgive and retain sins in John 20:23.

But that's unlikely because what Jesus commissions the apostles to do in John 20:22–23 is presented as something new. At no other time are we told that Jesus "breathed" on the apostles. Also, we're never told Jesus communicated the Holy Spirit to the apostles before this moment. Nor did Jesus ever use the words, "If you forgive the sins of any, they are forgiven; if you retain the sins of any, they are retained." Jesus *already* gave the apostles the role of preaching the forgiveness of sins. Here, Jesus is giving the apostles a role that they have not heretofore had: forgiving and retaining sins.

Finally, this objection fails to take into account the connection that Jesus makes between the mission that his Father sent him on and the mission he's sending the apostles on.

The Father didn't send Jesus merely to preach the forgiveness of sins. He sent Jesus to actually *forgive* them. For example, Jesus didn't tell the paralytic in Mark 2:5 about the forgiveness of sins; he told him, "Your sins are forgiven."

Jesus makes it clear that he is sending his ministers *on the same mission* as the Father sent him on: "As the Father has sent me, *even so* I send you" (John 20:21). And lest there be any ambiguity as to what that mission is, he tells them specifically that the mission involves forgiving and retaining sins.

Since Jesus' mission involved not merely preaching the forgiveness of sins, but the actual forgiving of sins, and since Jesus is unequivocal about his apostles doing the same thing that his Father sent him to do, we can conclude that Jesus doesn't intend that the apostles merely preach the forgiveness of sins, but that they actually forgive them.

This makes sense out of the command to forgive *or* retain. Like Jesus, the apostles are to judge whether to forgive or not to forgive. And since God doesn't ordinarily give his ministers the gift to read souls, this further implies that the penitent would need to confess his sins and express contrition.

"Luke clarifies what Jesus means by 'forgive and retain' in his parallel account in Luke 24:47."

Todd Baker argues that "the commission Jesus gave in John 20:23 is the same event recounted in Luke 24:46–48." Verse 47 is the key verse: "Then he opened their minds to understand the Scriptures, and said to them, 'Thus it is written . . . that repentance and forgiveness of sins should be *preached* in his name to all nations."

Since Baker thinks John and Luke describe the same event, he concludes that the instruction to forgive and retain sins in John 20:23 has the same meaning as the instruction in Luke 24:47: the disciples are to "go into the world and proclaim that the forgiveness of sins is offered in the name of Jesus Christ . . . whereby the forgiveness of God is offered through faith in Jesus Christ to those who repent and believe, but is withheld to those who do not believe."[131]

ANSWERING THE COMEBACK

It's true that Jesus' instruction in Luke's Gospel refers only to the *preaching* of the forgiveness of sins. But the objection assumes that the sequence of events in which this instruction is included (Luke 24:44–52) happened on Easter Sunday, and thus that it's the same as the instruction in John 20:23. A careful reading, however, indicates otherwise.

Several times in the verses preceding the sequence of events in question (Luke 24:44–52), Luke uses time cues to indicate that what he's recording took place on Easter Sunday: "On the first day of the week, at early dawn" (v. 1), "that very day" (v. 13), "that same hour" (v. 33).

But when Luke records the sequence of events that include the instruction to preach the forgiveness of sins, there are indications that he doesn't tie it to Easter Sunday. One could argue that earlier, in verses 41–42, Luke had already dropped chronological narration of the events that took place on Easter Sunday. Notice how he speaks about Jesus requesting from the disciples something to eat and them giving him "broiled fish." It's possible that Luke here is giving his version of the same tradition found in John 21:9–13, which John tells us is an event that occurred *after* Easter Sunday, sometime later when the disciples had returned to Galilee.

Moreover, the event described in Luke 24:39–40, where Jesus invites the apostles to handle him and he convinces them that he is not a ghost, may be Luke's presentation of the same tradition found in John 20:27, where Jesus allows himself to be handled and calls attention to his (wounded) hands and feet. Again, if this is the same tradition, John informs us that this occurred *after* Easter Sunday—exactly one week after.

It may be that for both events mentioned above John provides us a *chronological* placement, whereas Luke mixes them *topically* with other post-Resurrection material as evidence that Jesus has been physically raised. Topical arrangement is not uncommon for the biblical authors.

Now, someone may counter and say Luke *clearly* connects Easter Sunday with Jesus' appearance to the disciples and his invitation for them to handle him in verses 36–43, because Luke says Jesus appears *while* the disciples on the road to Emmaus are telling other disciples what happened, which for Luke occurred on Easter Sunday (see Luke 24:1, 13, 33).

Even if we grant for argument's sake that what Luke records in verses 36–43 occurred on Easter Sunday, Luke *does* seem to move on from this event and summarize a series of events that took place during the period of forty days that Jesus spent with his disciples prior to his ascension (Acts 1:3).

Notice that Luke connects Jesus' instruction to preach the forgiveness of sins with Jesus' instruction to preach his name "to all nations," and that they were to begin in Jerusalem (v. 47). He also includes the Father's promise to "send power from on high" (v. 49).

These are all items that Luke includes in his list of things that Jesus taught his disciples during the forty days before and on the day of his ascension (see Acts 1:1–10). Therefore, these instructions, including the instruction to preach the forgiveness of sins, likely were not given in the upper room on the night of Jesus' resurrection.

One could even read these instructions as given *on the day of* the Ascension, since it has to do with preaching to the nations (see Matt. 28:19–20), and Luke places them right before he records the Ascension.

"The Greek text reveals that the forgiveness and retainment of sins is something God has already done."

Protestants also try to justify their reading of John 20:23 by appealing to the Greek. Many argue that the Greek text reveals that the forgiveness and retainment of sins is something God has already done before the apostles declare it to be so.[132] Todd Baker's formulation of the argument is exemplary:

> The phrases Jesus spoke "are forgiven" and "are retained," are spoken in the perfect tense. The verse would then literally read: "If you forgive the sins of any, they are already forgiven them; if you retain the sins of any, they are already retained." Anyone familiar with Greek grammar here will know the perfect tense normally expresses a past action completed with ongoing results. Therefore, the forgiveness or the retainment of sins has already occurred prior to the disciples' ability to declare this to be so. The perfect tenses used in John 20:23 are in the passive voice and at once show it is God who is acting alone, either to forgive or retain the sins of the one being acted upon. Jesus is giving the authority for the disciple to affirm or deny this is the case, where God has already determined the results of either action.[133]

For Baker, the perfect tense of the Greek words translated "are forgiven" (*apheōntai*) and "are retained" (*kekratēntai*) implies an abiding state that began before the actions of "forgiving" and "retaining" are accomplished. This, Baker argues, implies that God is the one forgiving and retaining, not the apostles.

ANSWERING THE COMEBACK

We need to first point out that the question is not whether God is the one forgiving or retaining. The Catholic Church affirms that God forgives (and retains) in the sacrament of confession (CCC 1441). He just does so through the ministry of the apostles (1495). The real question at hand is *when* God does this.

The counter-argument is that the use of a perfect tense in the second part of a conditional statement—called the *apodosis* ("they are forgiven")—necessarily refers to an action that is prior to the first part of the conditional statement—called the *protasis* ("if you forgive the sins of any"). These are the grounds for interpreting the passage as meaning that the apostles merely declare what God has already done.

But the assumption here is false. Consider what John, the same author, says in 1 John 2:5: "Whoever keeps his word, in him truly love for God is perfected [Greek, *teteleiōtai*—perfect passive]."

This has the same structure as John 20:23:

	Protasis	Apodosis
John 20:23	"If you forgive the sins of any"	"they are forgiven [perfect passive]"
1 John 2:5	"Whoever keeps his word"	"in him truly love for God is perfected [perfect passive]"

In 1 John 2:5, John uses the perfect tense, *teteleiōtai*, in the apodosis, yet the perfection is accomplished not before

the keeping of Christ's word, but at the time of keeping Christ's word. Clearly, John's usage implies an action that occurs when the condition stated in the protasis is fulfilled.

The perfect tense in these passages is known as the *proleptic* or *futuristic perfect*, which "can be used to refer to a state resulting from an antecedent action that is future from the time of speaking."[134] The use occurs in the apodosis of a conditional clause and "depends on the time of the verb in the protasis."

Here are some other passages where the action of the perfect tense in the apodosis occurs not before the fulfillment of the protasis, but at the time thereof:

- James 2:10—"Whoever keeps the whole Law but fails in one point has become [Greek, *gegonen*—perfect active] guilty of all of it." The guilt is incurred at the time of failing in one point of the Law.

- Romans 7:2—"A married woman is bound by law to her husband as long as he lives; but if her husband dies she is discharged [Greek, *katērgētai*—perfect passive] from the law concerning the husband." The discharging from the law becomes real upon the woman's husband dying.

- Romans 13:8—"Owe no one anything, except to love one another; for he who loves his neighbor has fulfilled [Greek, *peplērōken*—perfect active] the law." The law is fulfilled when one loves his neighbor.

- Romans 14:23—"He who has doubts is condemned [Greek, *katakekritai*—perfect passive], if he eats." Condemnation takes effect when the doubt occurs.

In light of these passages, we can conclude with the late American Bible scholar Henry J. Cadbury, "One may simply assert that the action or condition implied in the perfect is not necessarily prior to that of the other clause."[135]

So the Protestant grammatical principle simply does not hold when compared to similar passages. But we can go further in defending the Catholic understanding.

Elsewhere in the Bible, the Greek word translated as "are forgiven," *aphiemi*, is used in the perfect tense and connotes sins being forgiven upon the action of the absolver. Consider, for example, Luke 5:20, wherein Jesus forgives the sins of the paralytic: "And when he saw their faith he said, 'Man, your sins are forgiven [Greek, *apheōntai*—perfect passive] you.'"

Another example is Luke 7:47. Jesus forgives the woman who anointed his head at the house of Simon the Pharisee: "Therefore I tell you, her sins, which are many, are forgiven [Greek, *apheoōntai*—perfect passive], for she loved much."

Luke did not intend to use the perfect tense of *aphiemi* in these passages to dissociate the forgiveness of sins from Jesus' declaration of the fact. Rather, Luke, like the bystanders, understood Jesus' words as a claim to forgive sins at the moment he said they were forgiven.

Consider what Luke records in both passages immediately following Jesus' pronouncements:

- Luke 5:21—"And the scribes and the Pharisees began to question, saying, 'Who is this that speaks blasphemies? Who can forgive sins but God only?'"

- Luke 7:49—"Then those who were at table with him began to say among themselves, 'Who is this, who even forgives sins?'"

If we're not going to dissociate the forgiveness of sins from Jesus' act of forgiving on account of the perfect tense of *aphiemi* in these passages from the Gospel of Luke, then we shouldn't do so for the apostles in John 20:23. As Cadbury writes: "Shall we accept a 'sacerdotalism' for Jesus from *apheōntai* in Luke and deny sacerdotalism for the apostles from the same word in John? Is it not better to treat the cases more alike?"[136]

"The apostles didn't absolve people; they preached the forgiveness of sins."

Some Protestants argue that we know that the disciples understood Jesus' instruction in John 20:23 to mean "preach the forgiveness of sins" because that's what they did, as recorded in the New Testament. They *didn't* go around absolving people's sins in a sacramental way. In the words of Baker:

> By letting Scripture interpret Scripture, we discover this commission was carried out and understood by the apostles and disciples to consist of the proclamation of the gospel to the world. . . . This is exactly what the apostles did, taught, and wrote in the New Testament.[137]

Baker appeals to several New Testament passages for evidence that the disciples preached the forgiveness of sins:

- Peter invites those present on Pentecost to "repent . . . for the forgiveness of sins" (Acts 2:28).

- Philip preached and called to the forgiveness of sins the Samaritans, the Ethiopian eunuch, and all the cities leading to Caesarea (Acts 8:5–7).[138]

- Paul preaches to the Gentiles that "everyone who believes in him receives forgiveness of sins through his name" (Acts 10:43).

- Paul declares, "Let it be known to you therefore, brethren, that through this man forgiveness of sins is proclaimed to you" (Acts 13:38).

- Paul defines the gospel that he preaches as "that Christ died for our sins in accordance with the Scriptures" (1 Cor. 15:3).

- Paul informs the Corinthians that he has been entrusted with "the ministry of reconciliation" (2 Cor. 5:18) and exercises it by saying, "We beg you on behalf of Christ, be reconciled to God" (5:20).

For Baker, that the early Christians didn't go around absolving people's sins in a sacramental way, but rather proclaimed the gospel message that through Jesus we have our sins forgiven gives evidence that the disciples understood Jesus' instruction in John 20:23 as a directive to preach the forgiveness of sins and not actually to forgive them.

ANSWERING THE COMEBACK

There are several ways we can respond to this comeback. First, although it is true that having New Testament records of the disciples absolving sins would make the sacramental interpretation of John 20:23 stronger, there is no need to reject the Catholic interpretation based on the lack of such evidence.

The first reason is that most preaching in the New Testament was directed to unbelievers, as is shown in many of the passages cited above (Acts 2:28, 7:51–52, 8:5–7, 10:43, 13:38). The message that sins are forgiven through Jesus was directed at people who were being called to conversion. That is why there's no mention of the sacrament of confession. Confession is only for those who've already been converted.

More fundamental, Acts is *a history of the early spread of the gospel.* It's a history of evangelization, not of pastoral care, so we don't see ordinary pastoral care of any sort on display in it: helping a convert who later has doubts, helping someone who's going through a dark time emotionally, helping people in problematic marriages, burying deceased parishioners, anointing sick ones, answering parishioners' moral questions, and discussions of goings-on in weekly worship services.

Second, the passages above that speak of the gospel message being directed to believers aren't necessarily exclusive of sacramental absolution. Christ's death for our sins, which Paul mentions in 1 Corinthians 15:3, isn't exclusive of the sacrament of confession because it's Christ's death that serves as the cause of the forgiveness of sins received in the sacrament.

The general gospel message that sins are forgiven through Christ can be inclusive of the means by which the merits of Christ's death are applied for post-conversion sins. A passing and summarized statement of the gospel message need not include the nuanced ways in which God forgives. Paul doesn't say anything about how God applies the merits of Christ's death to those who never come into contact with the gospel through no fault of their own. That Paul doesn't mention it doesn't mean that God has no way of reaching them with his grace.

The exhortation for the Corinthians to be reconciled back to God in 2 Corinthians 5:20 doesn't have any bearing on *how* that's accomplished. It could include sacramental absolution, or it could not.

A Protestant might say, "Well, the Bible says in 1 John 1:9, 'If we confess our sins, he is sure to forgive us.' So we know how it's done. It's done by confessing our sins to God, not to a priest."

But 1 John 1:9 doesn't *exclude* sacramental confession, either. The confessing of sins for John could easily refer to confession that involves an apostle or a presbyter. This is reasonable, given the fact that the same author records Jesus' words to the disciples: "If you forgive the sins of any, they are forgiven; if you retain the sins of any, they are retained."

Furthermore, the above appeal to 1 John 1:9 reads into the text the phrase "to God" with the idea of "to God exclusively." But the text in 1 John says *nothing* about whom the confession is to be made to or how it is to be done.

That Paul doesn't say in 2 Corinthians 5:20, "Be reconciled *by way of sacramental absolution*" could be due to the fact that it was such common knowledge that no explicit mention was needed.

A second way to respond to this argument is to challenge the assumption that there's no New Testament evidence that sins were forgiven in a sacramental way. It's true that there's no explicit statement that the *apostles* ever forgave sins in a sacramental way. But there is good evidence that at least the "presbyters" of the early Church did:

> Is any among you sick? Let him call for the elders (Greek, *presbuteros*) of the church, and let them pray over him, anointing him with oil in the name of the Lord; and the prayer of faith will save the sick man, and the Lord will raise him up; and if he has committed sins, he will be forgiven" (James 5:14–15).

Sins are forgiven through a prayer of faith prayed by a minister of the early Church. That sounds like the sacrament of confession.

Now, we can infer from this that the apostles likely would have performed the same duties, even though there is no direct evidence. The apostolic office, the *episkopē*—overseer (Acts 1:20)—is the fullness of the presbyterate (see Acts

20:28—the presbyters have the role of "guardian" [Greek, *episkopous*]). If the presbyters of the first-century Church anointed the sick with oil and forgave sins, it's reasonable to conclude that the apostles would have done so as well.

As a rejoinder to our appeal to James 5:14–15, a Protestant might object, "James 5:14–15 doesn't provide biblical support for the sacrament of confession because verse 16 says, 'Therefore, confess your sins to one another, and pray for one another.'" James here is simply giving instruction for a public disclosure of faults among Christians for the sake of making others aware of what they need prayer for."

The instruction to "confess your sins to one another" doesn't prove the sacramental interpretation wrong for two reasons. First, James's use of the word *therefore* indicates that he is connecting his instruction in verse 16 with what he said in verses 14 and 15.

When we look at verses 14 and 15, we see that the presbyters preside over the anointing and the prayer of faith. Since James asks us to understand his instruction to confess our sins in light of this, it's reasonable to conclude that he intends the presbyters to preside over this activity. The passage deals with sin and sickness and the use of rites presided over by presbyters to deal with both problems, which has continued in the Church as the sacraments of confession and anointing of the sick.

But what about the public aspect of this confession of sins? Doesn't that militate against seeing sacramental confession in this passage?

This question leads to our second reason why James's instruction to publicly confess our sins doesn't undermine a sacramental interpretation.

His instruction seems problematic for a believer in the sacrament of confession only if one assumes that private confession of sins is essential to the sacrament. But this is not the case. In the early years of Christianity, confession was ordinarily administered in public form. As the *Catechism* explains, private confessions didn't become common until around the seventh century (1447). James's instruction for public confession of sins coheres with an understanding of the sacrament of penance, so James here doesn't rob a believer in the sacrament of confession the right to appeal to this passage as biblical support for his belief.

> The seal of confession doesn't seem to be a divine law, since it was instituted after the institution of the sacrament and no pope since then has declared it to be a part of divine revelation. Neither does the seal seem to be merely ecclesiastical law, since it seems to be based on the right of every person to defend his reputation and privacy (cf. *Code of Canon Law*, can. 220). Some have called it a *mixed law*—an ecclesiastical law based on elements of divine law.

A third and final response is that the Protestant's argument unreasonably restricts the historical evidence to the New Testament. If we have good reason to think Luke shouldn't be expected to mention sacramental absolution since Acts is a history of evangelization rather than pastoral care, and those passages that speak of reconciliation can reasonably include sacramental confession, then there's no good reason to demand that evidence for the early Christian practice of sacramental confession come just from the New Testament.

We can reasonably look to extra-biblical Christian sources and see what they have to say.

Consider that early Christian sources testify that bishops succeeded the apostles in the apostolic office.[139] Early Christian sources also testify that bishops, as successors to the apostles, had the authority to forgive sins. One example is the prayer that a bishop of the early third century was to pray when conducting the ordination of a new bishop. Our record of the prayer comes from St. Hippolytus, in his *Apostolic Tradition* (c. 215):

> O God and Father of our Lord Jesus Christ . . . pour forth the power that is from you, of "the princely Spirit" that you delivered to your beloved child, Jesus Christ, and that he bestowed on your holy apostles, who established the Church that hallows you everywhere, for the endless glory and praise of your name. Father, "who knows the hearts [of all]," grant this servant, whom you have chosen for the episcopate, to feed your holy flock and serve as your high priest blamelessly night and day, and unceasingly turn away wrath from your face and offer to you the gifts of the holy Church. And *that by the high priestly Spirit he may have authority "to forgive sins" according to your command.*[140]

Given the instruction of James and the early Christian ordination prayer recorded by Hippolytus, the early Church clearly believed that presbyters and bishops had authority to forgive sins. And like what we've been arguing for in this chapter, they saw John 20:23 as evidence for this belief. St. John Chrysostom explains (c. 388): "It would not be wrong . . . to say that they received then the gift of a certain spiritual power, not to raise the dead and do miracles, but to remit sins."[141]

III
Mary and the Saints

CHAPTER 12

Mother of God
Luke 1:43

The belief that Mary is the mother of God is not unique to Catholicism. The vast majority of Christians accept this dogma, with only a minority of people in the Protestant community objecting.[142] One text that is appealed to in support of this belief is Luke 1:43. There, Elizabeth, inspired by the Holy Spirit, exclaims to Mary, who just arrived in her presence, "Why is this granted me, that the mother of my Lord should come to me?" Since Elizabeth was a good Jew, and Jews normally used the word *Lord* in the place of the tetragrammaton (God's name), YHWH, Elizabeth is calling Mary the mother of God. Therefore, we have a possible biblical foundation for the dogma of Mary, mother of God.

The Catechism of the Catholic Church appeals to Luke 1:43 as biblical support for the dogma of Mary, mother of God. See 448, 495, and 2677.

There are many comebacks that Protestants have to the belief in Mary as the mother of God. But there's really only one counter-argument made to using Luke 1:43 for scriptural justification of Mary as the mother of God. It targets the assumption that "lord" is intended by Elizabeth to refer to Almighty God.

There is a counter-argument that some Protestants make to the use of this text for Mary's sinlessness. But we can consider it here for our purposes of defending the appeal for Mary as mother of God, as will become evident below.

"Elizabeth simply uses the title *lord* in the sense of an earthly ruler. She's referring to the fruit of Mary's womb, Jesus, as her messianic king, not the divine messianic king."

Protestant Bible scholar Walter L. Leifeld argues that we shouldn't interpret this as a reference to Mary, "mother of God." His alternative interpretation is that Elizabeth was referring to Jesus as the *Messiah*. He writes:

> Nowhere in the [New Testament] is Mary called "mother of God." Deity is not confined to the person of Jesus (we may say, "Jesus is God," but not all of "God is Jesus"). She was, however, the mother of Jesus the Messiah and Lord.[143]

The evidence he gives is the fact that Luke frequently uses "Lord" as a title, 95 out of 166 occurrences in the synoptics. And not every one is charged with a divine meaning. Moreover, so Leifeld argues, Jesus is called "Lord" elsewhere in the Lukan birth narrative in a non-divine way ("For to you is born this day in the city of David a savior, who is Christ the Lord"—Luke 2:11).

169

ANSWERING THE COMEBACK

With regard to the use of "Lord" in reference to Jesus in Luke 2:11, it's not clear whether it's being used in a divine or non-divine way. There is nothing in the text that suggests either interpretation. Leifeld simply asserts its divine use without argumentation. Given such ambiguity, we can dismiss this text as evidence for Leifeld's conclusion.

There's no doubt, however, that the Greek word translated "Lord," *kurios,* is used in a non-divine way in the New Testament (e.g., 1 Cor. 8:5), even by Luke (e.g., 12:36, 37, 42, 43, 45, 46, 47). However, it's not the word *by itself* that indicates that Mary is the mother of God. It's how Luke sees Elizabeth using it.

There are several details that indicate that Luke is drawing a parallel between Mary and the Old Testament Ark of the Covenant. Take Elizabeth's words themselves, for example. They almost perfectly mirror David's in 2 Samuel 6:9, when he says in the presence of the ark: "How can the ark of the Lord come to me?" Other parallels include John the Baptist leaping for joy in the presence of Mary in Luke 1:44 and David "making merry" before the ark in 2 Samuel 6:5. According to Luke 1:39, Mary remains with Elizabeth for three months, similar to how the ark remained in the house of Obededom for the same amount of time according to 2 Samuel 6:11.

Now, since Luke is paralleling Elizabeth's "mother of my Lord" with David's "the ark of the Lord," it stands to reason that Luke intends for us to take Elizabeth's cry as a reference to almighty God. "Lord" in the phrase "ark of the Lord" wasn't a reference to the Messiah. The ark was the ark of almighty *God.* Therefore, we have good reason to interpret Luke 1:43 as a reference to Mary being the mother of God, contrary to Leifeld's claim.

"If you take some parallels with the ark, then you need to take all of them."

James White poses a challenge directed at the use of Mary as the new Ark of the Covenant for support for Mary's sinlessness. But since it's directed at Mary the new Ark of the Covenant, the counter-argument can be utilized for *whatever* inferences a Catholic might make from Mary being the new Ark of the Covenant, such as Mary, "Mother of God" in Luke 1:43.

White argues that if we draw parallels between Mary and the Ark of the Covenant, then we'll be pushed to affirm absurdities. He writes:

> Must Mary have been stolen by God's enemies for a time, so that she could be brought back to the people of God with great rejoicing (2 Sam. 6:14–15)? Who was Mary's Uzzah (2 Sam. 6:3–8)? [Catholic apologist Patrick] Madrid draws a further parallel between the three months the ark was with Obededom and the three months Mary was with Elizabeth. What, then, is the parallel with David's action of sacrificing a bull and a fattened calf when those who were carrying the ark had taken six steps (2 Sam. 6:13)?[144]

White charges that the use of Mary as the new Ark of the Covenant is violating rules of scriptural interpretation, since he perceives it as picking and choosing "those aspects of Mary's life [a Catholic] wishes to parallel in the ark and those which he does not." [145]

ANSWERING THE COMEBACK

Our response to this comeback is basically the same that we gave in a previous chapter concerning the interpretative context of the "key of the house of David" (Isa. 22:22) for the giving of the "keys of the kingdom" to Peter (Matt. 16:19). The premise—that some parallels require all parallels—is simply false. That's not how prophetic foreshadowing or intertextuality works.

As we pointed out before, the New Testament authors themselves don't honor the principle contained in this hidden premise. Consider the first two verses of Hosea 11:

> When Israel was a child, I loved him, and out of Egypt I called my son. The more I called them, the more they went from me; they kept sacrificing to the Baals, and burning incense to idols (1–2).

Matthew takes the phrase "out of Egypt I called my son" in the first statement as a prefigurement of the baby Jesus' return from the flight to Egypt (Matt. 2:15). Yet Matthew did not intend the latter part of the passage to refer to Jesus: Jesus did not go away from God, sacrifice to the Baals, and burn incense to their images.

There are numerous examples of this in the New Testament's use of the Old. Whenever prophetic foreshadowing is in play, some elements foreshadow, and some don't. There are continuities and discontinuities. If the New Testament authors employ this type of hermeneutic when relating the Old Testament to the New, it's legitimate for Catholics to do the same.

CHAPTER 13

Perpetual Virginity
Luke 1:34 & John 19:26–27

A minority of Protestants deny Mary's perpetual virginity by appealing to the biblical passages that speak of Jesus' "brothers" (Matt. 13:55; Mark 6:3).[146] On the other hand, there are a couple of passages that believers in this Marian dogma have appealed to for constructing a *positive* biblical argument for Mary as "ever-virgin."

The first is Luke 1:34. There, Luke records Mary's response to the angel Gabriel's revelation that she would bear the Messiah. Mary says, "How shall this be, seeing I know not a man?" (KJV). In Scripture, the term *know* (Greek, *gin ōskō*) commonly refers to sexual relations (see Gen. 4:1; Matt. 1:25). Luke 1:27 has already told us that Mary was "betrothed" to Joseph.

The angel tells Mary she will conceive a child, but Mary is puzzled as to how that could possibly happen. Why would Mary inquire as to how she is going to conceive a child if she were in a normal, soon-to-be-consummated marriage with Joseph? It suggests that she isn't planning on a normal marriage. This is why Gabriel's response explains the miraculous nature of the conception that will take place: "The Holy Spirit will come upon you, and the power of the Most High will overshadow you" (Luke 1:35).

A second passage believers in Mary's perpetual virginity appeal to for positive biblical support is John 19:26–27. "When Jesus saw his mother, and the disciple whom he loved standing near, he said to his mother, 'Woman, behold, your son!' Then he said to the disciple, 'Behold, your mother!' And from that hour the disciple took her to his own home." If Mary had other biological children, so the argument goes, Jesus wouldn't have entrusted Mary into John's care. The duty to care for Mary would have belonged to Jesus' brothers. And we know that Jesus cares about such a duty. In Mark 7:8–13, he condemns the Pharisees' *Corban* tradition, which held that if someone gives an offering to the Temple of the money saved to care for his elderly parents, he is excused from his obligation to care for them: they "leave the commandment of God [the Fourth Commandment]" (v.8) and "make void the word of God" (v.13).

Protestants have a comeback for each of the biblical passages that Catholics use to construct a positive argument for Mary's perpetual virginity.

Thomas Aquinas articulates four reasons why it was morally necessary that Mary remain a virgin.

1. The unique perfection of Jesus as the only-begotten Son of God;

2. The dignity of the Holy Spirit whose shrine was the virginal womb.

3. The dignity of Mary and her satisfaction with her divine Son.

4. The honor and chivalry of Joseph, who wouldn't dare to go into Mary who conceived by the Holy Spirit.[147]

"Mary's response refers to her being a virgin at the time of Gabriel's announcement, not to some vow of lifelong virginity."

James White argues that the angel was "speaking about an immediate conception,"[148] and therefore Mary's response has to do with her being a virgin at the time Gabriel announces to her that she is to bear the Messiah. To quote Ron Rhodes, her response basically amounts to, "I am a virgin, and my upcoming marriage will not take place for close to a year. So how will this pregnancy you speak of come to fruition?"[149]

White gives two reasons for his claim. First, he says Mary was "only engaged to Joseph, but not married." From this he infers that "at that time [Mary] could not possibly conceive in a natural manner, since she did not 'know a man.'" He thinks *that's* what prompts Mary's question.

White's second reason is "the present tense, 'I do not *know* a man.'" For White, if Mary had a vow of perpetual virginity, she would have said, "I have pledged *never to know* a man," or "I *will never* know a man." Since Mary doesn't say such things, White again concludes she must be thinking of not conceiving a child *at that time*.

ANSWERING THE COMEBACK

We can refute each of the reasons behind this argument. Let's take first the claim that Mary was "only engaged to Joseph, but not married." This simply is not true.

Consider, for example, Matthew 1:18. There Matthew writes, "When his mother Mary had been betrothed to Joseph, before they came together she was found to be with child of the Holy Spirit." Matthew uses the same Greek word for "betrothed" (*mnēsteuō*) as Luke does in Luke 1:27, right before Gabriel makes the announcement to Mary.

For Matthew, this "betrothal" was a *real* marriage. Immediately after, in verse 19, Matthew tells us Joseph sought to divorce Mary quietly. Why would Joseph seek to *divorce* her if they were not legally married? Couldn't he just leave her with no qualms about it?

Furthermore, in verse 19, for example, Matthew refers to Joseph as Mary's "husband" (Greek, *anēr*). *Anēr* also means "man," but the context concerning Joseph's contemplation of divorce confirms its marital sense. Then in verse 20, Matthew quotes the angel: "Do not fear to take Mary your *wife* (Greek, *gunē*[150])."

Now, some translations (ESV, NIV, NLV) translate verse 20 as "take Mary *as* your wife," allowing for the meaning that Mary is not Joseph's wife *yet*. But this directly contradicts verse 19 where Joseph is said to be Mary's "husband," a translation that both the ESV and NIV agree on. The NLV (*New Living Translation*), however, renders verse 19 as "Joseph, to whom she was engaged." But this is clearly an interpolation, since, as mentioned above, the Greek word for husband, *anēr*, is used to describe Joseph, and it's within the context of Joseph contemplating divorce. Joseph is Mary's "husband." Mary is Joseph's "wife." That's language of a real and legally binding marriage.

The point of Matthew's narrative is that Mary was found to be with child during the interim period between vows and consummation. It was customary in ancient Israel that a man and woman would become legally married, the husband would go off to prepare a place for his bride, and then come back to take his wife to begin their life together in one household, at which point consummation would occur. It's this interim period that both Matthew and Luke describe as "betrothal" (*mnēsteuō*).

Now that we have shown that Mary was legally married to Joseph at the time of the Annunciation, the significance of her question, "How shall this be?" comes into greater focus. Apologist Tim Staples explains the significance this way:

> Think about it: If you were a woman who had a rati-fied marriage and someone at your reception said—or "prophesied"—that you were going to have a baby, that would not really be all that much of a surprise. That is the normal course of events. You marry, consummate the union, and babies come along. You certainly would not ask the question, "Gee, how is this going to happen?" Mary never doubted; she simply asked a very valid ques-tion. She believed the message of the angel—that she was going to have a baby— but she did not know how it was going to happen. If she had been betrothed in the normal course, she would know precisely how it would happen because St. Joseph would have had a right to the marriage bed. Her question indicates she was not planning on the normal course of events in her future with her husband.[151]

What about the second point, regarding the present tense of *know*?

One response is that although Mary's statement, "I do not know man," is in the Greek present tense, it's a present tense that indicates an *ongoing* or *permanent* state of affairs (known as the habitual present).[152] On this reading, Mary's statement that she does not know man would suggest that she expects to remain a virgin on an ongoing basis. So, rather than the present tense undermining an appeal to this verse for support of Mary's perpetual virginity, it converges with it.

A second response is that the only way it would have entered into Mary's mind that the angel was speaking of an immediate conception is *if* the angel indicated she was to conceive immediately, or at least before she and Joseph consummated the marriage. But there's no such evidence. In fact, the evidence points in the opposite direction. The angel places everything he says prior to Mary's response (and even after) in the future:

> And behold, you *will* conceive in your womb and bear a son, and you *shall* call his name Jesus. He *will* be great, and *will* be called the Son of the Most High; and the Lord God *will* give to him the throne of his father David, and he *will* reign over the house of Jacob forever; and of his kingdom there *will* be no end (Luke 1:31–33).

It would be strange for Mary to think the angel was referring to an immediate conception when the future tense is used seven times *and* there's no revelation yet as to the supernatural nature of the conception. Mary would have every reason to think the angel was thinking of a regular conception that would occur after the consummation of her marriage with Joseph. The supernatural character of the conception doesn't come until *after* she queries, "How shall this be?"

Even if Mary's statement, "I do not know man," referred to her not knowing man during the interim period between the vows and consummation, still her question as to how she's going to conceive a child wouldn't make sense, given the fact that in normal circumstances, she would *eventually* consummate the marriage, after which a child would be conceived.

In the end, the Protestant who denies Mary's perpetual virginity is forced to read into the text something that is not there—namely, that Gabriel indicated an immediate conception (that is, one before she and Joseph begin living together as husband and wife). This is not stated by the text. You'd have to go beyond what the text says for this argument to work.

"There are other explanations for why Jesus entrusts Mary into John's care without having to say that Mary didn't have other biological children."

One alternate explanation White gives to rebut the Catholic's appeal to John 19:26–27 is that "his brothers were unbelievers,"[153] and wouldn't become believers until after the Resurrection. White appeals to John 7:5 for supporting evidence, where John tells us, "Even [Jesus'] brethren did not believe in him."

The other explanation White gives, and seemingly the one he prefers, is that the "brethren" "were not at the cross." For White, John would have been "far closer to Mary as a fellow believer than even her natural children," and that's the reason why Jesus entrusted Mary into John's care instead of her other biological children.

ANSWERING THE COMEBACK

With regard to the claim that Jesus' biological brothers weren't believers until after the Resurrection, that's not entirely clear. John 7:5 tells us that Jesus' brothers didn't believe in him *at the time of the Feast of Tabernacles*, which was quite a bit prior to the Crucifixion. And there's nothing in the New Testament that tells us they became believers after the Resurrection. The New Testament portrays them as believers after the Resurrection, but that doesn't mean that's the time when they *became* believers. Therefore, we cannot simply assert that none of his family members were believers at the time of the Crucifixion.

Another problem with this explanation of White is that it fails to consider Jesus' plans regarding what he would do after the Resurrection, which included appearing to his "brother" James. Even if we grant that his brothers didn't believe in him at the time of the Crucifixion, Jesus knew they would eventually come to believe in him within a matter of days. We're told in 1 Corinthians 15:7 that Jesus appeared to James, the chief of the brothers (referred to in the tradition as James "the Just"), and if James was not already a believer in Jesus, he became one then and went on to become a major leader in the early Church.[154]

Given this knowledge, Jesus' entrustment of Mary to John would have been only a temporary state of affairs, which would be fixed shortly thereafter, when James came to believe. But John 19:27 implies that Mary remained with John for an extended period of time, seemingly permanently: "And from that hour the disciple took her to his own home." There's nothing in the text to indicate that Mary was to stay with John just for a few days.

Since this explanation doesn't succeed in accounting for Jesus' entrustment of Mary to John, the best explanation remains that the brethren were not children of Mary's own womb.

Concerning the second explanation—that Jesus' brothers weren't present at the foot of the cross for Jesus to entrust Mary into their care—there are two things we can say in response. First, it may be that the brothers *were* present there on Golgotha. The idea that *only* women were there, with John being the exception, is false.

Luke tells us that all who knew Jesus were present: "And all his acquaintances [Greek, *pantes hoi gnōstoi autō*] and the women who had followed him from Galilee stood at a distance and saw these things" (23:49). We can assume that his acquaintances would include his family members. One reason is because at least one family member was there: Jesus' mother, Mary. A second reason is that this was at the time of Passover, an obligatory pilgrim feast for which observant Jews were required to travel to Jerusalem. We know that Jesus' family did travel to Jerusalem for these feasts, as we see Jesus' earthly parents doing in Luke 2 (2:41), and as we see the brethren doing in John 7 (7:2–10). Therefore, his brothers would have been in Jerusalem at the time of his crucifixion.

Now, someone might counter and say that perhaps they didn't know about Jesus' crucifixion and that's why they weren't there. But word of Jesus' crucifixion clearly reached the family as indicated by Mary's presence at the cross. Given this, it is unlikely that his brothers would not have come, and we should infer that they were there and were included under the statement in Luke 23:49. And if the "brothers" of Jesus were present at the foot of the cross, then Jesus' act of entrusting Mary into John's care indicates that they were not his biological brothers.

Second, Jesus didn't need to make arrangements for Mary's care from the cross if she had other children; it would have been *assumed* they would care for her, even if they weren't present at the Crucifixion. Moreover, making other arrangements would have been horribly insulting to her other children. And that goes against Jesus' strong view on God's law that children must care for their aging parents, as we saw above in Mark 7:8–13.

There's one last problem with this "Jesus had brothers" counter-argument, and it has to do with the overall claim that John would have been "far closer to Mary as a fellow believer than even her natural children," and for this reason Jesus entrusts Mary into John's care. This premise that the bond John had with Mary as a believer supersedes natural rights and obligations is problematic.

First, there is no reason to think this. The duty to care for an aging parent is a duty of the natural order, not the supernatural. Second, there's evidence that in Jesus' mind, the Christian bond would not supersede the natural duty of his brothers to care for their mother—that is, on supposition that his "brothers" are actually Mary's biological children. To suggest otherwise would conflict with Paul's instruction given in 1 Timothy 5:16: "If any believing woman has relatives who are widows, let her assist them; let the Church not be burdened, so that it may assist those who are real widows." Just as Paul expects families that have widows to take care of their own rather than burdening others in the Christian community, Jesus would have expected *Mary's own biological children* to take care of her rather than burdening an unrelated Christian like John.

We can further support Jesus' desire to uphold the natural obligation of children to care for their aging parents by appealing to what Jesus says in Mark 7:8–13 about the Pharisees' *Corban* tradition, which we mentioned above.

So not only is it unsupported speculation to argue that, for Jesus, the Christian bond between John and Mary would outweigh the natural duties of children to their parents, but there's evidence to the contrary.

In response to all of what was said above, someone could counter, "If Jesus' so-called 'brothers' weren't his biological brothers but were relatives of some sort, wouldn't Jesus have had to entrust Mary to them instead of John? If Jesus could have passed over them (perhaps for a reason like White suggests—a supernatural union that John had with Mary), then he could have done so for his biological brothers."

The problem here is that the Fourth Commandment and its imposed obligation pertains only to *children* caring for their aging parents: "Honor *your father* and *your mother.*" It's true that we can extend the Fourth Commandment to the general obligation to care for the elderly. But the Law itself didn't stipulate any sort of descending rank beyond the children who would be next in line to care for a deceased person's aging parents, such that if they were passed over it would be a violation.

In the end, Mary not having other children remains the best explanation of Jesus' entrustment of Mary to John's care. John 19:26–27, therefore, supports Mary's perpetual virginity.

CHAPTER 14

Immaculate Conception and Sinlessness
Genesis 3:14–15

Mary as the New Eve is an interpretative key for Catholics when it comes to explaining Mary's sinlessness, from conception to death. The primary basis for this belief is in Tradition rather than Scripture. However, there is a Bible passage that many have viewed as converging with this Catholic Tradition: Genesis 3:14–15. It reads,

> The Lord God said to the serpent, "Because you have done this, cursed are you above all cattle, and above all wild animals; upon your belly you shall go, and dust you shall eat all the days of your life. I will put enmity between you and the woman, and between your seed and her seed; he shall bruise your head, and you shall bruise his heel."

Scholars see in this passage the first announcement in the Old Testament of the coming of the New, which is why they commonly refer to it as the *protoevangelium*, which is Latin for "first gospel." And Christians since the first century have seen the "woman" in it as prophetically foreshadowing Mary. The woman is said to give birth to a male child who will defeat Satan, hence the good news. Jesus is a male child born of a woman and defeats Satan—the good news fulfilled. Therefore, seeing this woman as a reference to Mary in the spiritual sense is a legitimate interpretation.

With regard to the belief that Mary is the *New* Eve, and thus free from original and personal sin, the details revealed about the woman are relevant. God says he will put "enmity" between the woman and Satan, between her seed and Satan's seed, implying that neither the woman nor her seed would be of Satan's seed. Some have seen in this a reference to the woman not being part of fallen humanity— whether original or personal sin—*like Eve before the Fall.*

Like Eve, who was created without original sin, Mary as the *New* Eve is created without original sin. This is necessary at least for Mary as the New Eve to be on a par with the first Eve. But as the fulfillment of the type, Mary remains free from personal sin, unlike Eve, who fell into it.

Two of the three Protestant comebacks we'll consider here challenge the Catholic assumption that the woman is implied to be free from sin, both original and personal. The other targets the significance Catholics ascribe to Mary being the New Eve.

"The enmity is not total, as Mary's sinlessness would demand."

James White argues that this passage doesn't reveal the "complete enmity" between "the woman" (Mary) and the serpent (Satan) that Catholics need to support their belief. He tries to reduce the Catholic interpretation to absurdity:

> Since there is enmity between believers and the world, does that make all believers sinless? Does the fact that we still have sin in our lives mean that no enmity exists at all?[155]

Basically, White's argument is that Catholics can't appeal to the "enmity" spoken of in Genesis 3:15 because "enmity" doesn't necessarily entail *complete* enmity, which is what Catholics need to use this verse as biblical support for Mary's freedom from both original and personal sin. Enmity can exist between believers and Satan, so White argues, and at the same time believers will not be *completely* sinless as Catholics say Mary was.

ANSWERING THE COMEBACK

It's true that "enmity" doesn't *necessarily* entail complete enmity. As applied to Eve and her offspring, each will have some separation from the devil but not total separation. Eve is not totally separated because she sinned. However, there is some separation because, as tradition has it, she repented. Concerning Eve's offspring, we know they wouldn't be totally separated from the devil because they would be marred by both original and personal sin. But, like Eve, there would be *some* separation because some of Eve's offspring would have charity within their souls and be saved.

This lack of complete enmity, however, only holds on *this* level of interpretation. On a different level, a spiritual or prophetical level, complete enmity is a viable interpretation.

Consider, as mentioned above, that Christians throughout the centuries have viewed this text as the *protoevangelium*, seeing in the "seed of the woman" a prophetical reference to Jesus. On this prophetical view, the "enmity" that the woman's seed has with Satan ("I will put enmity between . . . your seed and *her seed*") is *complete*, given that Christians believe Jesus was free from both original and personal sin (Heb. 4:15).

Now, according to the inspired author, the enmity that Jesus has with Satan is equally applied to the woman: "I will put enmity between you and *the woman*, and between your seed and *her seed*." Since on this prophetical level of interpretation the enmity between Satan and Jesus is complete, which means freedom from both original and personal sin, it follows that on the prophetical view the enmity between Satan and the woman is also complete—the prophetical woman, Mary, is to be free from both original and personal sin.

Now, you might get a Protestant to concede that this passage doesn't give us the complete enmity between Jesus and Satan that we need for the belief that Jesus was entirely sinless and that we need to look elsewhere for such support. But this ironically would work in favor of a Catholic reading of the text.

Whatever other evidence we present for Jesus' complete sinlessness (no original or personal sin)—Hebrews 4:15, for example—would allow us to read the "enmity" between Jesus and Satan in Genesis 3:15 as complete. This follows the "Scripture interprets Scripture" principle advocated by Protestants. And since the enmity the woman has with Satan parallels the enmity between Jesus and Satan, we could read the enmity between the woman and Satan as complete as well.

Finally, the above counter-argument misses the *contrast* between the new woman and the first woman, Eve, in the spiritual sense of the text. If the enmity between the new woman and Satan were not to be complete and permanent, as a Protestant might argue, then there would be nothing new about the prophetical woman. She would be just like Eve in that she would eventually fall under Satan's dominion due to sin. Such an interpretation would undermine the biblical typology that God is intending to establish in the spiritual sense of the text.

"There's no prophecy that the woman would be victorious over the devil."

Ron Rhodes thinks it's a stretch to apply "the woman" to Mary. But he's willing to concede this for argument's sake. Even on this reading, Rhodes doesn't see the text as suggestive of Mary's sinlessness. He writes,

> For, indeed, the text indicates that while there will be *enmity* between the offspring of the woman and that of the devil, nevertheless the *victory itself* lies in the Messiah alone, who is one individual from among the woman's seed. It is never prophesied that "the woman" herself would be victorious, so any need for an immaculate conception of the woman vanishes. The woman's only significant role is to give birth to the human–divine Messiah.[156]

ANSWERING THE COMEBACK

This argument is based on the premise that if this passage is to converge with the Catholic Tradition that Mary was without sin, it would have to speak of the woman having victory over the serpent like the Messiah. But that's not true. Given our above argument that on the prophetical level the enmity between Satan and the woman is complete, the *enmity* that God puts between Satan and the woman is sufficient to affirm a convergence.

Moreover, even though the Hebrew text for this passage does indicate that the seed of the woman will crush the head of the serpent, it's also legitimate to see in the text the woman crushing the serpent's head, at least in an indirect way. The reason is that the woman, Mary, cooperated in the events that led to the serpent's head being crushed. She agreed to be the vessel for the male child to come into the world for the sake of crushing the serpent's head (Luke

1:38). She was struck by the serpent insofar as she suffered seeing her son hanging on the cross, which was prophesied by Simeon: "a sword will pierce through your own soul also" (Luke 2:35). Jimmy Akin sums it up nicely:

> Jesus *directly* crushed the serpent and was directly struck by the serpent, while Mary *indirectly* crushed it and was indirectly struck by it, due to her cooperation in becoming the mother of Christ.[157]

Given that Catholics have grounds to read in a spiritual way the woman crushing the serpent's head, Catholics could meet the above challenge and say, "The woman *does* have victory over the devil." And if victory over the devil is required to see a reference to the woman's sinlessness, and we can see the woman as a prophetical image of Mary, then Catholics can read the woman's victory as a reference to Mary's sinlessness.

CHAPTER 15

Bodily Assumption
Revelation 12:1–5

It's commonly recognized that Mary's bodily assumption is a belief that's not as explicit, biblically speaking, as, say, the belief that Mary is the mother of God. But there is one passage that some Catholics turn to for support: Revelation 12:1–5.[158]

> And a great sign appeared in heaven, a woman clothed with the sun, with the moon under her feet, and on her head a crown of twelve stars; she was with child and she cried out in her pangs of birth, in anguish for delivery. And another sign appeared in heaven; behold, a great red dragon, with seven heads and ten horns, and seven diadems upon his heads. His tail swept down a third of the stars of heaven, and cast them to the earth. And the dragon stood before the woman who was about to bear a child, that he might devour her child when she brought it forth; she brought forth a male child, one who is to rule all the nations with a rod of iron.

The first point of exegesis is that the "woman" is a *reference* to Mary. It's true that the woman can refer to other things, like Israel. But as Protestant author Gregory Beale explains,

"Most of Revelation's symbols have multiple associations or meanings and . . . the interpreter can never be sure that all the multiple meanings of a symbol have been discovered."[159] Are we as Catholics justified in seeing this as a reference to Mary? The answer is yes, because John describes her as giving birth to the male child, which is Jesus.

The second exegetical point is that this "woman," or Mary, is said to be in heaven with her body: "the moon under her *feet*, and on her *head* a crown of twelve stars." Given that the woman refers to Mary (even if not restricted to Mary), we have a biblical text that converges with the belief of Mary's bodily assumption, a Marian dogma that is known primarily from Tradition.

Protestants who challenge the Mariological reading of this text assert that the woman is not Mary. But not all appeal to the same details in the text to justify their assertion.

> In Revelation 12:17, the woman is said to be a spiritual mother: "Then the dragon was angry with the woman, and went off to make war on *the rest of her offspring*." Who are these offspring? Christians—"those who keep the commandments of God and bear testimony to Jesus."

"The woman is a symbol of Israel, not Mary."

Some Protestants argue for a restrictive view of the woman as referring *only* to Israel, thus excluding any possible Mariological reading. Ron Rhodes puts it plainly: "The 'woman' mentioned in this verse is not Mary, but is rather the nation of Israel."[160]

For support, Rhodes appeals to the patriarch Joseph's dream in the book of Genesis, in which he sees the sun, the moon, and eleven stars bowing down to him (Gen. 37:9). Rhodes thinks this Old Testament imagery of "sun, moon, and stars" is the interpretative context for Revelation 12:1, in which John describes the woman as "clothed with the *sun*, with the *moon* under her feet, and on her head a crown of twelve *stars*."

Steve Hays argues that we should interpret the woman as symbolic, since the satanic figure in Revelation 12 can "function as a synecdoche, not only standing for the devil but his entourage of fallen angels."[161] So if the dragon stands for all the fallen angels, then the woman should accordingly stand for all Israel.

ANSWERING THE COMEBACK

The reasons given above show that the woman can signify the nation of Israel. But the issue is not whether the woman signifies Israel. Rather, it's whether the "woman" is *only* a symbol of Israel (and *not* Mary).

Catholics recognize that the woman symbolizes the people of God. The bridal imagery of the woman (crown of twelve stars on her head) calls to mind the depiction of Israel as the Lord's bride in the Old Testament (Ezek. 16:8–21; cf. Jer. 3:1–2). The labor pains can be read as Israel giving birth to the Messiah. Jesus was born out of Israel.

But if the woman symbolizes Israel, that doesn't mean John *does not also* intend for us to understand the woman to be Mary. As we mentioned above, scriptural images can have multiple layers of meaning, especially in the book of Revelation.

A similar example is "the rock" in Matthew 16:18. Some Protestants think the rock *can't* be Peter and instead must be

Peter's confession. But the *Catechism of the Catholic Church* recognizes the rock as representing both Peter (881) and Peter's confession of faith (424).

This counter-argument, therefore, creates a false dichotomy: either Israel *or* Mary. But there's no contradiction to say the woman in Revelation refers to both. Protestant scholar Ben Witherington concurs: "This figure is both the literal mother of the male child Jesus and also the female image of the people of God. Again, the text is multivalent!"[162] Peter Leithart, president of the Theopolis Institute for Biblical, Liturgical, and Cultural Studies, also agrees: "If not only Mary, the woman is also Mary, Mary as eschatos in a line of miracle mothers, as the embodiment of the virginity of Israel's labor, all of it necessary to form Christ in this world."[163]

"The Mariological reading gets the chronology wrong."

Steve Hays counters the Mariological reading of this text by claiming that it conflicts with the proper chronology of events described.

> In terms of Catholic Mariology, the chronology is backwards. Mary is assumed into heaven at the end of her life. But in Revelation 12, the woman is up there at the outset, then comes down to earth. In Catholic theology, Mary is not a celestial being who originates in heaven. Rather, she's an earthling who ascends to heaven. But the imagery and sequence of Revelation 12 are just the opposite.[164]

For Hays, the sequences of events must be a one-to-one match to justify a Mariological reading of this text.

ANSWERING THE COMEBACK

The first thing we can say in response is that the multiple layers of meaning for images throughout the book of Revelation give us justification not to demand a perfect parallel between where "the woman" and Mary start and where they end up. Just like a perfect parallel doesn't exist between Mary and "the woman" in Genesis 3:15 (see above), at least on one level of interpretation, so too in Revelation 12:1–5 there doesn't need to be a perfect match between Mary and "the woman," especially since there are multiple levels of interpretation. On the level that "the woman" refers to Mary (she gives birth to the male child who is Jesus) and she's seen to be in heaven in a vision received most likely at a time when Mary's earthly life had finished, Revelation 12:1–5 convergences with the Catholic dogma that Mary was bodily assumed.

Now, someone may counter, "Well, if you're going to appeal to the symbolic nature of the book of Revelation, then perhaps the bodily imagery is just that—symbolic." Yet this would work in our favor, since an appeal to the symbolic nature of the book of Revelation would allow us to get out of the demand for an exact account of the sequence of events. Furthermore, the bodily depiction of "the woman" in Revelation 12:1–5 stands in contrast with the disembodied "souls of those who had been slain for the Word of God and the testimony they had borne" in 6:9.[165] This converges with the Catholic belief that Mary was an exception to the general rule that no soul receives its glorified body until the final judgment—excluding Jesus, and perhaps Enoch (Gen. 5:24) and Elijah (2 Kgs. 2:9–10).

A second response is that the demand for accurate chronology causes problems no matter how one interprets the woman. Consider, for example, the view that the woman represents Israel, a view that many Protestants hold (see above). How could Israel be present in heaven before being established by God here on earth? Surely, Israel too is "not a celestial being who originates in heaven."[166] If the "imagery and sequence of events" can't conflict with one's interpretation of the woman, then we'd have to say that the woman can't refer to Israel on any level of interpretation whatsoever.

"The woman can't be Mary because she has birth pains."

Another detail that some Protestant apologists think conflicts with the view that "the woman" refers to Mary is that the woman is "with child" and cries out "in her pangs of birth, in anguish for delivery." For example, Ron Rhodes writes, "The fact that this woman was pregnant and cried out in pain goes against the Roman Catholic claim that Mary suffered virtually no pain during the birth of Jesus."[167] "It makes far more sense," Rhodes concludes, "that Israel as a nation metaphorically gave birth to Jesus as the promised Jewish Messiah."[168]

It's true that according to common Catholic belief, Mary didn't experience pains when she gave birth to Jesus.[169] But the imagery of the woman having birth pains doesn't disprove that the woman can represent Mary.

ANSWERING THE COMEBACK

Note that we don't disagree with Rhodes that the birth pains can be seen as a metaphor for the nation of Israel giving us Jesus as the promised Jewish Messiah, since images in Scripture can have multiple meanings. What we disagree with is Rhodes's assertion that the woman *cannot* refer to Mary and his reason for this assertion: birth pains.

We're on solid ground taking the "pangs of birth" metaphorically. First, the book of Revelation is loaded with metaphors—beasts, lions, winged creatures, golden streets, harlots, etc. From that fact alone, we can at least be more favorable to a non-literal interpretation of this imagery.

Second, birth pains *are* used metaphorically in Scripture—for example, in some translations of Galatians 4:19 (NIV, KJV) and in several Old Testament passages (Isa. 26:17; Mic. 4:9, 5:3). One significant Old Testament passage is Micah 5:3. There the prophet Micah prophesies that when she who gives birth is in travail, God will release his people from exile and captivity, and the Messiah will come and be born in Bethlehem. Therefore, it's possible that John describes "the woman" in Revelation with the "pangs of birth" to signify the fulfillment of Micah's prophecy.

Finally, as apologist Tim Staples points out in his book *Behold Your Mother*, it's possible that the pain described here signifies the suffering Mary experienced from the special knowledge she had concerning her son. She would know the suffering Jesus as the Messiah is to endure. She even knows from the beginning that she will suffer when the prophet Simeon tells her a sword will pierce her soul (Luke 2:35). And we see this fulfilled when she witnesses her own son dying on the cross (John 19:25–30).

Given this unique knowledge that Mary has of her son and his role in salvation history, it is no surprise that her suffering in connection with the son she brought into the world would be described as "pangs of birth" in Revelation 12:2. Just as Jesus describes the martyrdom his apostles will endure with the image of a "woman in travail" (John 16:20–22), so too John describes Mary's spiritual martyrdom with the image of birth pains.

Therefore, the Mariological reading of the woman does not conflict with "the pangs of birth" image, as Rhodes thinks it does. As such, a Catholic doesn't need to give up Revelation 12:1–5 as a biblical reference to Mary's bodily assumption.

CHAPTER 16

Intercession of the Saints
Revelation 5:8

Catholics, along with other Christians who believe in the intercession of the saints, such as the Eastern Orthodox, often appeal to Revelation 5:8 as biblical support for the intercession of the saints.

> And when he had taken the scroll, the four living creatures and the twenty-four elders fell down before the Lamb, each holding a harp, and with golden bowls full of incense, which are the prayers of the saints.

Since the Bible reveals that the saints in heaven offer our prayers to God, it's reasonable to pray to them—that is, to make our requests known to them and ask them to pray to God for us.

Most Protestants don't accept this interpretation of Revelation 5:8, and they offer several comebacks. Some challenge the assumption that "prayers of saints" refers to *petitions* that *Christians on earth* make. Others concede this assumption but challenge inferences to justify the *practice* of entreating the saints in heaven to pray for us.

"The 'saints' aren't Christians on earth."

Matt Slick is one Protestant who challenges the assumption that the term "saints" refers to Christians on earth. He argues that the referent for the term is ambiguous and that "their identity can't be precisely demonstrated."[170] Slick favors the view that the term "saints" refers to either the four living creatures or the twenty-four elders who surround the throne of the Lamb.

His reasoning is that in verse 9, John says, "They sang a new song." Slick asks, "Who is the 'they'?" Slick answers, "It would have to be either the four living creatures and/or the twenty-four elders since 'prayers of the saints' don't sing; 'creatures' and 'elders' do the singing."

ANSWERING THE COMEBACK

It's true that the "they" in verse 9, those who sing the new song, are the four living creatures and the twenty-four elders. John lists the activity of singing along with other activities these heavenly inhabitants perform: falling down before the Lamb, holding harps, and offering the golden bowls full of incense. But his phrase "prayers of the saints" is separated from, or not included in, what the four living creatures and twenty-four elders are doing. John identifies "prayers of the saints" with the *incense* that the elders offer. The offering that the elders make is *distinct from* the "prayers of the saints," so the twenty-four elders are not the "saints" John speaks of.

We can complement the above negative approach with a more positive one and give reasons to think "saints" refers to Christians on earth. Consider that in the New Testament, the term *saint* overwhelmingly refers to human beings on earth, and there are no unambiguous instances where the New Testament uses the term *saint* to refer to a human being in heaven. This gives us reason at least to be inclined to think that "saints" in Revelation 5:8 refers to Christians on earth.

Another reason is that the Bible directly associates the prayers of the faithful on earth with incense. For example, the Psalmist writes, "Let my prayer be counted as incense before thee, and the lifting up of my hands as an evening sacrifice!" (Ps. 141:2). If the Bible describes prayers being offered in heaven under the form of incense (Rev. 5:8), and the Bible explicitly associates prayers on earth arising to God with incense (Ps. 141:2), then we have biblical grounds for identifying the prayers of Christians on earth with the "prayers of the saints."

One more point: This phrase, "prayers of the saints," would have been familiar to any Jew who read the book of Tobit. It comes from Tobit 12:15, where the angel Raphael says, "I am Raphael, one of the seven holy angels who present the prayers of the saints and enter into the presence of the glory of the Holy One."

The context reveals that the "prayers of the saints" included the prayer of Tobit and his daughter-in-law. In verse 12, Raphael tells Tobit, "When you and your daughter-in-law Sarah prayed, I brought a reminder of your prayer before the Holy One." And so here we have explicit scriptural evidence that the phrase "prayers of the saints" includes prayers of God's righteous *on earth*.

Now, you're probably thinking, "But Protestants don't accept Tobit as inspired." That's true. But Tobit still is a historical source for Jewish belief, and thus, it is acceptable for trying to discern what a Jew, like John, would have had in mind when he wrote "prayers of the saints."

Our appeal to Tobit becomes even more reasonable when we read in Revelation 8:3–4 that the "prayers of the saints," which are mingled with incense, *also* rise to God from the hand of an *angel*. Perhaps Raphael?

"The 'prayers' aren't petitions; they're praises."

Slick has another comeback:

> In verse 11–12 the angels, the creatures, and the elders who were all around the throne (which means they are in heaven) were *praising* God directly. In verse 13 it says every created thing in heaven and earth was *praising* God, then the elders fell down and worshiped, v. 14.[171]

Slick appears to be saying verses 11–13 are the key to interpreting "prayers" (in the phrase "prayers of the saints") not as petitions, but rather as *praises* that these heavenly inhabitants offer to God.

ANSWERING THE COMEBACK

This appeal to the "prayers" being praises doesn't help restrict the "saints" to heavenly inhabitants. John tells us in Revelation 5:13 that among those praising God and the Lamb were "every creature in heaven *and on earth* and under the earth and in the sea, and all therein." If the "prayers" are praises, then the elders are presenting the praises of Christians on earth to God, which would serve as yet another reason to number Christians on earth among the saints in Revelation 5:8.

This leads us to our second response: if the twenty-four elders can present the *praises* of Christians on earth to the throne of God, then it seems reasonable to say that they could present their *petitions*. There is no good reason to think they couldn't.

A third response is that there is good reason to think the "prayers" would at least include petitions, if not be restricted to them. Here are some reasons why.

First, although Christians commonly understand prayer to include praise, the common biblical use for the term is as a petition. A look in a biblical concordance reveals as much. Moreover, the Greek word for "prayers" here in Revelation 5:8, *proseuchē*, specifically connotes petitionary prayer rather than praise,[172] for which there are other words (*aineō, epaineō, eulogeō*).[173] The word itself, therefore, *points us to* petitionary prayer.

Second, the elders are depicted as *priests*, which gives us insight to the nature of the prayers being offered. Their status as priests is suggested by the number "twenty-four," which calls to mind the twenty-four divisions of Levitical priests (1 Chron. 24–25) and the offering of incense, which was a priestly duty (Exod. 30:1; Num. 7:84–86, 16:8, 10–11).

Inasmuch as they are priests, they "act on behalf of men in relation to God" (Heb. 5:1) in imitation of Jesus, the true priest, "who always lives to make intercession" for those "who draw near to God through him" (7:25). God's people relate to him not just by offering praises. They also relate to him by making petitions: "in everything by prayer and supplication with thanksgiving let your requests be made known to God" (Phil. 4:6).

If the elders in Revelation 5:8 are priests, and their job is to act on behalf of men in relation to God, and God's people relate to God not only by way of praise, but by way of petition, then we can conclude that the prayers of the saints that the elders make present before God involve petitions.

In his work *Prayer* (ca. A.D. 233), Origen wrote of souls in heaven praying for Christians on earth: "But not the high priest [Christ] alone prays for those who pray sincerely, but also the angels . . . as also the souls of the saints who have already fallen asleep."

201

Finally, the motif of prayers being presented before God's throne calls to mind Tobit 12:15 and the description of Raphael presenting the prayers of Tobit and his daughter-in-law to God. Both of their prayers were petitionary (see Tobit 3:1–6, 11–15).

As mentioned above, Protestants won't accept this story as inspired. Nevertheless, it does show that the motif of petitionary prayers being presented before God is a part of the Jewish tradition. And given that John the revelator was Jewish, it makes sense that his reference to the prayers of the saints being presented before the throne of God would refer to petitionary prayers.

"We can't be sure that the saints in heaven hear the prayers."

Slick offers another counter-argument worth considering. This one concedes for argument's sake that "prayers of the saints" refers to petitions offered by Christians on earth. Slick's target for this counter is the view that the twenty-four elders actually "hear" (or know) the prayers of Christians on earth. He states his case plainly:

> Nothing in that verse [referring to Rev. 5:8] says that anyone hears the prayers of the saints. . . . The saints in heaven offering the prayers doesn't mean that they can hear the prayers of people on earth.[174]

For Slick, since the text doesn't say anything about the twenty-four elders actually hearing (knowing) our prayers, "the Roman Catholic Church has read a doctrine into the text," thereby violating "biblical truth."

ANSWERING THE COMEBACK

Even if we concede for argument's sake that the elders don't "hear" (have knowledge of) the prayers, the belief in the intercession of the saints is not threatened. First, we know *that* they intercede (through Revelation 5:8), and intercession can be made even without knowledge of what the petitions are. As Catholics, we pray for the intentions of the pope all the time even though we might not know what they are. Second, we could still make our requests known because God would hear them and direct the elders to intercede for them. The bottom line is that whether the elders "hear" (have knowledge of) the prayers or not, if they bring them, they're interceding.

Now, there are reasons to challenge Slick's key premise that the elders don't actually "hear" (or know) the prayers. One reason is that the incense is simply a symbol for the prayers, which by nature are *immaterial*. And even more particular, they're immaterial *ideas*. It's not like the contents of the prayers are enclosed within an envelope that the elders lay a hold of and carry to the Lamb as heavenly mailmen. Since the prayers can only be immaterial ideas, the only way that the elders could possibly present the prayers to Jesus would be to *know* them.

What's more, as we noted above, the elders are *priests*. Jewish priests knew the contents of the prayers that Jews offered to the Lord when they interceded for them, whether it was the particular sin that a sin offering was offered for (Lev. 5:5–6; cf. Lev. 6), or the thanksgiving given to God with the peace offering (Lev. 7:11–13). Given that the elders are exercising an active *priestly* role in heaven, it's reasonable to think they would know the contents of the prayers.

Finally, recall from Tobit 12 (see above) that Raphael, "one of the seven holy angels who present the prayers of the saints" (v.15), seems to *know* the contents of the prayers of Tobit and his daughter-in-law: "When you and your daughter-in-law Sarah prayed, I brought *a reminder of your prayer* before the Holy One" (v.12). Both Tobit and Sarah's petitionary prayers are recorded in Tobit 3:1–6 and 11–15.

Perhaps it could be that Raphael only tells God, "Hey God, remember *that* Tobit and Sarah said a prayer." But this doesn't seem to fit the *precise knowledge* that Raphael has of the earthly affairs of Tobit and Sarah: he knows that they "buried the dead" (v.12), he knows that they "did not hesitate to rise and leave" dinner "in order to go out and lay out the dead" (v.13), and he knows the physical ailments that both Tobit and Sarah suffered—"now God sent me to heal you and your daughter-in-law Sarah" (v.14). To say that Raphael didn't know the contents of the prayers is a bit out of place.

Given that we can read Revelation 5:8 in light of Tobit 12:12–15, as discussed above, it's reasonable to think that the elders in Revelation 5:8 know the contents of the prayers offered, just like Raphael seemingly knows the contents of the prayers offered by Tobit and Sarah.

"Even if the elders hear us and intercede for us, we're still not justified in praying to them."

Slick makes another attempt to undermine the appeal to Revelation 5:8. Rather than targeting some aspect of the doctrine, like the saints *hearing* (knowing) our prayers, this counter-argument challenges the practice of invoking the saints to pray for us. He writes, even if "those in heaven can hear the prayers of those on earth does not mean that is okay to pray to saints."[175]

There seem to be two reasons Slick gives to justify this claim. The first is that "there is nothing [in Revelation 5:8] suggesting that those on earth are requesting the prayers or intercession of those in heaven." His second reason is that "there is no biblical teaching at all that states we are to pray to those who once were alive on earth and are now in heaven."

ANSWERING THE COMEBACK

It's true that Revelation 5:8 doesn't explicitly say we should request the prayers of the saints, nor does the Bible say that anywhere else. But that doesn't mean we can't infer from the text that we *can* request their prayers.

For example, nowhere does the Bible give explicit instruction to pray to the Holy Spirit. But given that Paul says the Holy Spirit intercedes for us (Rom. 8:26–27), we can infer that it's appropriate to pray to him. Many Protestants agree.

We can take a similar approach with Revelation 5:8 and the intercession of the saints. When Revelation 5:8 is combined with other things the Bible teaches, we can infer that it's good and appropriate for us to ask the saints to pray for us.

The Bible approves of requests made to other Christians for intercessory prayer. For example, Paul asks the Romans to pray for him to God on his behalf: "I appeal to you, brethren, by our Lord Jesus Christ and by the love of the Spirit, to strive together with me in your prayers to God on my behalf" (Rom. 15:30). He then informs the Romans about that which he wishes to obtain from their intercession: "that I may be delivered from the unbelievers in Judea, and that my service for Jerusalem may be acceptable to the saints" (v.31).

If it's acceptable to entreat other Christians to intercede for us for some specific purpose, and the saints in heaven are Christians, who not only are *able* to intercede for us but in fact *do* intercede for us, then it's reasonable to infer that we're justified in making our requests known to them.

Finally, that God reveals the saints in heaven interceding for us gives reason for us to ask for their intercession. It doesn't make sense that God would reveal this to us if he didn't intend for us to make our requests known to the saints.

> The language of "praying to the saints" is actually never used by the Catholic Church's Magisterium. Rather, the more common language in official Church documents is "the invocation of the saints." However, a Catholic is still justified in using the language, since the term "prayer" can be used simply to refer to a request, even if the request is made of another human being.

With regard to the contention that the text doesn't say the Christians on earth actually make their requests known to the elders in heaven—it's true that the practice was not common around the end of the first century, when John had the vision. The early Christians would have known that deceased saints *could* pray for them, as indicated in 2 Maccabees 15:12–14, where Judah Maccabee has a vision of the deceased Jeremiah interceding for the people of Israel. But the practice of asking the saints in heaven to pray for them wouldn't become common until after the early Christians reflected upon the implications of the revelation that had been given to them. That said, the absence of an explicit biblical example for a practice doesn't mean that the practice is wrong—as Protestants, who have many such practices, should know well.

"Even if the saints hear us, the Bible doesn't say how they hear us."

There's one more comeback Slick makes to undermine the practice of invoking the saints' intercession. He draws our attention to the lack of information as to *how* the saints intercede for us. He writes, "If the people in heaven are aware of the prayers, it doesn't say how they are aware."[176] Based on this premise, Slick concludes, "The Roman Catholic Church is stretching the verse beyond its intent and not being logical in its examination." [177]

ANSWERING THE COMEBACK

It's true that Revelation 5:8 doesn't reveal *how* the saints in heaven are aware of our prayers. But why should that matter?

We don't know *how* God made the world, but we know that he did. And from that knowledge, we can relate to him as the Creator. Similarly, just because we don't know *how* the saints in heaven are aware of our prayers, it doesn't follow that we can't relate to them by asking for their intercessory prayers, since we know they do intercede for us.

This is consistent with our everyday lives. Most people don't know how cell phones work, but that doesn't stop them from using them to talk to other people. We don't have to know how the saints hear our prayers. As long as they do, it's reasonable for us to talk to them.

Another critical question to ask in response is, "Why must we restrict our source of evidence to Revelation 5:8?" There's an entire Bible that we can look to for clues as to how the saints in heaven might be aware of our prayers.

Take, for example, the Old Testament story in Daniel 2 involving Daniel's interpretation of King Nebuchadnezzar's dream. According to the narrative, Nebuchadnezzar had a troubling dream and asked his sorcerers and wise men to interpret it. But Nebuchadnezzar made it more difficult by demanding that his wise men first tell him his dream, something the wise men recognized that only the gods could do: "The thing that the king asks is difficult, and none can show it to the king except the gods, whose dwelling is not with flesh" (v.11). All of the wise men failed to fulfill the king's request.

We then read in verse 19 that "the mystery was revealed to Daniel in a vision of the night." Afterward, Daniel was able to articulate the dream (and then interpret it) for Nebuchadnezzar. In other words, God revealed to him the interior thoughts of a man. If God can reveal knowledge of Nebuchadnezzar's dream to Daniel, surely he can reveal to the saints in heaven the interior prayer requests of Christians on earth.

There's also the New Testament revelation of the beatific vision. Contrasting the knowledge we have in this life with the knowledge we will have in the next, Paul writes, "For now we see in a mirror dimly, but then *face to face*. Now I know in part; then I shall understand fully, even as I have been fully understood" (1 Cor. 13:12).

The "face to face" bit refers to what Christians have come to call the *beatific vision*. In that vision, Paul teaches that we're going to be enhanced cognitively to understand things fully. If God *in fact* enhances the saints' cognitive abilities to know him and understand things fully, then it's reasonable to think God would in fact enhance the saints' cognitive abilities such that they could be aware of the requests made to them by Christians on earth.

IV
Scripture and Tradition

Hold to the Traditions
You Were Taught
2 Thessalonians 2:15

The Second Vatican Council, in its Dogmatic Constitution on the word of God *Dei Verbum,* taught that the Church "does not derive her certainty about all revealed truths from the holy scriptures alone" (9). Consequently, the council concludes, "Both Scripture and Tradition must be accepted and honored with equal sentiments of devotion and reverence." This teaching was reaffirmed by the *Catechism of the Catholic Church* (82).

A key Bible passage that Catholics have turned to for support of this teaching is 2 Thessalonians 2:15. Right after he speaks of the Thessalonians being saved through "belief in the truth" to which they were called through the "gospel," Paul writes, "Stand firm and hold to the traditions [Greek, *paradoseis*] which you were taught by us, either by word of mouth or by letter." For Paul, the truth of Jesus' gospel is to be found in Sacred Tradition along with Sacred Scripture.

Since Paul nowhere says this command is only for the Thessalonians, we can apply the principle to all Christians and say that holding fast to the apostolic traditions is essential to a Christian's salvation and thus is binding for a Christian.

Protestant responses to the Catholic argument from 2 Thessalonians 2:15 can be grouped into two broad categories: 1) responses that deny the existence of oral traditions distinct from Scripture and 2) responses that affirm the existence of oral traditions but deny some Catholic inference.

"The traditions spoken of are identical to what was put in writing."

One comeback says the traditions Paul speaks of *are the same as* the written word of God. Ron Rhodes takes this route, arguing, "The apostles for a time communicated their teachings orally until those teachings could be permanently recorded in written form."[178] He quotes nineteenth-century Bible expositors Jamieson, Fausset, and Brown for support:

> Inspired tradition, in Paul's sense, is not a supplementary oral tradition completing our written word, but it is identical with the written word now complete; then the latter [written word] not being complete, the tradition was necessarily in part oral, in part written, and continued so until, the latter [written word] being complete before the death of St. John, the last apostle, the former [oral tradition] was no longer needed.[179]

Geisler and MacKenzie follow suit when they argue, "The traditions (teachings) of the apostles that were revelations were written down. . . . There is no evidence that all the revelation God gave [the apostles] to express was not inscripturated in the twenty-seven books of the New Testament."[180]

ANSWERING THE COMEBACK

The major problem with this Protestant comeback is that it just *assumes* that everything was written down, making the oral teaching identical to the apostolic writings. But there is simply no evidence for this claim. Neither Jesus, Paul, nor the other apostles ever tell us that everything we must believe as Christians would be written down someday, and that those writings alone would be taken as our only guide for the Faith. But this is what a Protestant would need in order to justify his belief that the oral traditions Paul speaks of are identical to the written Word.

For a Protestant, Scripture alone serves as the infallible source for Christian belief, a doctrine known as *sola scriptura* (Latin, Scripture alone). Anything not found within the confines of the written word should not be accepted as Christian doctrine. But this principle is self-defeating: since the belief "the apostolic preaching is identical to the written word" is not found within the confines of Scripture, a Protestant must not accept it as a Christian doctrine. To do so would be to violate the principle of *sola scriptura*.

Finally, there is evidence that some apostolic traditions aren't identical to the sacred writings. Consider, for example, Paul's statements concerning the "man of lawlessness" or "son of perdition" in 2 Thessalonians 2:3–6. Paul writes,

> Let no one deceive you in any way; for that day will not come, unless the rebellion comes first, and the man of lawlessness is revealed, the son of perdition, who opposes and exalts himself against every so-called god or object of worship, so that he takes his seat in the temple of God, proclaiming himself to be God. Do you not remember that when I was still with you I told you this? And you know what is restraining him now so that he may be revealed in his time.

Notice the last line, "And you know what is restraining him now." This is listed among several things concerning "the man of lawlessness" (v.3) that Paul says he taught them when he was still with them (v.5). Yet, it's not identified in his writings.

There are also some things that Protestants believe to be essential to Christian faith that aren't found in the Bible. The canon of Scripture is one example. Nowhere does the Bible teach which books we must consider inspired by God.

Also, Protestants, along with Catholics, believe that public revelation ceased with the death of the last apostle. But nowhere does the Bible say, "When the last apostle dies divine revelation will cease." And if a Protestant appeals to Jude 3—"the Faith [has been] once for all delivered to the saints"—then he'll have to reject the epistle of Jude itself, or at least all the verses that come after verse 3, since all Christian doctrine would have already been delivered complete by the time they were written.[181] But a Protestant isn't going to do that.

In sum, not only do Protestants have no evidence that all of the important, necessary-for-salvation teachings that the apostles taught by word of mouth found their way into Scripture, but we have positive evidence that the two are not strictly identical.

"Paul identifies the oral traditions as 'the gospel' and therefore restricts the oral traditions to that which eventually would be included in the written word."

The previous counter simply asserted without justification that the oral traditions that Paul speaks of are identical to the word of God in written form. But some Protestants do give justification. James White is one example. He argues,

What does the term "orally" refer to? We first note that the context of the passage is the gospel. The verses that immediately precede verse 15 speak of the gospel and its work among the Thessalonians. The traditions Paul speaks of are not traditions about Mary or papal infallibility. Instead, the traditions Paul refers to have to do with a single topic, one that is close to his heart. He is encouraging these believers to stand firm—in what? In oral traditions about subjects not found in the New Testament? No, he is exhorting them to stand firm *in the gospel*.[182]

ANSWERING THE COMEBACK

Here the traditions Paul is discussing get lumped in with "a single topic" that is close to Paul's heart: the gospel. However, in this passage, White doesn't explain what the "gospel" contains. When the New Testament discusses "the gospel," it connects it with a limited number of subjects—principally God, his son Jesus Christ, and his kingdom—indicating that the gospel would be a small subset of Christian teaching. On the other hand, some Christians speak as if the gospel is identical to the full range of Christian truths.

Let's suppose White interprets "gospel" to mean a subset of Christian teachings connected with the basic message about God, his son Jesus Christ, and his kingdom. On this supposition, we know that Paul doesn't intend to limit the traditions he had in mind to those identified with the gospel.

Consider, for example, the tradition that Paul speaks of in the next chapter: "Now we command you, brethren, in the name of our Lord Jesus Christ, that you keep away from any brother who is walking in idleness and not in accord with the *tradition* that you received from us" (2 Thess. 3:6). Which tradition is Paul referring to? He tells us in verse 10: "For even when we were with you, we gave you this command: If anyone will not work, let him not eat." Some of the brethren were mooching off others and "not doing any work."

This tradition is not offered as mere opinion. Rather, it's something Christians *must* hold fast to: "Now we command you, brethren, *in the name of our Lord Jesus Christ.*"

Now, working for a living is a matter of Christian *ethics*, not part of the gospel of God, his son, and his kingdom. Moreover, it's unlikely that Paul envisions this tradition as part of the "gospel" that he and others preached because he often speaks of the "gospel" within a context that wouldn't have included this tradition.

For example, in Galatians 2:2, Paul tells us that he went up to Jerusalem sometime after his conversion to lay before the apostles "the gospel" (Greek, *euangelion*) that he preached among the Gentiles. Surely, Paul didn't have in mind the instruction to work for a living, since that wasn't a problem he had to deal with until his interaction with the Thessalonians.

Another example is Galatians 2:7, where Paul informs his readers that he was "entrusted with the *gospel* [*euangelion*] to the uncircumcised, just as Peter had been entrusted with the *gospel* [*euangelion*] to the circumcised." Paul's referring to a time *before* he had to deal with the problem of Christians mooching off others and not working, yet he speaks of the "gospel."

Since the tradition of working for a living is a matter of Christian ethics, and since Paul speaks of the "gospel" (*euangelion*) within contexts that wouldn't include the binding tradition in 2 Thessalonians 3:6, we can conclude that Paul didn't envision all the traditions he speaks of in 2 Thessalonians 2:15 as identical to the "gospel." Sure, Paul intends the Thessalonians to stand firm in the gospel. But he *also* intends the Thessalonians to stand firm in the traditions that go beyond the basic truth about God, his son, and his kingdom.

Suppose now that we interpret "gospel" as referring to a completed body of Christian truths. There are a few things we can say on this front.

First, it's not clear from the *context* that Paul intends to limit the traditions he had in mind to a body of Christian truths that's complete. The language he uses—stressing the bindingness of both what the Thessalonians heard from him "by word" on his initial three-week visit (Acts 17:2) and the ongoing letters he has begun writing them—suggests that the traditions he wants them to adhere to are not a closed, restricted body, but would include any binding tradition he might deliver to them in the future.

The fact that Paul was able to spend only three weeks in Thessalonica before a riot drove him from the city (Acts 17:5–10) means that he could not possibly have given the Thessalonians a full course of instruction in Christian doctrine, and so delivering supplemental traditions (such as by letter) would be necessary.

Second, some Catholic teachings that Protestants might think aren't part of this "gospel," like teachings about Mary, may not have been revealed yet. Paul was writing at a time when revelation was still being received. Furthermore, it's likely that Mary was still alive at the time Paul was writing his letters to the Thessalonians. If that's the case, then there would have been no revelation yet about Mary's bodily assumption. Such teachings about Mary may not have been part of the "gospel" at the time Paul penned his letters. But that doesn't mean they couldn't become part of the "gospel" before public revelation was complete.

Third, the exclusion of papal infallibility from the body of apostolic truth simply begs the question against the Catholic. Although it's true that the doctrine was not articulated in the precise way that we articulate it today (neither was the Trinity), Catholics believe that this teaching is part of the sacred deposit of truth that Christ revealed to us. You can't simply assert that it's not included in this deposit of truth since what we're debating in the first place is whether such traditions can be included within the body of truth that Christ revealed to us—the "gospel."

Furthermore, there's nothing in the text that would lead us to conclude that such traditions are *not* part of the contents of what Paul calls "our gospel." So the argument that these Catholic traditions are not part of the "gospel" is no argument at all, but merely an assertion.

"Paul doesn't say traditions and letter, but rather traditions *or* letter."

Another reason some Protestants give to justify their claim that the oral traditions were identical to the written Word is that Paul uses "or" instead of "and" when speaking of traditions and the apostolic letters. Protestant apologist Eric Svendsen makes this argument in his book *Evangelical Answers: A Critique of Current Roman Catholic Apologetics.* He writes,

> Paul does not say "by word of mouth *and* by letter" (which would be expected if each one was a different tradition and both were necessary); instead, Paul says "by word of mouth *or* by letter" (Greek, *eite*), implying that one or the other is equally sufficient to convey Paul's message, and that both are essentially the same.[183]

ANSWERING THE COMEBACK

One problem here is equating the value of the *means* of transmitting what Paul and the other apostles taught with the identity of the *content* transmitted via the means. Compare this parallel command that I might give to my kids as my wife and I leave for a date:

> "Kids, obey whatever instructions we give you, whether we tell you in person (before we leave for our date) or by phone (when we're on our date and they call to bug us about who did what to whom)."

The implication here is that whatever means my wife and I use to give the kids an instruction, they must obey. Each means of conveying an instruction is of equal value to bind our children to obedience.

The *and* versus *or* argument, applied to 2 Thessalonians 2:15, would have us conclude that since the means of conveying the instructions are equal in value, it follows that the instructions my wife and I give in person are identical to the instructions we give by phone. But that's simply not true. In fact, often they're different. They *could* be identical, but it's not necessary that they are.

Another problem is that citing the Greek *eite* is selective and misleading. *Eite* does not simply mean "or." It is a particle used in a series to signal alternatives, and it is commonly translated "if."[184]

Paul doesn't say to hold to the traditions "by word of mouth or [*eite*] by letter," as Svendsen presents it. The construction he uses is "*eite* by word *eite* by letter from us." Literalistically, this would be an instruction to hold to the traditions "if by word, if by letter from us." However, English does not favor the "if . . . if . . ." construction, and translators typically use a "either . . . or

. . ." construction. Thus, the RSV renders the statement "either by word of mouth or by letter."

Like "either . . . or . . .," the *eite . . . eite . . .* construction indicates the equal legitimacy of both alternatives. In context, the construction indicates that Paul's readers are to hold to the traditions he gives them regardless of the means by which they are given.

There's one last problem with *and* versus *or.* The conclusion that Paul's message given by word of mouth and by letter is "essentially the same" doesn't fit the historical account. Recall the riot that shortened Paul's time with the Thessalonians to three weeks (Acts 17:2, 5–10). His subsequent letters to them, therefore, were meant to *supplement* what he taught them in person.

Now, the mere fact that Paul's letters are supplementary gives us good reason to conclude that the content he preached while in person is not entirely contained within his letters. Moreover, it's unlikely that Paul would have been able to fit three weeks of content within just two short letters. Since Svendsen's interpretation doesn't fit the historical evidence, we have good reason to reject it.

"The oral traditions were authoritative but not inspired or infallible."

This comeback acknowledges distinct oral traditions present in the first century but argues they didn't have the authority Catholics say they had. In reference to the oral traditions spoken of in 2 Thessalonians 2:15, Geisler and MacKenzie write, "It is not necessary to claim that these oral teachings were inspired or infallible, only that they were authoritative."[185] Geisler and MacKenzie give three lines of evidence to support their claim:

1. "The believers were asked to 'maintain' them [the traditions] (1 Cor. 11:2) and 'stand fast in them' (2 Thess. 2:15)."

2. "Oral teachings about Christ (not the words of Christ) and the apostles' affirmations were not called inspired or unbreakable or the equivalent unless they were inscripturated in the Bible (2 Tim. 3:16).

3. "The apostles were living authorities, but not everything they said was infallible. Catholics understand the difference between authoritative and infallible, since they make the same distinction with regard to non-infallible and [infallible (*ex cathedra*)] statements made by a pope."

ANSWERING THE COMEBACK

There are a few general comments to make before we address each argument.

First, what do we mean by "inspired" and "infallible"? These are words that have taken on technical theological meanings within various theological communities. For example, Catholics would not say the traditions Paul speaks of are *infallible*, since that's a term used only in connection with post-biblical magisterial acts. However, Catholics would say these traditions are *true* and *without error* (inerrant) because they come from God, and thus are binding for Christians.

Similarly, *for Catholics*, the term *inspired* is a technical term applied *only* to Scripture and not Sacred Tradition. *Inspiration* for Catholics means that everything "asserted" by the biblical authors is "asserted" by the Holy Spirit (*Dei Verbum* 11). We believe that this applies to Scripture because we believe that everything asserted by the biblical authors is asserted by the Holy Spirit.

> There is debate among some Catholic theologians as to whether inspiration covers *every word* in Scripture. *Dei Verbum* does not say that every "word" is inspired, but rather that whatever is "asserted" by the biblical authors is "asserted" by the Holy Spirit (sec. 11). The question is whether we ought to include every *word* within the category of what the authors intended to *assert*.

We don't believe that this applies to the apostolic preaching, since we don't believe that every *word* spoken by the apostles in their preaching was intended by the Holy Spirit.[186] But even though the *words* that made up the apostolic preaching may not have been inspired, the substance of what they preached—what they asserted to be true—was. God can "inspire" Paul and the apostles to know certain revealed truths without inspiring them to choose the exact words he desires to communicate those truths.

Now, your Protestant friend might respond that he's using *inspired* in the sense that Paul does in 2 Timothy 3:16—"God-breathed" (Greek, *theopneustos*). But we cannot know precisely how Paul was using this term, since this is the only occurrence of the word *theopneustos* in the Bible. We have no other uses by which to judge precisely what Paul meant.

Paul *could* have meant by the term that every word used by the biblical authors is intended by the Holy Spirit. But he *also* could have meant simply that Scripture conveys God's revelation and thus can be said to be "God-breathed." Paul doesn't give us any indication one way or the other.

So, without clarification, Geisler and MacKenzie run the risk of anachronistically imposing categories on Paul's thought. The real question is whether Paul thought the oral traditions that he speaks of were just as binding for Christians as Scripture was.

We already saw above that he thought this concerning the tradition of avoiding idleness. Recall, Paul instructs the Thessalonians "in the name of Jesus Christ" to hold fast to that tradition. That suggests they're bound to believe it based on *Jesus'* authority.

> **Paul is very disciplined in letting his readers know when he's giving his own opinion and when he's giving something from the Lord. See 1 Corinthians 7:10–12.**

That Paul believed that the oral traditions were binding for Christians is further confirmed in 1 Thessalonians 2:13, where Paul tells the Thessalonians that they received the oral traditions not as the "word of men," but as the "word of God." He writes,

> We also thank God constantly for this, that when you received the word of God which you *heard* from us, you accepted it not as the word of men but as what it really is, the word of God.

Notice that Paul views the oral traditions he delivered to the Thessalonians as the word of God. If the oral traditions were considered to have their origin in God, then surely, they are binding for Christians—that's to say, the oral traditions were something that Christians had to believe.

Let's now consider the three supporting arguments listed above. First, Paul merely exhorts the Thessalonians to "maintain" and "stand fast" in the traditions, the assumption being that the exhortation to maintain and stand fast doesn't connote a binding authority equivalent to Sacred Scripture. Perhaps this is true if considered on its own. But we have contextual evidence to suggest otherwise.

Consider, for example, that Paul *also* exhorts the Thessalonians to "maintain" and "stand fast" in the traditions they were taught in his letters, which are Scripture. If Geisler and MacKenzie's argument worked, it would prove too much—namely, that Scripture is just authoritative but not binding for Christian faith. But that's absurd.

Moreover, we've shown above with 2 Thessalonians 3:6 and 1 Thessalonians 2:13 that the exhortation to "maintain" and "stand fast" is one that involves the necessity to believe the oral traditions as they were to believe Sacred Scripture.

Finally, in the verses preceding 2 Thessalonians 2:15, Paul reminds the Thessalonians that they were "saved through the sanctification by the Spirit and belief in the truth," and that God called them to this salvation through the "gospel" that Paul and the other apostles preached. It's immediately after this that Paul says, "So then, brethren, stand firm and hold to the traditions which you were taught by us, either by word of mouth or by letter."

The "so then" (Greek, *ara oun*) connects the exhortation to stand firm in the traditions to the preceding statements about "belief in truth" and the "gospel" preached. For Paul, the traditions (teachings) that he taught the Thessalonians, whether by word of mouth or letter, *are identical to* the "truth" and "gospel" preached.

Now, it's *that* truth and gospel that brought salvation to the Thessalonians. And since whatever pertains to our salvation and truth is binding for us, it follows that the oral traditions he taught have just as much binding authority as the traditions found in the letters.

So Paul's exhortation to "maintain" and "stand fast" in the oral traditions does not provide evidence that the binding authority of the oral traditions was not equivalent to the binding authority of Sacred Scripture.

The second argument is that the oral teachings about Christ weren't called "inspired" unless "inscripturated in the Bible." The scriptural support here is 2 Timothy 3:16: "All Scripture is inspired by God."

One problem here is that this is a positive statement rather than a negative one. It states that all Scripture is inspired, but it does not state that no traditions are inspired or that only Scripture is inspired.

Second, as we mentioned before, whether something is considered inspired will depend on the meaning one attributes to the term, and we cannot know precisely how Paul was using it, since this is the only occurrence of the word "inspired" (*theopneustos*) in the Bible.

We have no other uses by which to judge precisely what Paul considered inspired, and—although modern Catholic usage applies this term only to Scripture, Paul may have considered the oral traditions to be "God-breathed" given the fact that he recognized the apostolic traditions concerning Jesus as part of the "word of God" (cf. 1 Thess. 2:13).

Therefore, it's futile to argue that the oral traditions were never called "inspired" as Scripture was. That the oral traditions may not have been inspired in the way the written traditions were doesn't take away from the fact that the oral traditions contained divine revelation and therefore bound Christians to stand firm in them.

Finally, there's the appeal to the fact that not everything the apostles said was infallible. To say something was said *infallibly* means that God protected the person saying it from error, and the apostles did not always enjoy this charism. This is true. But that can't possibly be evidence that the *traditions spoken of in 2 Thessalonians 2:15* were not binding parts of Christian truth. We have already seen that Paul regarded these traditions as part of "the word of God" that had been delivered to the Thessalonians.

"The oral tradition was only for the first century. The oral tradition/Scripture paradigm changed when the last apostle died."

Unlike the comebacks we've considered so far, there's one response that acknowledges *both* that there were oral traditions in the first century *and* that they were binding on first-century Christians. What makes this counter unique is that it claims that the oral tradition/Scripture paradigm was only for the first century. Once all the apostles died off, so it's argued, the paradigm changed to Scripture alone.

There are a few ways in which a Protestant apologist might try to justify this claim. Steve Hays, for example, appeals to the fact that Paul addresses his letters to the *Thessalonians* and *not* to Christians in general. From this, Hays concludes that Paul didn't intend for Christians beyond the boundaries of Thessalonica to adhere to his instructions concerning the oral traditions.[187]

Another justification, given by Geisler and MacKenzie and Ron Rhodes,[188] is that apostolic authority resided in only the apostles. Since they're all dead, the only apostolic authority we have is the inspired record of their teaching.

A third argument that a Protestant might give is to say that the Catholic idea that these traditions are always binding is an inference that's not supported by the text. There's nothing in the text itself, it might be argued, that says Christians were *always* to depend on those oral traditions.[189]

ANSWERING THE COMEBACK

The first reason given above to justify the claim that the Tradition-Scripture paradigm is no longer applicable fails when we consider that the oral traditions are put on a par with the written traditions. If the exhortation to stand firm in the oral traditions doesn't apply anymore because it was addressed only to the Thessalonians, then it wouldn't apply to the written traditions, either. Such logic, in fact, would entail that no epistle in the New Testament applies anymore since they were all written for specific Christian communities in the first century.

The second justification above is problematic on two fronts. First, it's unclear as to what the implication is. Does the claim that there is no more apostolic authority imply that no more revelation can be given, whether in oral or written form? If that's the case, then we agree as Catholics. Sacred Tradition for Catholics does not entail the belief that public revelation was given after the time of the apostles. As we mentioned above, the Catholic Church teaches, along with Protestants, that public revelation ceased with the death of the last apostle.

Now, if the implication is that there is no more apostolic authority to *preserve* that which the apostles taught, then we have a problem, since the Bible and extra-biblical Christian sources make it clear that one way the Holy Spirit preserved the apostolic traditions was by leading the apostles to appoint men to succeed them in their apostolic ministry, and they charged such men to preserve what the apostles had taught. For example, before his death, Paul made arrangements for the Apostolic Tradition to be passed on in the post-Apostolic Age. He tells Timothy: "What you have *heard* from me before many witnesses entrust to faithful men who will be able to teach others also" (2 Tim. 2:2).

We also have evidence from extra-biblical Christian sources that the apostles appointed men to succeed them for the sake of preserving what they taught. Clement of Rome's first-century letter to the Corinthians (c. A.D. 70) is one example. He writes,

> Our apostles also knew, through our Lord Jesus Christ, that there would be strife on account of the office of the episcopate. For this reason, therefore, inasmuch as they had obtained a perfect foreknowledge of this, they appointed those [ministers] already mentioned [bishops—at Chapter 42], and afterward gave instructions, that when these should fall asleep, other approved men should succeed them in their ministry.[190]

Irenaeus of Lyons, a bishop of the late second century, affirms that the apostolic traditions were preserved in this line of succession from the apostles. Here's what he writes in his classic work *Against Heresies*:

> It is within the power of all, therefore, in every church, who may wish to see the truth, to contemplate clearly the tradition of the apostles manifested throughout the whole world; and we are in a position to reckon up those who were by the apostles instituted bishops in the churches, and [to demonstrate] the succession of these men to our

own times; those who neither taught nor knew of anything like what these [heretics] rave about.[191]

For Irenaeus, the truth of Apostolic Tradition is preserved
in the succession of bishops from the apostles. This is what
we find in Scripture.

For these reasons, we can reject the second justification given for the claim that the oral tradition-Scripture
paradigm shifted once the apostles died off. The apostolic
authority didn't die with the apostles. It continued in the
men they chose to succeed them, called bishops.

Now we come to the third reason that might be given in
support of the paradigm shift—namely, there's nothing in
Paul's affirmation of first-century Christians depending on
oral traditions to say they would *always* be dependent on it.

The problem here is that the logic would equally apply
to the written traditions, since Paul speaks of the oral and
written traditions together as that which the Thessalonians
need to maintain and stand firm in. If a Protestant thinks the
lack of an explicit exhortation to always stand firm in the
oral traditions favors the oral tradition-Scripture paradigm
shift, then he must be willing to say Christians don't always
have to depend on the written traditions (Scripture), since
Paul says nothing in 2 Thessalonians 2:15 about Christians
always depending on them. Perpetual dependence on the
written traditions has to be inferred. And if we can do that,
then we can reasonably make the same kind of inference for
the oral traditions.

V
Salvation

CHAPTER 18

Not by Faith Alone
James 2:24

James 2:24 is a popular text that Catholics appeal to when they talk to Protestants about faith and works:

> You see that a man is justified by works and not by faith alone.

Catholic apologists often say, "The only time in the Bible when the words 'faith alone' appear, the words 'not by' are in front it." Since James says we're justified by works, so Catholics argue, then works must play *some* role in our justification.

Since there's no room for ambiguity as to *what* James says in James 2:24 ("we're justified by works"), Protestants can respond only by challenging the meaning of *justification*. Catholics assume that *justification* means justification in sight of God. But Protestants who counter a Catholic's appeal to this passage argue that James is speaking of justification not in the sight of God, but rather in the sight of men.[192] In other words, it's argued that our works prove *to men* that our claim to faith is genuine. The late American Reformed theologian R.C. Sproul writes, "Our works 'justify' our claim to faith in the eyes of human beholders. Such 'justification' or vindication is not necessary for God."[193]

Since the Catholic target is very small with James 2:24, dealing with just four words ("we're justified by works"), the above comeback is pretty much the only one you find among Protestant apologists. However, there are a few different ways in which Protestants try to justify this claim.

"James is speaking of justification in the sight of men—because he says so in James 2:18."

Above, we quoted R.C. Sproul as representative of the general claim that James is speaking of justification in the sight of men. He's also representative of the lines of justification that Protestants use for this claim. For example, he appeals to James 2:18 as a supporting text: "Show me your faith apart from your works, and I by my works will show you my faith." Given this context of manifesting faith to others through good works, Sproul infers that James must be speaking about justification in the sight of men.

ANSWERING THE COMEBACK

The first problem with this argument is that it fails to consider the salvific context in which James places his teaching about works. James 2:14 sets it up: "What does it profit, my brethren, if a man says he has faith but has not works? Can his faith *save* him?"

The context doesn't suggest that James is speaking of salvation in a temporal sense. He doesn't mention being saved from physical enemies, or of our salvation being confirmed in the sight of men. He is speaking of the actual gift of salvation that God grants us. And there are a few reasons to believe this.

First, James tells us that "faith by itself, if it has no works, is dead." Notice that James doesn't say, "dead *in the sight of men*." He says faith *itself* is dead. In fact, he makes the point vividly by comparing it to a corpse: "For as the body apart from the spirit is dead, so faith apart from works is dead" (v. 26).

If James meant that our works justify us merely in the sight of men, then our lack of works would have no negative effect on our faith itself. It would only be *seen* as dead. But that would run contrary to what James actually tells us. Moreover, it would make the parallel to a body without the spirit unintelligible. In what sense can the absence of the spirit have no negative effect on the body?

Also, the three other times when James uses the word "save" (Greek, *sōzō*) in his epistle, he uses it in reference to the salvation that God grants our souls (1:21, 4:12, 5:20). In light of such context, it's reasonable to conclude that James is using the word in the same way in James 2:14.

Finally, it's interesting to note that the works James lists as necessary for having a saving faith (clothing the naked and feeding the hungry) are of the same type that Jesus says will merit eternal life: "inherit the kingdom prepared for you . . . for I was hungry and you gave me food . . . I was naked and you clothed me" (Matt. 25:35–36).

It's not unreasonable to conclude that James had this teaching in mind when he spoke of the corporal works of mercy. And if so, then the justification he has in mind is not one that is relative to the sight of men, but one that is wrought by God.

The claim that James is speaking of justification merely in the sight of men also fails because it doesn't jibe with James's use of Abraham's offering of Isaac as an exemplary case of justification by works (2:21–23). There was no one around with Abraham and Isaac on Mt. Moriah for Abraham to be justified in the sight of! (Neither James nor the author of Genesis gives us any indication that Abraham was justified in the sight of *Isaac*).

Perhaps a Protestant might respond and say Abraham is justified in *our* sight. After describing Abraham's offering of Isaac, James begins his concluding sentence about Abraham's faith with "you see": "*You see* that faith was active along with his works" (v. 22a). Perhaps James is saying Abraham's offering of Isaac confirms for *us* that he had faith—not that his works justified him in the sight of God.

The problem with this is that James explicitly teaches that Abraham's *faith* was "completed by works" (v. 22b) by offering Isaac. The Greek word used for "complete," *teleioō*, means "to complete, bring to an end, finish, accomplish . . . to make perfect."[194] How can Abraham's faith be made complete if he is justified merely in the sight of men? If Abraham's work of offering Isaac confirmed merely for us that he had faith, then Abraham's work would have no effect whatsoever upon his faith, and still less make it "complete." But this contradicts what James teaches in verse 22.

Furthermore, James's emphasis on Abraham's *faith* being made perfect indicates that it's the *same* faith that justified him when he first believed. James speaks of Abraham being justified by his obedience in verse 21 and then indicates that his faith was completed by works in verse 22. And without breaking his train of thought, James quotes Genesis 15:6 in verse 23: "Abraham believed God, and it was reckoned to him as righteousness." All Protestants agree that this event refers to Abraham being justified in God's sight.

James quotes Genesis 15:6 in direct connection with Abraham's justification by works and gives no indication that the two must be viewed in contrast with each other. This tells us that the justification James has in mind in verse

21 (Abraham's justification by works) is the same justification spoken of in Genesis 15:6 ("Abraham believed God, and it was reckoned to him as righteousness"). It's a justification in the sight of God, not men.

Abraham's justification in the sight of God is further confirmed by Abraham being called "the friend of God" as a result of his obedient action. For James, Abraham's offering of Isaac set off a chain reaction. His faith was "completed by his works," the "Scripture was fulfilled" whereby Abraham was reckoned as righteous, and he was called "the friend of God."

We know that God is the one valuing what was done, because after the angel intervenes and stops Abraham from killing Isaac, God says, "For now *I* know that you fear God, seeing you have not withheld your son, your only son, from me" (Gen. 22:12). God valued what Abraham had done, and thus Abraham stood justified in God's sight. God reiterates his approval of Abraham in Isaiah 41:8, when he calls Abraham "*my* friend."

So if Abraham was justified in the sight of God by offering Isaac, and our justification by works that James speaks of (2:24) is like Abraham's justification, then it follows that justification by works is a justification in the sight of God.

Given the context of salvation, and the parallel between our justification and Abraham's justification in the sight of God, we can conclude that this counter-argument lacks persuasive force. There's no need for a Catholic to stop using James 2:24 to justify his belief that works play a role in our justification.

"Abraham was justified without works."

Sproul thinks the appeal to Abraham gives reason to think James is *not* talking about justification in the sight of God. His reason? James would be in conflict with Paul.[195]

Here's Paul in Romans 4:1–5. The key verses are 1–3:

> For if Abraham was justified by works, he has something of which to boast, but not before God. For what does Scripture say? "Abraham believed God, and it was accounted to him for righteousness."

Sproul concludes,

> Abraham was justified *before* he performed works. He was justified as soon as he had faith (in Gen. 15). Abraham was reckoned or counted as righteous (a forensic declaration) before and without a view to his works.[196]

For Sproul, James can't be speaking of justification in the sight of God when he speaks of "justification by works" (v. 24), lest his parallel with Abraham fall apart, since Abraham was justified before works.

ANSWERING THE COMEBACK

One problem with this reasoning is that he doesn't consider that there could be multiple aspects of Abraham's justification, as Catholics believe. The Catholic Church distinguishes between different stages of justification.

In the tenth chapter of its decree, "The Increase of the Justification Received," the Council of Trent speaks of those who have "been thus justified and made the friends and domestics of God," thereby recognizing an initial stage of justification in which we first come into relationship with Christ. The council excluded the justifying role of works from this stage. Chapter eight of its *Decree on Justification* reads, "None of those things which precede justification—whether faith or works—merit the grace itself of justification."

The council then says that such justified Christians "increase in that justice received through the grace of Christ and are further justified" through the "observance of the commandments of God and of the Church" and by "faith cooperating with good works." This "increase in justice" that makes a Christian "further justified" signifies an ongoing stage of justification.

It's here where works play a positive role in our justification. Immediately after the above statements, the decree quotes James 2:24 as biblical support.

Canon 24 of the decree adds a *preserving* role for works: "If any one saith, that the justice received is not *preserved* and also increased before God through good works; but that the said works are merely the fruits and signs of justification obtained, but not a cause of the increase thereof; let him be anathema."

Finally, in Canon 32, the council teaches that works merit our *final justification*—that's to say, they truly merit eternal life. The canon reads: "If anyone says . . . that the said justified, by the good works which he performs through the grace of God and the merit of Jesus Christ, whose living member he is, does not truly merit increase of grace, *eternal life*, and the attainment of that *eternal life*—if so be, however, that he depart in grace—and also an increase of glory; let him be anathema."

The view that justification is *not* a one-time event in the past but has multiple dimensions is justified by Scripture. James equates Abraham's justification by works in verse 21 with his justification in Genesis 15:6. This proves that there are multiple stages or dimensions to justification and that it's not a one-time event in the past.

Even aside from this connection, we know that Genesis 15:6 was not the only time Abraham was considered justified.

Abraham had already been justified many years before when he followed God's call to leave his home in Haran and journey to a then unknown land promised to him (Gen. 12:1–3).

The author of Hebrews is our guiding light here. In Hebrews 11, we discover that Abraham obeyed God's call "by faith," and the type of faith that he had was a faith "without [which] it is impossible to please God" (v. 6) and a faith by which "men of old received divine approval" (v. 2). This means that Abraham responded to God's call with a faith that justifies—a saving faith.

So the righteousness that was reckoned to Abraham later, when he believed God's promise in Genesis 15:6, was not his initial stage of justification. It was a new act of belief that God reckoned as a new act of righteousness.[197] The New American Bible translation brings this point out better, saying the Lord "attributed it to him [Abraham] as an act of righteousness."

Further scriptural warrant that justification is not a one-time event of the past is found in Paul's writings. Consider, for example, what he says in Romans 2:13: "For it is not the hearers of the law who are righteous before God, but the doers of the law who will be justified." The future tense, "will be justified," suggests that justification doesn't merely occur in the past.

Another example of this future dimension of justification is Romans 6:16. Here Paul juxtaposes sin and obedience and teaches that obedience "leads to righteousness [Greek, *eis dikaiosunēn*]." And he's not just talking about obedience prior to faith—he's talking about obedience leading to righteousness after we already have believed.

In Galatians 5:5, Paul writes, "For through the Spirit, by faith, we wait for the hope of righteousness (Greek, *dikaiosunēs*)." Paul's use of hope indicates that there is some aspect to our justification that is not yet complete, since you can only hope for that which you don't yet possess (see Rom. 8:24). Moreover, Paul speaks of those who have such hope as having faith and already being in the Spirit. How could Paul speak of justified Christians having a hope of righteousness if there were not some future aspect to our justification?

Using Abraham to refute the Catholic position on faith and works is only as good as the assumption underlying the argument—namely, that justification is a one-time event in the past. Since we have good reason to reject this assumption, the appeal to Abraham fails to support the claim that James is speaking of justification in the sight of men.

"The term *justification* is used elsewhere in Scripture for vindication."

There's another move that Sproul makes to bolster his claim that James is *not* speaking of justification in the sight of God. He appeals to Matthew 11:19, where the Greek verb for "to justify" (Greek, *dikaioō*) is used to connote the idea of vindication: "Wisdom is justified by her deeds."[198]

Sproul then gives his thoughts on this verse as it applies to the issue at hand (emphasis added):

Jesus is obviously not saying that wisdom is reconciled to God by having babies. He is saying that true wisdom is made *manifest*, or *demonstrated* to be true wisdom, by the fruit it yields.[199]

Sproul sees in Matthew 11:19 a possible key to interpreting James, for he writes, "Perhaps this [the way *justified* is used in Matthew 11:19] is close to what James means when he speaks of Abraham as 'justified' by his works."[200] For Sproul, James is using "justified" to convey the idea that faith is manifest or demonstrated through good works, not that good works constitute Abraham being just before God. And if James is using justification in that sense for Abraham, then that's how he's using it in verse 24, when he says we're justified by works and not by faith alone.

ANSWERING THE COMEBACK

All this argument shows is that the Greek word *dikaioō* can be used for vindication. But this doesn't give us any reason to think that's how *James* is using the word.

We have to appeal to other details in the context to determine whether James is using *dikaioō* simply to convey the idea of vindication or in the way Christians use it concerning their standing before God. And given the contextual details that we enumerated in response to the above counters, we can say James is using it in the salvific sense: Abraham's obedience to God's command (his good work) constitutes him being *just*, having a rightly ordered relationship with God.

CHAPTER 19

Work Out Your Salvation
Philippians 2:12

Discussions between Catholics and Protestants about the topic of salvation sometimes involve a reference to Philippians 2:12, a passage fondly quoted by Catholics in support of their view that good works play a role in achieving our final salvation and that it's possible for a Christian to lose his salvation. Paul writes, "Work out your own salvation with fear and trembling."

"What else could Paul mean?" the Catholic asks. Since Paul connects salvation with works, works must play a role in attaining salvation—that is, our *final* salvation. And if that's the case, then a Christian's salvation, or justification, is not eternally secure.

There are basically three comebacks that Protestants make to the Catholic argument from Philippians 2:12. All three target the Catholic assumption that Paul is talking about *salvation* in the eternal sense. Each comeback argument proposes a different understanding of the word.

The work spoken of in Philippians 2:12 is not meant to be understood as something done apart from God's grace. Paul says in the very next verse, "For God is at work in you, both to will and to work for his good pleasure" (v.13). The good that we do has a double agency: us and God.

"Paul is speaking of a corporate salvation of the Philippian community, a salvation that's temporal and experiential."

Ron Rhodes writes,

> This church as a unit was in need of "salvation" (that is, salvation in the temporal, experiential sense, not in the eternal sense). It is critical to recognize that *salvation* in this context is referring to the *community* of believers in Philippi and not to *individual* believers. Salvation is spoken of in a *corporate* sense in this verse. The Philippians were called by the apostle Paul to "keep on working out" (continuously) the "deliverance of the church into a state of Christian maturity."[201]

For Rhodes, since "salvation" in Philippians 2:12 is not referring to an individual's salvation in the eternal sense, surely a Catholic can't appeal to this verse for support of its belief that works play an essential role in attaining eternal life.

ANSWERING THE COMEBACK

The first thing to point out in response is that it goes against the grain in the New Testament to read salvation in a temporal sense. Throughout the New Testament, including Paul's writings, the Greek word translated here as "salvation," *sōtēria*, is normally used in reference to eternal salvation. So a natural reading of Philippians 2:12 would be as such.

To interpret *sōtēria* in a temporal sense, you have to shoulder the burden of proof to justify such an unnatural reading. You'll see that's difficult to do!

Maybe the Protestant you're talking to will argue, as Rhodes does, that the exhortation to "work out your salvation" is a response to "the particular situation of the church in Philippi." The church's situation there, the reasoning goes, was plagued by 1) rivalries and personal ambitions (Phil. 2:3,4; 4:2); 2) the teaching of Judaizers (who said circumcision is necessary for salvation—3:1–3); 3) perfectionism (attain sinless perfection in this life—3:12–14); and 4) influence of *antinomian libertines* (people who took excessive liberty in how they lived their lives, ignoring or going against God's law—3:18, 19).

The problem here is that each item listed above doesn't pull its weight in proving the point. Take rivalries and personal ambitions. Here's what Philippians 2:3–4 says: "Do nothing from selfishness or conceit, but in humility count others better than yourselves. Let each of you look not only to his own interests, but also to the interests of others."

That Paul exhorts the Philippians to refrain from sinful behavior doesn't mean they're actually guilty of it. It's simply a part of Paul's general moral exhortation that begins in Philippians 1:27—"only let your manner of life be worthy of the gospel of Christ, so that . . . I may hear of you that you stand firm in one spirit, with one mind striving side by side for the faith of the gospel." Any type of moral exhortation is going to involve an exhortation to avoid sin, regardless of if a person is guilty of that sin or not.

Philippians 4:2 reads, "I entreat Euodia and I entreat Syntyche to agree in the Lord." This is as close as Rhodes gets to identifying problems in the Philippian church. But notice it's directed to only two people. It's not the whole church "as a unit," to use the words of Rhodes.

Next, there's the appeal to the teaching of the Judaizers, whom Paul identifies as those "who mutilate the flesh" (Phil. 3:2). But he warns the Philippians, "Look out . . . for those who mutilate the flesh," implying they're not numbered among the Judaizers. Then he writes, "For *we* are the true circumcision, who worship God in spirit, and glory in Christ Jesus, and put not confidence in the flesh" (3:3). The Philippians are numbered with Paul among those of the true circumcision, not the Judaizers.

Then there's Philippians 3:12–14, in which Paul acknowledges that he has not yet attained the resurrection of the dead and that he is not yet perfect, and he presses on to make the resurrection of the dead and perfection his own, looking forward "toward the goal for the prize of the upward call of God in Christ Jesus." That Rhodes sees perfectionism as an active problem in the Philippian community from Paul's acknowledgment that he's not perfect yet is a stretch, to say the least.

The purpose of Paul's statements is to remind the Philippians that they too haven't yet attained the resurrection of the dead or perfection, and that they too should be pressing forward to make it their own. This is an exhortation to be holy and a sober reminder that they could fail to achieve salvation, not an identification of church problems they need to be saved from.

The last passage to touch on here is Philippians 3:18–19: "For many, of whom I have often told you and now tell you even with tears, live as enemies of the cross of Christ. Their end is destruction, their god is the belly, and they glory in their shame, with minds set on earthly things."

You might think this could refer to Christians in the Philippian community, but the next verse shows that this is not so. Paul writes, "But *our* commonwealth is in heaven, and from it we await a Savior, the Lord Jesus Christ" (v. 20). Christians in the Philippian community are not the ones identified as the "enemies of the cross of Christ"; they are clearly distinguished from them.

So, the evidence fails to support the temporal view of salvation for the Philippian church. But is there any positive evidence that Paul intended to speak of salvation in the eternal sense in Philippians 2:12?

In both the preceding and subsequent context of Philippians 2:12, Paul speaks of eternal salvation. Consider, for example, Philippians 1:27–28, where Paul contrasts the "salvation" the Philippians receive from God with the "destruction" of their enemies:

> Only let your manner of life be worthy of the gospel of Christ . . . not frightened in anything by your opponents. This is a clear omen [Greek, *endeixis*, demonstration, proof, or sign] to them of their destruction, but of your salvation [Greek, *sōtērias*], and that from God.

The destruction that Paul speaks of can't refer to a temporal destruction that the Philippians might bring upon their enemies, since Paul is exhorting the Philippians to have no fear and remain faithful when their enemies persecute them. Therefore, the destruction of their enemies must refer to an eternal destruction—their damnation.

Also, Paul speaks of the Philippians living a life "worthy of the gospel of Christ" and the Philippians' salvation as coming "from God." Both these details strongly indicate that Paul is speaking of eternal salvation here.

Now, if Paul contrasts the Philippians' salvation with their enemies' destruction, and that destruction refers to eternal damnation, then it follows that Paul intends salvation to be understood in the eternal sense. And it's that salvation that Paul speaks of in Philippians 2:12 when he says, "work out your salvation."

We can also look to Philippians 2:14–16, where Paul identifies what "working out your own salvation" involves: "Do all things without grumbling or questioning, that you may be blameless and innocent, children of God without blemish in the midst of a crooked and perverse generation . . . holding fast the word of life."

Paul then gives the reason in verse 16 why he exhorts the Philippians to do such things: "So that in the day of Christ I may be proud that I did not run in vain or labor in vain." The implication is that if *on the day of Christ*, the Philippians are found to be blameworthy, not innocent, and with blemish, then he would have run in vain. In other words, his preaching would have been for nothing.

Paul is not exhorting the Philippians to be "blameless and innocent" and "without blemish" merely in the sight of men. Rather, he's calling them to a state of holiness that is a condition to receive their salvation at the Final Judgment. If that's not a reference to eternal salvation for believers, then nothing is.

So not only does the evidence for the Protestant argument fail to support a temporal view of salvation in Philippians 2:12, but we also have contextual evidence that Paul did *not* intend salvation to be taken in a temporal sense. Paul was speaking of our final salvation to be received at the Final Judgment, and by way of extension at our particular judgment. And since Paul says we need to put effort into bringing about *that* salvation, and that we should do so with fear and trembling,

Catholics are justified in appealing to this passage for support of their belief that good works do play a role in our final salvation and that it's possible to lose it in the end.

"The salvation that Paul speaks of is successful endurance of persecution, not salvation from eternal damnation."

Protestant author and executive director of The Grave Evangelical Society Robert Wilkin also denies the eternal sense of "salvation" in Philippians 2:12.[202] For support, Wilkin appeals to what he thinks is a parallel between the Philippians' "salvation" [Greek, *sōtērian*] in 2:12 and *Paul's* salvation spoken of in Philippians 1:19. There, Paul expresses confidence that through the prayers of the Philippian church and the Holy Spirit, his persecution "will turn out for [his] salvation" [Greek, *eis sōtērian*]."

Wilkin argues that Paul is not talking about salvation "from hell or union with Christ," but rather him "successfully enduring the persecution he was undergoing during his Roman imprisonment."[203] For Wilkin, this parallel proves that the salvation Paul speaks of in Philippians 2:12 "refers to the believers in Philippi successfully enduring their persecution at the hands of unbelievers,"[204] like Paul.

Wilkin goes on to explain what Paul means by "fear and trembling":

> The reason why Paul refers to "fear and trembling" is because he is reminded of the Judgment Seat of Christ, where, though eternally secure, believers will nevertheless be held accountable for their works and will be rewarded accordingly, hopefully experiencing confidence before the Lord and not shame.[205]

So Wilkin says "work out your own salvation with fear and trembling" has nothing to do with being saved in the eternal sense.

ANSWERING THE COMEBACK

One response is to provide the positive evidence that we looked at in our previous comeback that Paul intended to speak of salvation in the eternal sense (see above).

Another is to assume the legitimacy of the parallel that Wilkin draws between the Philippians' "salvation" in 2:12 and *Paul's* salvation spoken of in 1:19 but challenge the claim that Paul's salvation spoken of in 1:19 ("this will turn out for my salvation") doesn't refer to salvation in the eternal sense.

We can agree that Paul is requesting prayers from the Philippians that he may *succeed* in enduring the imprisonment and persecution. But that success, for Paul, is his "salvation" [Greek, *sōtērian*]. So the question becomes, "What does Paul have in mind as to the nature of this 'salvation'?"

You can't just say, "Paul's salvation is successful endurance during persecution," because we're inquiring as to what that success entails—something eternal or merely temporal. Wilkin, for his part, argues that it *can't* refer to salvation in the eternal sense. But the reason he gives just begs the question. He writes, "That salvation [salvation from hell or union with Christ] was already accomplished by faith in Christ, apart from works."[206]

This begs the question because what's being debated is whether Philippians 2:12 is evidence that salvation, at least final salvation, is accomplished through works. You can't use the belief that salvation is accomplished apart from works as a reason to reject the Catholic claim that Philippians 2:12 teaches that salvation, at least final salvation, is accomplished through works. You'd be assuming your doctrine to be true in order to argue for the truth of your doctrine.

Not only does this reason for interpreting "salvation" in a temporal sense not work, but nothing in Philippians 1:19, or its context, suggests what "salvation" could mean in a temporal sense. For example, if there were an indication that Paul would be set free from his imprisonment, then we'd have grounds for interpreting "salvation" in a temporal sense. But nothing of the sort is found in the text.

"Paul is speaking about sanctification, not justification or salvation."

Geisler and MacKenzie make an argument that Paul's phrase "work out your salvation" falls under the category of *sanctification*, not *salvation*. As such, they conclude that this passage has nothing to do with works meriting final salvation. It only has to do with works manifesting a Christian's sanctification.

Their reason? "Works-for-reward come under sanctification. They are what we do as a result of being saved, not what we do in order to be saved (i.e., to receive the gift of eternal life)."[207]

ANSWERING THE COMEBACK

If by "in order to be saved," we're talking about the initial state of salvation, whereby we first enter a saving relationship with Christ, then, as we've seen above from the Council of Trent, we as Catholics agree with Protestants—we do not perform good works to be initially saved.

Furthermore, we agree that "works-for-reward come under sanctification." But that doesn't mean that works-for-reward can't *also* fall under salvation. Given what we've seen above, James 2:24 teaches that we are justified by works of charity, parallel to Abraham's justification in the sight of God. We're also going to see below in our next Catholic argument from Matthew 25:31–46 that eternal life is given as a reward for good works.

Finally, there's some begging the question here. Notice the preconceived idea that salvation is not attained by works, used here in order to argue that Philippians 2:12 doesn't speak of attaining salvation by works. But if the Catholic argument is sound, then the belief that salvation is not attained by works in any sense would be falsified. You can't assume your belief to be true when that's what is being debated—in this case, with Philippians 2:12.

CHAPTER 20

The Sheep and the Goats
Matthew 25:31–46

Catholics believe we will be judged based on our works. And there's no better argument for this belief than one that appeals to Jesus' teaching about judgment in Matthew 25:31–46. The text reads,

> When the Son of Man comes in his glory, and all the angels with him, then he will sit on his glorious throne. Before him will be gathered all the nations, and he will separate them one from another as a shepherd separates the sheep from the goats, and he will place the sheep at his right hand, but the goats at the left. Then the king will say to those at his right hand, "Come, O blessed of my Father, inherit the kingdom prepared for you from the foundation of the world; for I was hungry and you gave me food, I was thirsty and you gave me drink, I was a stranger and you welcomed me, I was naked and you clothed me, I was sick and you visited me, I was in prison and you came to me." Then the righteous will answer him, "Lord, when did we see you hungry and feed you, or thirsty and give you drink? And when did we see you a stranger and welcome you, or naked and clothe you? And

when did we see you sick or in prison and visit you?" And the king will answer them, "Truly, I say to you, as you did it to one of the least of these my brethren, you did it to me." Then he will say to those at his left hand, "Depart from me, you cursed, into the eternal fire prepared for the devil and his angels; for I was hungry and you gave me no food, I was thirsty and you gave me no drink, I was a stranger and you did not welcome me, naked and you did not clothe me, sick and in prison and you did not visit me." Then they also will answer, "Lord, when did we see you hungry or thirsty or a stranger or naked or sick or in prison, and did not minister to you?" Then he will answer them, "Truly, I say to you, as you did it not to one of the least of these, you did it not to me." And they will go away into eternal punishment, but the righteous into eternal life.

The difference between the sheep and the goats is what they did and did not do. Performing the works of charity merited eternal life, and failure to perform works of charity led to damnation. For a Catholic, it doesn't get much clearer than this.

There are two major Protestant comebacks to this Catholic argument. Both reinterpret the role that works play at the Final Judgment.

"Jesus is talking about ruling with him in the kingdom, not entrance into the kingdom."

Robert Wilkin argues that it's "erroneous"[208] to equate Jesus' statement, "inherit the kingdom prepared for you," with "entering it" or "that these people have eternal life." He interprets Jesus to be saying, "They will be rewarded with the privilege of reigning with him forever."[209] Protestant author Joseph Dillow takes the same line as Wilkin, writing, "'To inherit the kingdom' is a virtual synonym for rulership in the kingdom and not entrance into it."[210]

ANSWERING THE COMEBACK

For our first response, let's concede for argument's sake that "inherit the kingdom" is equivalent to "reigning with Christ forever." By itself, this doesn't exclude the Catholic view that serving Christ in others is a condition for *entrance* into the kingdom.

Consider, for example, the contrast Jesus makes between those who "inherit the kingdom" and those who do not. Those who don't inherit the kingdom depart from Christ "into the eternal fire prepared for the devil and his angels . . . they will go away into eternal punishment." "Eternal fire" and "eternal punishment" both convey the nature of the individual's *experience* as he departs from Christ.

But it would be ridiculous to think this somehow excludes the idea that the goats don't ever enter the kingdom because of their failure to practice love in serving Christ in others. Jesus explicitly says, "Depart from me, you cursed, into the eternal fire . . . *for* I was hungry and you gave me no food." Jesus' statements about *what* the damned will experience also involves exclusion from the kingdom.

Since "eternal fire" and "eternal punishment" involve *both* what the damned will experience being separated from Christ *and* that they are excluded from the kingdom, and Jesus explicitly contrasts "eternal fire" and "eternal punishment" with "inheriting the kingdom," it's reasonable to conclude that "inheriting the kingdom" would involve not only what the saved will experience in heaven (e.g., ruling with Christ forever), but also *entrance* into the kingdom. And since serving Christ in others is a condition for ruling with Christ (assuming that "inheriting the kingdom" refers to ruling with Christ), it follows that serving Christ in others is also a condition of *entering* the kingdom.

A second response is that the word *inheritance* implies entering a new state that you didn't have before. For example, if I were to say to my son, "You will inherit my money when I die," I would mean that my son would eventually enter a state of possessing my money that he doesn't have now, before my death. Another example is the Israelites' inheritance of the promised land. Given that the term *inheritance* signifies entering a new state, we can interpret Jesus' statement about Christians "inheriting the kingdom" to mean Christians *entering* the kingdom of heaven.

A third response is that we have *biblical* grounds for thinking the phrase "inherit the kingdom" refers to receiving eternal life.[211] First, Jesus explicitly identifies the sheep who "inherit the kingdom" as "the righteous" who "go . . . into eternal life." Eternal life here is not to be equated with merely a reward, such as ruling with Christ, since it's contrasted with "eternal punishment." Jesus is contrasting two *eternal destinies*: one for the righteous and the other for the unrighteous.

Moreover, as R.T. France points out,[212] the phrase "eternal life" is already familiar to the reader of Matthew's Gospel as being equated with being saved or entering the kingdom of *heaven*. For example, in Matthew 19:16, the rich young man asks Jesus, "What good deed must I do, to have eternal life?" Then, in verses 28–29, Jesus makes clear that the eternal life the rich young man asked about refers to the life the righteous will receive at the Final Judgment: "Truly, I say to you . . . when the Son of Man shall sit on his glorious throne . . . everyone who has left houses or brothers or sisters or father or mother or children or lands, for my name's sake [what the rich young man didn't do], will receive a hundredfold, and inherit eternal life."

Second, Matthew elsewhere in his Gospel records Jesus' teaching about the kingdom, and it specifies that entrance into the kingdom is conditioned on whether Jesus' followers perform loving actions. For example, in Matthew 7:21, Jesus is clear that only those who *do* the will of his Father will "enter the kingdom of heaven." Doing God's will is the essence of the theological virtue of charity.

Matthew records Jesus two chapters earlier: "For I tell you, unless your righteousness exceeds that of the scribes and Pharisees, you will never enter the kingdom of heaven" (Matt. 5:20). Jesus goes on to list a variety of things that make up this righteousness:

- making amends with someone we've offended before we offer our sacrifice

- avoiding lust

- refusing to divorce or to attempt marriage after divorce

- not swearing

- turning the other cheek and being generous

- loving enemies

Notice that each item in the above list involves charity. And it's this charity, manifest in deeds or the avoidance thereof, that is necessary to have the righteousness required to "enter the kingdom of heaven" and be called "sons of your Father who is in heaven" (v. 45). Therefore, charity, and the behaviors associated with it, is a necessary condition for *entrance* into the kingdom.

Given this context of Matthew's Gospel concerning entrance into the kingdom and its relation to charity, as shown both in Matthew 5:20–47 and Matthew 7:21, it makes sense to think that when Jesus speaks of "inheriting the kingdom" based on charitable actions in Matthew 25, he has in mind the same teaching he gave concerning *entrance* into the kingdom based on charity in Matthew 5 and 7.

In sum, this counter-argument fails on multiple grounds. It doesn't jibe with Jesus' teaching on the kingdom and its relation to charity elsewhere in Matthew's Gospel. Nor does it succeed even if we grant for argument's sake that "inherit the kingdom" refers to ruling with Christ. As such, this comeback shouldn't cause a Catholic to stop using Matthew 25:31–46 for biblical support of the belief that works play an essential role in entering heaven.

"The works are not causative of entrance into the kingdom. They're merely evidential."

Protestant Bible scholar D.A. Carson offers an alternative explanation for the role works play in Matthew 25:31–46. He proposes the idea that the works mentioned are merely evidence of one's saving relationship with Christ and that they play no causal role. [213] It's not that the righteous are entering the kingdom *because* they committed good works; rather, those who deserve to enter the kingdom will *just happen* to have committed good works, and those good works can serve as the proof that these people are in the right place. Carson thinks this interpretation is "suggested by the surprise of the righteous."[214]

ANSWERING THE COMEBACK

One problem with this interpretation is that it contradicts the plain sense of the text. When Jesus tells the sheep they will "inherit the kingdom" prepared for them, he says, "*for* [Greek, *gar*, "marker of cause or reason"[215]] I was hungry and you gave me food" (v.35). In other words, the sheep will inherit the kingdom *because* they exercised charity. Charity is the reason for entrance into the kingdom. That's not merely evidential; it's causative.

Similarly, the goats do not inherit the kingdom, and thus are sent into "eternal fire," *because* they did not exercise charity. Jesus says, "Depart from me, you cursed, into the eternal fire . . . *for* I was hungry and you gave me no food" (v.41–42).

Jesus makes it clear: if charitable deeds, then entrance into the kingdom; if no charitable deeds, then no entrance into the kingdom. How can charitable works not have a causal role when they are a necessary condition for entering the kingdom?

A second problem lies with the surprise of the righteous. Those who receive eternal life are not surprised at getting into the kingdom. Rather, they are surprised at the fact that when they served others, they somehow served Jesus. Furthermore, the surprise that the righteous experience in discovering they were serving Christ in serving others doesn't take away from the *fact* that loving service of others is grounds for their entrance into heaven. In other words, there's a difference between the righteous *knowing* the reasons they are saved and the reality that they are saved for those reasons. Really, the former can't possibly undermine the latter!

CHAPTER 21

Abide in Me or Be Burned
John 15:5–6

A go-to passage for evidence from Jesus that Christians can lose their salvation is John 15:5–6. Jesus says,

> I am the vine, you are the branches. He who abides in me, and I in him, he it is that bears much fruit, for apart from me you can do nothing. If a man does not abide in me, he is cast forth as a branch and withers; and the branches are gathered, thrown into the fire, and burned.

Obviously, that a branch can be cut off from the vine implies that it once was a part of the vine, living with the life of the vine. And when it's cast forth, it dies.

Just as branches live with the life of the vine when united to it, so too Christians live with the life of Jesus when united to him. And just as branches can be separated from the vine and die, so too Christians can be separated from Jesus and die spiritually, since to be separated from Jesus is not to have salvation. Therefore, Jesus teaches that Christians can lose their salvation.

There aren't many comebacks Protestants make to a Catholic's appeal to John 15:5–6. John Calvin argued that Jesus speaks of those who merely appeared to be Christians but were not in reality.[216] Since this reading is so contrary to the plain sense of the text (Jesus says, "he who abides in me," not "he who appears to abide in me"), most Protestants don't use it.

There is one comeback, however, that some Protestants use . . .

> It's interesting that the only other place where Jesus speaks of abiding in him is with reference to the Eucharist: "He who eats my flesh and drinks my blood abides in me, and I in him" (John 6:56). The Eucharist is key to remaining on the vine and not being burned.

"Jesus is not talking about eternal punishment. Rather, he's talking about temporal punishment."

Robert Wilkin counters by targeting the Catholic assumption that Jesus is talking about *eternal* judgment. He argues Jesus is speaking about *temporal* judgment. Wilkin supports his claim by appealing to what Jesus doesn't say. Wilkin writes,

> Since the Lord did not use the verb *to be burned up,* but rather the less intense verb *to be burned,* He is holding open the possibility that the unproductive believer may respond to the burning and return to fruitfulness."[217]

For Wilkin, the image of the branch burning *up* would have to be present if Jesus intended his teaching to mean that a Christian can be definitively separated from Jesus and receive eternal damnation. Since Jesus doesn't use that image, but rather simply says the branch will burn, Wilkin concludes that Jesus isn't talking about eternal judgment.

ANSWERING THE COMEBACK

One glaring problem with this argument is that it doesn't fit with the viticultural imagery.[218] As Catholic Bible scholar Michael Barber argues, "Why would a vinedresser cut off and 'burn' a branch in order to restore it?"[219] Burning a branch doesn't restore the branch; it destroys it.[220]

A second problem is that the language "burned" doesn't suggest something temporary. The same language jibes just as easily with the view that Jesus is talking about the Final Judgment and the everlasting burning that someone separated from Jesus will experience. That person will be forever "burned." Given this ambiguity, anyone using the "burned but not burned up" argument would have to provide further evidence to defend his claim that this is a temporary burning. Until he does, this counter-argument is an assertion without evidence.

Finally, consider the Greek. First, there's nothing there to suggest that this is a temporary burning. Second, there's only one other time in the New Testament where the Greek word translated as "burned" (*kaiō*) is Matthew 13:40. It's used in relation to judgment, and it's used for the *Final* Judgment, which implies an everlasting burning: "Just as the weeds are gathered and burned [Greek, *kaietai*] with fire, so will it be at the close of the age. The Son of Man will send his angels, and they will gather out of his kingdom all causes of sin and all evildoers, and throw them into the furnace of fire, where there will be weeping and gnashing of teeth."

CHAPTER 22

Severed from Christ
Galatians 5:4

Galatians 5:4 is a go-to text for Catholics when it comes to defending the belief that Christians can lose their salvation:

> You are severed from Christ, you who would be justified by the law; you have fallen away from grace.

Notice that St. Paul says the Galatians were "severed from Christ" and that they have "fallen away from grace." Both statements imply that the Galatians had been saved, since to be in Christ and in grace is to be free from condemnation (Rom. 8:1). Yet, these Galatians, who were looking to be justified by the Old Law, are no longer in Christ and in grace. As such, they are currently subject to condemnation, which means they lost that initial saving relationship they had with Christ.

For some Protestants, the Catholic take on Paul in Galatians 5:4 is based on a fundamentally flawed assumption. Basically, Catholics don't understand what Paul is talking about here!

"Paul is not talking about a loss of salvation. He's talking about a loss of sanctification."

Norman Geisler argues that this text refers to sanctification, not salvation. In the chapter he wrote for the book *Four Views on Eternal Security*, he writes, "they have not lost their true salvation but only their sanctification . . . they have fallen from grace as a means of living a sanctified (holy) life."[221]

Geisler gives two reasons for this claim. First, "they are already saved,"[222] since they are called "brothers" (6:1) and have placed their "faith" in Christ (3:2). Second, Paul mentions only the threat of the "yoke of slavery" (5:1) and not eternal torment in hell.[223]

ANSWERING THE COMEBACK

Our first response is directed toward the overall interpretation here. An immediate glaring problem is that it clashes with the plain sense of the text. Paul doesn't say, "You who would seek to be *sanctified* by the law." Rather, he says, "You who would seek to be *justified* by the law." The Greek word for "justified" is *dikaioō*, the same word that Paul uses when he speaks of justification by faith in Romans 3:28, a text that all Protestants acknowledge refers to justification in the sight of God.

Now we can turn our attention to the two points in support of Paul talking about sanctification. Galatians 5:4, the argument goes, can't refer to salvation because "they are already saved," since they are called "brothers" and have "faith" in Christ. The problem here is the assumption that "already being saved" (being a Christian) necessarily entails being eternally secure in that salvation.

The status of "already being saved" (having faith in Christ and being called a "brother") can just as easily be read within the Catholic framework of salvation. On the Catholic view, a believer is truly saved when he initially comes to faith in Christ and enters the body of Christ via baptism. Being a member of Christ's mystical body constitutes all Christians as spiritual brothers and sisters. It's just that on the Catholic view, the saving relationship with Christ that we initially enter through baptism can be lost by mortal sin.

> The *Catechism* teaches that mortal sin "destroys charity in the heart of man" (1855) and that "to die in mortal sin without repenting and accepting God's merciful love means remaining separated from him forever by our own free choice" in a state of existence that we call "hell" (1033). This means that a Christian (someone initially saved) who commits a mortal sin can lose his salvation.

Since the "already saved" status of the Galatians can fit within the Catholic framework, just as it can within an "eternally secure doctrine" framework, a Protestant can't appeal to the Galatians' "saved" status to counter the Catholic interpretation of Galatians 5:4.

What about the "yoke of slavery"? Why not hell? Well, Paul mentions the yoke (i.e., the Old Testament Law) several verses earlier, and after doing so, he says, "If you receive circumcision, Christ will be of no advantage to you" (5:2). What advantage does Christ give us? Salvation! Therefore, Paul is saying that to go back to the Old Covenant—i.e., circumcision—is to cut oneself off from salvation. The reason is because Christ *alone* is our source of salvation (Acts 4:12). It is in this light that we must understand Paul when he says, "You have been severed from Christ" and "you have fallen away from grace."

So, in fact, Paul *does* threaten the Galatians with damnation. As such, Paul teaches it's possible for a Christian to lose salvation.

CHAPTER 23

Lest I Be Disqualified
1 Corinthians 9:27

1 Corinthians 9:27 is a powerful text for Catholics since it seems that Paul himself doesn't think his saving relationship with Christ is eternally secure. He writes,

> I pommel my body and subdue it, lest after preaching to others I myself should be disqualified.

In context, the disqualification refers to the race Paul runs in order to attain the "imperishable" wreath (v. 25), which is eternal life.

For Catholics, it's clear. Paul thinks he can be disqualified from the race to attain eternal life, which means he thinks his relationship with Christ is not eternally secure.

The major Protestant comeback to the Catholic argument from 1 Corinthians 9:27 challenges the assumption that Paul is talking about salvation.

"Paul is talking about losing heavenly rewards, not salvation."

Norman Geisler argues, "Paul is speaking here of loss of reward, not of salvation."[224] There's one reason Geisler gives to defend his claim: "[Paul] speaks of it [the imperishable wreath—v. 25] as a 'prize' to be won, not a 'gift' to be received (Rom. 6:23)."

ANSWERING THE COMEBACK

The first thing we can say in response is that this argument assumes the truth of a hidden premise. The conclusion is that Paul in 1 Corinthians 9:27 is not speaking of losing the prize of salvation. The premise that undergirds this conclusion is that Paul speaks of making an effort to receive the prize, the assumption being that salvation *in no way* can be won as a prize. The reasoning here, therefore, seems to be as follows:

Premise 1: If the prize were a reference to eternal life, then Paul would be espousing the view that we can merit eternal life.

Premise 2: But Paul can't espouse the view that we can merit eternal life.

Conclusion: Therefore, the prize that Paul speaks of can't be a reference to eternal life.

It's premise 2 that we can challenge. Although we affirm that Paul views eternal life as a gift, he *also* views eternal life as a reward. Consider, for example, what he writes in Galatians:

Do not be deceived; God is not mocked, for whatever a man sows, that he will also reap. For he who sows to his own flesh will from the flesh reap corruption; but he who sows to the Spirit will from the Spirit *reap eternal life*. And let us not grow weary in well-doing, for in due season we shall reap, if we do not lose heart (Gal. 6:7–9).

For Paul, eternal life is given as a reward for those who sow to the Spirit and continue in doing good.

Paul teaches the same thing in Romans 2:5–7: "On the day of wrath God's righteous judgment will be revealed. He will render to every man *according to his works*: to those who by patience in well-doing seek for glory and honor and immortality, he will give *eternal life*."

From the above two passages, it's clear that Paul believes that eternal life can be given as a reward for doing good. As such, it's false to say Paul can't espouse the view that we can merit eternal life. Since premise 2 is false, it follows that the conclusion—Paul can't be referring to the prize as eternal life—must be false.

A second response is that the context of 1 Corinthians 9:27 is about salvation. Paul starts off talking about how he adapts his ministry according to his audience. When he ministers to the Jews, he becomes a Jew. For those outside the law, he becomes as one outside the law. When the weak are his audience, he becomes weak.

Now, Paul tells us he relates to his different audiences in order that he might "win" them. What might Paul be winning them over to? His answer is salvation: "I have become all things to all men, that I might by all means *save* some" (1 Cor. 9:22).

It's within this context that Paul gives the instruction to run as to attain "the prize." The only thing that separates Paul's concept of salvation and the "prize" is him telling us he adapts to different audiences to share in the gospel's blessings, which include salvation.

Given the context, therefore, we can conclude that the "prize" refers to salvation. And if the prize refers to salvation, then the disqualification from receiving that prize that Paul talks about in verse 27 must refer to losing the gift of salvation.

CHAPTER 24

Those Who Spurn the Son of God
Hebrews 10:26–31

The evidence for the Catholic belief that we can lose our salvation is also found in the letter to the Hebrews. One passage many Catholics turn to is Hebrews 10:26–31.

> For if we sin deliberately after receiving the knowledge of the truth, there no longer remains a sacrifice for sins, but a fearful prospect of judgment, and a fury of fire which will consume the adversaries. A man who has violated the Law of Moses dies without mercy at the testimony of two or three witnesses. How much worse punishment do you think will be deserved by the man who has spurned the Son of God, and profaned the blood of the covenant by which he was sanctified, and outraged the Spirit of grace? For we know him who said, "Vengeance is mine, I will repay." And again, "The Lord will judge his people." It is a fearful thing to fall into the hands of the living God.

Notice the markers that indicate that the individual was saved to begin with:

- *"after* receiving the knowledge of the truth," implying that the individual had such knowledge

- "there *no longer* remains a sacrifice for sins," which implies the individual had a sacrifice for his sins—namely, the sacrifice of Jesus

- "the blood of the covenant by which he *was sanctified*," which implies that the individual was saved. How can someone be holy and not be in a saving relationship with Christ?

According to the author of Hebrews, it's this kind of person who can be subject to the "fearful prospect of judgment," a punishment by a "fury of fire" that is worse than the capital punishment passed down by Moses. That sounds a lot like damnation. And if damnation, then we can say the author of Hebrews teaches that a saved Christian can lose his salvation.

Generally, there are two comebacks that some Protestants give to the argument from Hebrews 10:26–31. One dodges the conclusion; the other tries to turn the tables.

"The author is talking about the loss of rewards, not salvation."

Geisler argues that Hebrews 10:26–31 is referring not to salvation, but rather to the loss of rewards.[225] He defends his position by appealing to verse 39, where the author writes, "We are not of those who shrink back and are destroyed, but of those who have faith and keep their souls." For Geisler, the author can't be referring to salvation in the prior verses because in verse 39, he says "we" are not among those who lose our souls. The author, Geisler concludes, is simply "affirming with confidence that believers will not be lost."[226]

ANSWERING THE COMEBACK
Geisler fails to interact with the data in the passage that suggest

that salvation is the focal point. Consider, for example, the consequence for those who "sin deliberately after receiving knowledge of the truth": "there no longer remains a sacrifice for sins, but a fearful prospect of judgment, and a fury of fire" (v.1) that consumes. Moreover, the author reveals in verses 28–29 that harsh punishment awaits these people.

Missing out on rewards doesn't fit with most of the consequences enumerated by the inspired author. For example, no longer to have a sacrifice for sins is to not miss out on rewards, but *salvation*. Only Jesus' sacrifice is the source of salvation. Without access to it, there is no salvation.

Consider also the consequence of not receiving mercy and undergoing a punishment by a "fury of fire," which the author says is worse than capital punishment. Moreover, such punishing fire is for "adversaries," indicating that the author sees those who "sin deliberately" as enemies of Christ.[227]

All these details are antithetical to someone being saved, which Geisler's view necessarily entails. How can someone who is saved be said to have no mercy? How can someone who is an enemy of Christ be numbered among the saved?

Since all these warnings are about damnation and not the loss of rewards, and all these warnings are directed to Christians, including the inspired author ("for if *we* sin deliberately"), then it follows that this passage reveals it's possible for us to lose our salvation.

Now, concerning verse 39, which Geisler appeals to for support of his claim, it must be read in context. We already argued above that the warnings the author issues in the preceding verses are directed to Christians and that these warnings are about damnation. This, in itself, lends support to the idea that verse 39 is not an expression of absolute certitude that all believers will be finally saved, but one of hope.

Further support is found in verses 35–36. The author writes,

> Therefore, do not throw away your confidence, which has a great reward. For you have need of endurance, so that you may do the will of God and receive what is promised.

If the author thought all believers were eternally secure in their salvation, then his exhortation to "not throw away" their confidence would be unintelligible. The exhortation implies that it's possible for them to *lose* their confidence in Christ. And not to have confidence in Christ is not to be in a saving relationship with him.

Moreover, the author exhorts them to endure in doing the will of God. Why is there a need to *endure* in doing God's will if they're eternally secure?

Geisler might respond, "But you're assuming that the need to keep confidence and endurance in doing God's will is to receive final salvation. These things fit just as easily with my rewards view. In fact, the author says, 'Do no throw away your confidence, which has a great *reward*' (v. 35)."

In response, we've already given reason to think the author in the preceding context is not talking about mere rewards. Also, verse 39 is evidence that the "great reward" in verse 35 is salvation.

Notice that immediately after the author exhorts his Christian readers to remain confident and endure in doing God's will, he speaks of being "destroyed," not having faith, and losing one's soul. That's damnation talk.

So when he says in verse 39 that they aren't among those who "shrink back" and are "destroyed," he's talking about Christians not being among the damned. And since we know from the context that this is an expression of hope and not absolute certitude, we can conclude that the author has hope that his Christian readers are numbered not among the damned, but rather among the elect.

This is the same kind of language used in diplomacy when one encourages a dialogue partner not to do something by expressing confidence that he will not do it. For example, "some leaders embark on needless wars, but of course you would never do that" is an exhortation not to embark on a needless war. In the same way, "we are not among those who shrink back to destruction" is an aspirational exhortation not to shrink back.

> "There are no limits to the mercy of God, but anyone who deliberately refuses to accept his mercy by repenting, rejects the forgiveness of his sins and the salvation offered by the Holy Spirit. Such hardness of heart can lead to final impenitence and eternal loss" (CCC 1864).

"The passage cuts against Catholic belief, since the author teaches that the sinner can't be restored, no longer having a sacrifice for sins."

Geisler argues that Hebrews 10:26–31 can't be used to support the belief that a Christian can lose his salvation because, in his words, "it says those who commit this sin cannot be restored again, for 'no sacrifice for sins is left' (Heb. 10:26)."[228]

ANSWERING THE COMEBACK

The first thing we can say in response is that the RSV translation "if we sin deliberately" does not reflect the fact that the Greek word rendered "sin" is a present participle, which in Greek conveys the idea of ongoing action. Thus, other translations render this statement "If we go on sinning deliberately" (ESV), "if we deliberately keep on sinning" (NIV, NET), "if we go on sinning willfully" (NASB), "if we willfully persist in sin" (NRSV). The passage thus envisions not a single sin or fall into sin, but an ongoing pattern of willful sin that has not been repented of.

For our second response, we can affirm the author's statement, "There no longer remains a sacrifice for sins." But this doesn't mean a person can *never* repent and be restored. It means that as long as the person *remains* an apostate, he can't have the merits of Christ's death on the cross applied to him. In other words, if we refuse what God has provided for our salvation, then we're left with no means of salvation at all. As W. Leonard puts it, such a person has "incapacitated himself for the reception of ministrations by the paralyzing ingratitude of his rejection of Christian riches and by his complete break away from all contact with the source of salvation."[229]

Conclusion

In my book *Meeting the Protestant Challenge: How to Answer Fifty Biblical Objections to Catholic Beliefs*, I addressed challenges that target Catholic *beliefs*, all of which took the form "How can the Catholic Church teach X when the Bible says Y?" Such a defense of *beliefs* provides Catholics with confidence that our beliefs stand up to biblical scrutiny and do not contradict Scripture. But such a defense doesn't provide *positive evidence* to persuade a Protestant to believe such doctrine.

In this book, we took on Protestant challenges to Catholic *arguments* for those beliefs, which take on a slightly different significance. Given that a Protestant will believe only what's found in the Bible, only Catholic arguments that provide biblical grounds for a belief will have persuasive force. But those arguments won't be effective if a Protestant is persuaded by counter-responses. Hence the need for Catholics to answer those comebacks.

Knowing there are biblical grounds for a Catholic belief, and knowing that the challenges to those biblical texts are not effective, a Protestant will be more inclined at least to take a new look at the classic Catholic arguments. And who knows? He may just start to "get it" and be persuaded to become Catholic.

There are a few more things we can take away from this book, all of which apply to us as Catholics. First, the arguments presented in this book in support of our Catholic beliefs give Catholics the confidence that our beliefs are scripturally justified. With such arguments in hand, there's no need for a Catholic to get stuck thinking the Bible is "Protestant territory" and thus too intimidating to argue about.

These arguments and their defenses also exclude any fear a Catholic might have in using these texts in conversations. I know from my own personal experience that there have been times when I feared to use a text to justify a particular belief because I wasn't sure how a Protestant would respond. And not wanting to be stumped *due to my pride*, I shied away from sharing the passage. By knowing which comebacks a Protestant might make, a Catholic can confidently share the passage and be ready to go further in discussions about the text.

Finally, the answers given in this book go a long way for Catholics who might fear using a biblical text because they're not able to, so to speak, swim in the deep waters of exegesis, having encountered only cursory treatments of these texts in pop apologetics. It's often the case that literature in popular Catholic apologetics contains only supporting citations, without any explanation as to *how* these texts support such beliefs. After reading the Catholic answers covered in this book, a Catholic can shake off his exegetical aquaphobia.

The days of sitting back and thinking Protestants won't convert because they've heard these age-old arguments are done and over. Let's get out there and tell our Protestant friends something they don't already know. A *new* springtime of conversions from Protestantism to Catholicism awaits your contribution.

Postscript

There's one last takeaway from this book that requires its own section. Here it is: the Protestant comebacks that we've covered in this book *can help Catholics view Protestants with a renewed sense of respect.*

Recall from the introduction that folks who express to me their joy in doing apologetics often say things along the lines of, "Why don't Protestants get it? The evidence for the Catholic faith is so clear!"

Well, as we've seen in this book, for many Protestants, it's not so clear. And it's not that they're closed-minded or stubborn. Protestants actually do have respectable reasons for remaining Protestant in the face of Catholic arguments. And such reasons challenge any rash judgment a Catholic may have made about a Protestant who seemingly just doesn't "get it." Hopefully, awareness of these reasons can foster respect for our Protestant brothers and sisters.

It's important for us Catholics not to fall into the trap of *triumphalism*, which is "the spirit of arrogance or pride with respect to belonging to the Church."[230]

This must not be confused with a *proper* sense of pride, such as, "I'm proud to be Catholic." It's rather an *exaggerated* or *disordered* sense of pride—for example, "I belong to the One True Church, and you don't; therefore, you're inferior to me."

Such arrogance is poisonous to the work of evangelization. Pope St. Paul VI picked up on this idea in his 1975 apostolic exhortation *Evangelii Nuntiandi,* where he stressed the importance of being a witness first in our evangelistic endeavor, using the term *witness* thirty-six times. Having respect for those to whom we minister, as Christ did, is what wins converts. The arguments are necessary. But they're simply a "noisy gong or a clanging cymbal" if there's no charity in them (1 Cor. 13:1).

A triumphalistic attitude is antithetical not only to the work of evangelization but also to our own salvation. The Bible reveals that charity is what puts us into communion with God, a charity that involves love of God *and* neighbor. The arrogance involved in Catholic triumphalism is directly opposed to this love of neighbor, since it doesn't lead to sharing the Catholic faith as a good that God desires the other to have and experience, but rather as something with which I can lord it over the other.

We as Catholics often lament anti-Catholicism. But we need to check ourselves that we don't follow suit and become anti-Protestant.

May this renewed sense of respect for our Protestant brothers and sisters guide our conversations and inspire love within our hearts—love that hopefully will be contagious and lead all Christians to unite and gather around the one altar of Christ's sacrifice in the Mass.

About the Author

Karlo Broussard, a native of Southern Louisiana, left a promising musical career to devote himself full-time to the work of Catholic apologetics.

As a staff apologist and speaker for Catholic Answers, he travels the country and the world giving talks on apologetics, biblical studies, theology, and philosophy.

Karlo has published articles on a variety of subjects in *Catholic Answers Magazine*, is a regular guest on *Catholic Answers Live*, and is an active writer for *Catholic Answers Magazine Online* at catholic.com.

Karlo holds undergraduate and graduate degrees in theology from Catholic Distance University and the Augustine Institute, along with master's degree in philosophy from Holy Apostles College and Seminary.

He also worked for several years in an apprenticeship with nationally known author and theologian Fr. Robert J. Spitzer at the Magis Center of Reason and Faith.

Karlo is one of the most dynamic and gifted Catholic speakers on the circuit today, communicating with precision of thought, a genuine love for God, and an enthusiasm that inspires.

You can view Karlo's online videos at KarloBroussard.com.

Endnotes

1   James G. McCarthy, *The Gospel According to Rome: Comparing Catholic Tradition and the Word of God* (Eugene, OR: Harvest House Publishers, 1995), 242.

2   McCarthy, *The Gospel According to Rome,* 243.

3   Ron Rhodes, *Reasoning from the Scriptures with Catholics* (Eugene, OR: Harvest House Publishers, 2000), 103–104, emphasis added. See also William Cathcart, *The Papal System* (Philadelphia: Griffith and Rowland Press, 1872), 76.

4   D.A. Carson, "Matthew," in *The Expositor's Bible Commentary: Matthew, Mark, Luke,* Vol. 8 (Grand Rapids, MI: Zondervan, 1984), 368.

5   R.T. France, *The Gospel of Matthew,* The New International Commentary on the New Testament (Grand Rapids, MI: Wm. B. Eerdmans, 2007), 621.

6   France, *The Gospel of Matthew,* 624.

7   This line of reasoning is taken from Steven D. Greydanus, "The Petrine Fact, Part 7: And Upon This Rock, cont.", http://www.jimmyakin.org/2009/09/the-petrine-fact-part-7.html.

8   France, *The Gospel of Matthew,* 624.

9   This line of reasoning is taken from Greydanus, "The Petrine Fact, Part 7."

10 Todd Baker, *Exodus from Rome: A Biblical and Historical Critique of Roman Catholicism* (Bloomington, IN: iUniverse, 2014), Chap. 2; Kindle Edition.

11 Carson, "Matthew," 368.

12 Craig Keener, *The IVP Bible Background Commentary of the New Testament* (Downers Grove, IL: IVP Academic, 2014), 90.

13 Oscar Cullman, "Rock," in *Theological Dictionary of the New Testament,* Vol. 6, ed. by Gerhard Kittle and Gerhard Friedrich (Grand Rapids, MI: Wm. B. Eerdmans, 1968), 98.

14 See Dave Armstrong, "Primacy of St. Peter Verified by Protestant Scholars," April 21, 2018, https://www.patheos.com/blogs/davearmstrong/2018/04/primacy-of-st-peter-verified-by-protestant-scholars.html.

15 Rhodes, *Reasoning from the Scriptures with Catholics,* 105.

16 For a Protestant who agrees with this line of argument, see Carson, "Matthew," 368.

17 See Jimmy Akin, *A Daily Defense: 365 Days (plus one) to Becoming a Better Apologist* (El Cajon, CA: Catholic Answers Press, 2016), 186.

18 See James White, *The Roman Catholic Controversy: Catholics and Protestants—Do the Differences Still Matter?* (Minneapolis, MN: Bethany House Publishers, 1996), 118. See also Steve Hays, "Catholic Prooftexts," *Triablogue,* December 17, 2017, http://triablogue.blogspot.com/2017/12/catholic-prooftexts.html; Norman L. Geisler and Ralph E. MacKenzie, *Roman Catholics and Evangelicals: Agreements and Differences* (Grand Rapids, MI: Baker Academic, 1995), 207.

19 James White, *Answers to Catholic Claims: A Discussion of Biblical Authority* (New York: Crowne Publishing, 1990), Chap. 7; Electronic Edition.

20 J. Knox Chamblin, "Matthew," in *Evangelical Commentary on the Bible* (Grand Rapids: MI: Baker, 1989), 742.

21 James White, "Robert Sungenis and evpi.tau,th," May 30, 2008, https://www.aomin.org/aoblog/roman-catholicism/upon-this-rock-jesus-is-speaking-to-peter-about-the-rock/.

22   Richard T. France, "*The Gospel According to Matthew: An Introduction and Commentary*," Tyndale New Testament Commentaries, ed. Leon Morris (Grand Rapids, MI: Wm. B. Eerdmans, 1985), 254.

23   See Jimmy Akin, "Peter the Rock," November 1, 1998, https://www.catholic.com/magazine/print-edition/peter-the-rock-0.

24   Geisler and MacKenzie, *Roman Catholics and Evangelicals*, 208.

25   Ibid.

26   Jason Engwer, "The Pillars of Roman Catholicism," *Triablogue*, October 8, 2020, http://triablogue.blogspot.com/2020/10/the-pillars-of-roman-catholicism.html.

27   This is not James the brother of John. That James was killed by Herod around the time when Peter was arrested and put in prison, A.D. 44 (Acts 12:2). So, Paul is referring to James, the "brother of the Lord." That this James became a leader in the Jerusalem Church is confirmed by the early Church: "Then James, whom the ancients surnamed the Just on account of the excellence of his virtue, is recorded to have been the first to be made bishop of the church of Jerusalem. This James was called the brother of the Lord." Eusebius, *Church History*, Bk. 2, Chap. 1. Jerome teaches the same thing: "James was at once ordained by the apostles bishop of Jerusalem." Jerome, *Lives of Illustrious Men* 2.

28   F.F. Bruce, *The Epistle to the Galatians: A Commentary on the Greek Text*, The New International Greek Testament Commentary (Grand Rapids, MI: Wm. B. Eerdmans, 1982), 121–122.

29   See *The Ignatius Catholic Study Bible: The New Testament* (San Francisco: Ignatius Press, 2010), 333.

30   Hays, "Catholic Prooftexts."

31   See Gen. 1:1; Ezra 4:6; Prov. 20:21; Wis. 14:6; Sir. 15:14, 24:9, 36:15, Jer. 26:1, 27:1, 49:34; Amos 7:1; Phil. 4:15; Heb. 1:10.

32   W.F. Albright and C.S. Mann, *Matthew,* The Anchor Yale Bible (Garden City, NY: Doubleday, 1971), 196.

33   Jason Engwer, "Does Combining Isaiah 22 with Matthew 16 Lead Us to a Papacy?," *Triablogue,* August 23, 2006, http://triablogue.blogspot.com/2006/08/does-combining-isaiah-22-with-matthew.html.

34   Jason Engwer, "Re: The Gates of Hell Shall Not Prevail [Blog Comment]," *Triablogue,* August 30, 2017, http://triablogue.blogspot.com/2017/08/the-gates-of-hell-shall-not-prevail.html?showComment=1504144283696#c6591148820319584669.

35   White, *The Roman Catholic Controversy,* 249, footnote 18.

36   See A.S. Wood, "Key," in *The International Standard Bible Encyclopedia, Revised,* ed. Geoffrey W. Bromiley (Grand Rapids, MI: Wm. B. Eerdmans, 1979–1988), 10–11.

37   For a list of these scholars, see Dave Armstrong, *Biblical Proofs for an Infallible Church and Papacy* (Dave Armstrong, 2012), 126–136.

38   Walter C. Kaiser Jr., Peter H. Davids, F.F. Bruce, and Manfred T. Brauch, *Hard Sayings in the Bible* (Downers Grove, IL: InterVarsity Press, 1996), 385.

39   Jason Engwer, "Opening Statement," Debate between Mark Bonocore and Jason Engwer "Was the Papacy Established by Christ," http://www.biblicalcatholic.com/apologetics/debate15.htm.

40   See Geisler and MacKenzie, *Roman Catholics and Evangelicals,* 208; Ron Rhodes, *Reasoning from the Scriptures with Catholics,* 111.

41   See Kaufmann Kohler, "Binding and Loosing," *Jewish Encyclopedia,* www.jewishencyclopedia.com.

42   See Ibid; Flavius Josephus, *The Jewish War* 1.111.

43   Engwer, "Opening Statement," Debate "Was the Papacy Established by Christ."

44   Geisler and MacKenzie, *Roman Catholics and Evangelicals*, 207.

45   Rhodes, *Reasoning from the Scriptures with Catholics*, 106.

46   Geisler and MacKenzie, *Roman Catholics and Evangelicals*, 207.

47   This structure is taken from Jimmy Akin, *A Daily Defense*, 256.

48   Hays, "Catholic Prooftexts."

49   *A Greek-English Lexicon of the New Testament and Other Early Christian Literature*,
      3rd ed., eds. Frederick W. Danker, Walter Bauer, William F. Arndt, and F. Wilbur
      Gingrich (Chicago: University of Chicago Press, 2000), 213.

50   I am grateful to Joe Heschmeyer for this line of reasoning. See Joe Heschmeyer, *Pope
      Peter: Defending the Church's Most Distinctive Doctrine in a Time of Crisis* (El Cajon, CA:
      Catholic Answers Press, 2020), Chap. 4.

51   Joseph A. Fitzmyer, *The Gospel According to Luke X-XXIV*, Anchor Bible Series, Vol.
      28A (Garden City, NY: Doubleday and Company, 1985), 622.

52   See R.T. Kendall, *The Parables of Jesus: A Guide to Understanding and Applying the Stories
      Jesus Told* (Grand Rapids, MI: Chosen Books, 2006), 144; Geisler and MacKenzie,
      Roman Catholics and Evangelicals, 211.

53   Albright and Mann, *Matthew*, 195.

54   Rhodes, *Reasoning with Catholics from the Scriptures*, 115.

55   Baker, *Exodus from Rome*, Chap. 2.

56   I am grateful to Heschmeyer for this line of argumentation. See Heschmeyer, *Pope
      Peter*, Chap. 4.

57   See Ibid.

58   See Craig A. Evans, *From Jesus to the Church* (Louisville, KY: Westminister John
      Knox, 2014), 27.

59   I am grateful to Jimmy Akin for pointing out to me this particular progression in the
      narrative. See Akin, *Daily Defense*, 276.

60   White, *The Roman Catholic Controversy*, 115. White notes the Greek word *stērizein* on
      page 246, footnote 8.

61   See Ibid., 113; Rhodes, *Reasoning from the Scriptures with Catholics*, 116–117; Baker,
      Exodus from Rome, Chap. 2; Jason Engwer, "Abusing Peter's Weaknesses to Establish
      A Papacy," January 23, 2020, http://triablogue.blogspot.com/2020/01/abusing-
      peters-weaknesses-to-establish.html.

62   Geisler and MacKenzie, *Roman Catholics and Evangelicals*, 212.

63   Bradford Baine Jr., *Peter in the Gospel of John: The Making of an Authentic Disciple*
      (Boston, MA: Brill Academic Publishers, 2007), 170.

64   Veselin Kesich, "Peter's Primacy in the New Testament and the Early Tradition," in
      The Primacy of Peter, ed. John Meyendorff (Crestwood, NY: St. Vladimir's Seminary
      Press, 1992), 43.

65   See White, *The Roman Catholic Controversy*, 113; Baker, *Exodus from Rome*, Chap.
      2; Jason Engwer, "Abusing Peter's Weaknesses"; Ron Rhodes, *Reasoning from the
      Scriptures*, 116–117; Geisler and MacKenzie, *Roman Catholics and Evangelicals*, 211.

66   David A. de Silva, *An Introduction to the New Testament: Contexts, Methods and Ministry
      Formation* (Downer's Grove, IL: InterVarsity Press, 2004), 432.

67   Joachim Jeremias, "ποιμην, αρχιποιμην, ποιμαινω," in *Theological Dictionary of the New
      Testament*, vol. 6, ed. Gerhard Friedrich (Grand Rapids, MI: Wm. B. Eerdmans,
      1968), 498.

68   See Ibid.

69   Hays, "Catholic prooftexts."

70   Geisler and MacKenzie, *Roman Catholics and Evangelicals*, 284.

71   Hays, "Catholic prooftexts."

72   See White, *The Roman Catholic Controversy*, 112.

73   This line of argument is taken from Scott Butler, Norman Dahlgren, and David Hess, *Jesus, Peter and the Keys* (Santa Barbara, CA: Queenship Publishing, 1996), 96–97.

74   For a similar argument, see Hugh Pope, "The Papacy in the New Testament" in Cuthbert Lattey, S.J., *The Papacy* (Cambridge, England: W. Heffer and Sons, 1924), 23.

75   See 1 Corinthians 8:8–9 where Paul gives permission to eat meat offered to idols.

76   *A Greek-English Lexicon of the New Testament and Other Early Christian Literature*, 567–568.

77   Rhodes, *Reasoning with Catholics from the Scriptures*, 166.

78   *The Ignatius Catholic Study Bible*, 166.

79   George R. Beasley-Murray, *John*, Word Biblical Commentary, Vol. 36, revised ed. (Dallas, Texas: Word Books Publisher, 1999), 49.

80   See Baker, *Exodus from Rome*, Chap. 11.

81   See Rhodes, *Reasoning from the Scriptures with Catholics*, 163–164.

82   See Karlo Broussard, *Meeting the Protestant Challenge: How to Answer Fifty Biblical Objections to Catholic Beliefs* (El Cajon, CA: Catholic Answers Press, 2019), 111.

83   This line of argumentation was taken from C.S. Dessain, "The Acts of the Apostles," in *A Catholic Commentary on Holy Scripture*, eds. B. Orchard and E.F. Sutcliffe (New York: Thomas Nelson, 1953), 1022.

84   *The Shepherd of Hermas* 2:4:3.

85   I am grateful to Jimmy Akin for this line of reasoning.

86   Baker, *Exodus from Rome*, Chap. 11.

87   Other passages that Baker cites are Acts 10:47–48; 16:14–15, 31–33; 18:8; 19:4–5.

88   See Thomas Aquinas, *Summa Theologiae* I–II:113:4; III:85:6; II–II:6:2. One passage that Baker cites, Acts 10:47–48, likely doesn't involve imperfect fact. But we dealt with this passage above.

89   Baker, *Exodus from Rome*, Chap. 11.

90   *A Greek-English Lexicon of the New Testament and Other Early Christian Literature*, 362. See also B.M. Newman Jr., *A Concise Greek-English Dictionary of the New Testament* (Deutsche Bibelgesellschaft: United Bible Societies, 1993), 67.

91   "A formal request, *appeal*." *A Greek-English Lexicon of the New Testament and Other Early Christian Literature*, 362. "That which is asked for—'request, appeal.'" J.P. Louw and E.A. Nida, *Greek-English Lexicon of the New Testament: Based on Semantic Domains* (Deutsche Bibelgesellschaft: United Bible Societies, 1996), 406.

92   Baker, *Exodus from Rome*, Chap. 11.

93   B.M. Newman Jr., *A Concise Greek-English Dictionary of the New Testament*, 46. See also *A Greek-English Lexicon of the New Testament and Other Early Christian Literature*, 249.

94   See Robert Zins, *Romanism—The Relentless Roman Catholic Assault on the Gospel of Jesus Christ!* (Huntsville, AL: White Horse Publications, 1995), 118; See also Baker, *Exodus from Rome*, Chap. 10; Rhodes, *Reasoning from the Scriptures with Catholics*, 197.

95   Other passages include Matthew 13:11 and Matthew 16:5–12.

96   See W. Webster, *The Church of Rome at the Bar of History* (Carlisle, PA: Banner of Truth, 1997), 130; John W. Riggs, *The Lord's Supper in the Reformed Tradition* (Louisville, KY: Westminster John Knox Press, 2015), 62; Matt Slick, "Transubstantiation and the Real Presence," December 3, 2008, https://carm.org/

roman-catholicism/transubstantiation-and-the-real-presence/; Baker, *Exodus from Rome*, Chap. 10.

97   Slick, "Transubstantiation and the Real Presence," emphasis added.

98   See James White, "John 6 For Roman Catholics," January 10, 2017, video, https://www.aomin.org/aoblog/roman-catholicism/john-6-roman-catholics/.

99   See D.A. Carson, *The Gospel According to John,* The Pillar New Testament Commentary (Grand Rapids, MI: Wm. B. Eerdmans, 1991), 303; Leon Morris, *The Gospel According to John,* The New International Commentary on the New Testament (Grand Rapids, MI: Wm. B. Eerdmans, 1995), 342; *A Greek-English Lexicon of the New Testament and Other Early Christian Literature,* 297–298; Daniel B. Wallace, *Greek Grammar Beyond the Basics: An Exegetical Syntax of the New Testament* (Grand Rapids, MI: Zondervan, 1996), 371–372.

100   See Baker, *Exodus from Rome*, Chap. 10; Andreas J. Kostenberger, *John,* Baker Exegetical Commentary on the New Testament (Grand Rapids, MI: Baker Book House, 2004), 207.

101   Baker, *Exodus from Rome,* Chap. 10.

102   L. Goppelt, "τρώγω," in *Theological Dictionary of the New Testament,* eds. Gerhard Kittle and Gerhard Friedrich, Vol. VIII (Grand Rapids, MI: Wm. B. Eerdmans, 1972), 236. See also R.L. Thomas, *New American Standard Hebrew-Aramaic and Greek Dictionaries* (La Habra, CA: Foundation Publications, Inc., 1998), Electronic Edition; *The Lexham Analytical Lexicon to the Greek New Testament* (Logos Bible Software, 2011).

103   See Loraine Boettner, *Roman Catholicism* (Phillipsburg, NJ: Presbyterian and Reformed Publishing Company, 1962), 178.

104   Slick, "Transubstantiation and the Real Presence."

105   Geisler and MacKenzie, *Roman Catholics and Evangelicals,* 262.

106   See Baker, *Exodus from Rome,* Chap. 10.

107   Zins, *Romanism,* 117.

108   Eric Svendsen, *Evangelical Answers A Critique of Current Roman Catholic Apologists* (Lindenhurst, New York: Reformation Press, 1999), 179.

109   White, *The Roman Catholic Controversy,* 170.

110   See Ibid.; Eric Svendsen, *Evangelical Answers,* 180.

111   White, *The Roman Catholic Controversy,* 17

112   Baker, *Exodus from Rome,* Chap. 10.

113   See Rhodes, *Reasoning from the Scriptures with Catholics,* 197.

114   Other passages that are appealed to include Psalm 34:8, Psalm 119:103, Isaiah 55:1, Jeremiah 15:16, Ezekiel 3:1–3.

115   Baker, *Exodus from Rome,* Chap. 10.

116   White, *The Roman Catholic Controversy,* 174.

117   Eusebius, *Church History* 3:39:14–15; emphasis added.

118   Thomas Aquinas, *Catena Aurea: Commentary on the Four Gospels, Collected out of the Works of the Fathers: St. Matthew,* Vol. 1, ed. J.H. Newman (Oxford: John Henry Parker, 1841), 897.

119   White, *The Roman Catholic Controversy,* 176, emphasis added.

120   See Albert Barnes, "Commentary on 1 Corinthians 10:4," in *Barnes' Notes on the Whole Bible,* 1870, https://www.studylight.org/commentaries/bnb/1-corinthians-10.html; Matthew Poole, "Matthew Poole's Commentary," https://biblehub.com/commentaries/poole/1_corinthians/10.htm.

121   See Brant Pitre, *Jewish and the Jewish Roots of the Eucharist: Unlocking the Secrets of the Last Supper* (New York: Doubleday, 2011), Chap. 4; Electronic Edition.

122 *Against Heresies* 4:33:2

123 Protestant apologist Eric Svendsen makes the argument this way: "The Greek word used in John 6 to designate that which we are to eat is (σαρξ [*sarx*]; translated "flesh"), while the Greek word used in the Last Supper texts is always *sôma* (σῶμα; translated "body"). The differences between these words suggests that if a connection between John 6 and the Eucharist is made, it must at best be a loose one. This fits well with the symbolic understanding of John 6." Svendsen, *Evangelical Answers*, 182.

124 Baker, *Exodus from Rome,* Chap. 10.

125 Ibid.

126 See Merrill C. Tenney "The Gospel of John," in *The Expositor's Bible Commentary, Volume 9 (John-Acts),* ed. Frank E. Gaebelein (Grand Rapids, MI: Zondervan Publishing House, 1981), 160; Leon Morris, *The Gospel According to John*, The New International Commentary on the New Testament (Grand Rapids, MI: Wm. B. Eerdmans, 1995), Electronic Edition.

127 See Craig S. Keener, *The Gospel of John: A Commentary,* Vol. 1 (Grand Rapids, MI: Baker Academic, 2003), 1046–1047; Colin G. Kruse, *John,* Tyndale New Testament Commentaries (Nottingham, England: Inter-Varsity Press, 2003), Electronic Version.

128 See White, *The Roman Catholic Controversy,* 176; emphasis added.

129 Zins, *Romanism*, 100.

130 Rhodes, *Reasoning from the Scriptures with Catholics,* 223.

131 Baker, *Exodus from Rome,* Chap. 11; Electronic edition.

132 See J.R. Mantey, "The Mistranslation of the Perfect Tense in John 20:23, Matthew 16:19, and Matthew 18:18," *Journal of Biblical Literature*, 58 (1939): 243–249; Tenney, "The Gospel of John," 193; Matt Slick, "Does John 20:23 mean that Catholic priests can forgive sins?", June 1, 2012, https://carm.org/roman-catholicism/does-john-2023-mean-that-catholic-priests-can-forgive-sins/.

133 Baker, *Exodus from Rome,* Chap. 11; emphasis in original.

134 Daniel B. Wallace, *Greek Grammar beyond the Basics: An Exegetical Syntax of the New Testament* (Grand Rapids, MI: Zondervan, 1996), 581.

135 Henry J. Cadbury, "The Meaning of John 20:23, Matthew 16:19, and Matthew 18:18," *Journal of Biblical Literature*, 58, n. 3 (1939): 251–254.

136 Ibid., 254.

137 Baker, *Exodus from Rome,* Chap. 11.

138 Geisler and MacKenzie make this same counter-argument and appeal to Philip and the Ethiopian eunuch in Acts 8. See Geisler and MacKenzie, *Roman Catholics and Evangelicals,* 289.

139 Clement of Rome, *First Letter to the Corinthians*, Chap. 44, https://www.newadvent.org/fathers/1010.htm.

140 St. Hippolytus, *Apostolic Tradition*, 2–3; emphasis added.

141 St. John Chrysostom, Homily 86, in Thomas Aquinas, *Catena Aurea: Commentary on the Four Gospels, Collected out of the Works of the Fathers: St. John*, Vol. 4, 607).

142 The title "Mother of God" is accepted by Eastern Orthodox Christians, Oriental Orthodox Christians, Lutherans, and Anglicans.

143 Walter L. Liefeld, "Luke," in *The Expositor's Bible Commentary: Matthew, Mark, Luke,* Vol. 8 (Grand Rapids, MI: Zondervan, 1984), 834.

144 White, *The Roman Catholic Controversy,* 205.

145 Ibid.

146 See Broussard, *Meeting the Protestant Challenge,* Chap. 32.

147 *Summa Theologiae* III:28:3.

148 James White, *Mary—Another Redeemer?* (Minneapolis, MN: Bethany House Publishers, 1998), Chap. 3, Electronic Edition.

149 Rhodes, *Reasoning with Catholics from the Scriptures,* 297.

150 *Gune* also means simply "woman," but like marital context indicates "wife" as the appropriate translation.

151 Tim Staples, *Behold Your Mother: A Biblical and Historical Defense of the Marian Doctrines* (El Cajon, CA: Catholic Answers Press, 2014), 134–135.

152 See Daniel B. Wallace, 521–522; cf. Manual Miguens, *The Virgin Birth, an Evaluation of the Scriptural Evidence* (Westminster, MD, 1975), 81; William H. Carroll, *A History of Christendom,* Vol. I (Front Royal, VA: Christendom Press, 1985), 310.

153 James White, *Mary—Another Redeemer?,* Chap. 3, Electronic Edition.

154 See Eusebius, *Church History,* Bk. 2, Chap. 1; Jerome, *Lives of Illustrious Men,* 2.

155 White, *The Roman Catholic Controversy,* 204.

156 Rhodes, *Reasoning from the Scriptures with Catholics,* 292–293.

157 Jimmy Akin, "Who Will Crush the Serpent's Head?" September 1, 1997, https://www.catholic.com/magazine/print-edition/who-will-crush-the-serpents-head.

158 Although Pope Pius XII didn't specify which passages support the revealed truth that Mary was bodily assumed when he defined the dogma of Mary's Bodily Assumption, he does affirm that it's "based" on Scripture. This doesn't mean that there is a particular prooftext. Rather, it's meant to suggest that when certain things in Scripture are taken collectively we can see a convergence with the Tradition of Mary's Bodily Assumption. He writes, "This truth [Mary's Bodily Assumption] which is based on the Sacred Writings, which is thoroughly rooted in the minds of the faithful, which has been approved in ecclesiastical worship from the most remote times, which is completely in harmony with the other revealed truths, and which has been expounded and explained magnificently in the work, the science, and the wisdom of the theologians." Pope Pius XII, Apostolic Constitution Defining the Dogma of The Assumption *Munificentissimus Deus* § 41, https://www.vatican.va/content/pius-xii/en/apost_constitutions/documents/hf_p-xii_apc_19501101_munificentissimus-deus.html. The *Catechism of the Catholic Church,* however, in paragraph 2853, does reference "the woman" of Revelation 12:1–5 in reference to Mary's bodily assumption.

159 Gregory K. Beale, *John's Use of the Old Testament in Revelation* (Sheffield, United Kingdom: Sheffield Academic Press, 1998), 59.

160 Rhodes, *Reasoning with Catholics from the Scriptures,* 320.

161 Steve Hays, "Marian Prooftexts," March 9, 2020, http://triablogue.blogspot.com/2020/03/marian-prooftexts.html.

162 Ben Witherington III, *What Have They Done With Jesus: Beyond Strange Theories and Bad History –Why We Can Trust the Bible* (San Francisco: Harper Collins Publishing, 2006), 130.

163 Peter Leithart, *Revelation 12–22,* International Theological Commentary (New York: Bloomsbury T&T Clark, 2018), 23.

164 Hays, "Marian Prooftexts,"

165 For this line of reasoning, see Staples, *Behold Your Mother,* 200.

166 Hays, "Marian Prooftexts."

167 Ron Rhodes, *Reasoning with Catholics from the Scriptures,* 321.

168 Ibid.

169 There is debate among theologians as to whether Mary's freedom from labor pains is official non-infallible Catholic teaching or simply a matter of theological opinion. There are two potential magisterial sources for this teaching to be classified as official non-infallible Catholic teaching. The first is a statement by Pope Alexander III, who writes in an 1169 letter, "[Mary] indeed conceived without shame, gave birth without pain." Pope Alexander III, Letter *Ex litteris tuis* to the Resident Sultan in Iconium, in Heinrich Denzinger, *Enchiridion Symbolorum Definitionum et Declarationum De Rebus Fidei et Morum: Compendium of Creeds, Definitions, and Declarations on Matters of Faith and Morals*, ed. Peter Hünermann, Robert Fastiggi, and Anne Englund Nash, 43rd ed. (San Francisco: Ignatius Press, 2012), 245, DH 748. It's argued that since this statement is merely a letter directed to a private individual, and *not* the universal Church, it doesn't carry the magisterial weight needed to be classified as official Catholic teaching. The second potential magisterial reference comes from *The Catechism of the Council of Trent*, which reads, "From Eve we are born children of wrath; from Mary we have received Jesus Christ. . . . To Eve it was said: In sorrow shalt thou bring forth children. Mary was exempt from this law, for preserving her virginal integrity inviolate she brought forth Jesus . . . without experiencing, as we have already said, any sense of pain." *The Catechism of the Council of Trent*, trans. J. Donovan (New York: The Catholic Publication Society), 41. Although this is a legitimate expression of the Church's magisterium, some theologians argue that it has dropped to the level of theological opinion given the seemingly intentional avoidance of this issue when modern magisterial documents address Mary's sinlessness and/or perpetual virginity (*Catechism of the Catholic Church* 490–493, 499). See Steven D. Greydanus, "*The Nativity Story* and Catholic Teaching," https://decentfilms.com/articles/nativitycritics.

170 Matt Slick, "Is Praying to the Saints Biblical?" December 6, 2008, https://carm.org/roman-catholicism/is-praying-to-the-saints-biblical/.

171 Slick, "Is Praying to the Saints Biblical?"

172 "Petition addressed to deity, prayer." *A Greek-English Lexicon of the New Testament and Other Early Christian Literature*, 878.

173 See *A Greek-English Lexicon of the New Testament and Other Early Christian Literature*, 27, 357, 408.

174 Matt Slick, "Can Mary Hear Our Prayers," June 10, 2016, https://carm.org/roman-catholicism/can-mary-hear-our-prayers.

175 Slick, "Is Praying to the Saints Biblical?"

176 Slick, "Can Mary Hear Our Prayers."

177 Ibid.

178 Rhodes, *Reasoning from the Scriptures with Catholics*, 79–80.

179 Robert Jamieson, David Brown, and Andrew Robert Fausset, *A Commentary, Critical, Experimental, and Practical, on the Old and New Testaments*, 1882, https://biblehub.com/commentaries/jfb/2_thessalonians/2.htm.

180 Geisler and MacKenzie, *Roman Catholics and Evangelicals*, 188.

181 Some apologists have pursued this line of argument using 2 Peter, since "most scholars now believe that 2 Peter depends on Jude, questioning whether Jude would have written his letter otherwise, since he restated much of 2 Peter." Thomas Schreiner, *1, 2 Peter, Jude: An Exegetical and Theological Exposition of Holy Scripture* (Nashville, TN: B&H Publishing, 2003), 417–418. I am grateful to apologist Trent Horn for this research. See Trent Horn, *The Case for Catholicism: Answers to Classic and Contemporary Protestant Objections* (San Francisco, CA: Ignatius Press, 2017), footnote 108.

182 White, *The Roman Catholic Controversy*, 96–97.

183 Eric Svendsen, *Evangelical Answers*, 84.

184 "89.69 εἴτε . . . εἴτε: (normally a doublet, but in 1 Cor 14:27 occurring singly) a double or multiple marker of condition (equivalent in meaning to εἰα 'if,' 89.65)—'if . . . if, whether . . . or.' εἴτε δὲ θλιβόμεθα . . . εἴτε παρακαλούμεθα 'if we are in difficulty . . . if we are encouraged' 2 Cor 1:6; εἴτε Παῦλος εἴτε Ἀπολλῶς εἴτε Κηφᾶς εἴτε κόσμος εἴτε ζωὴ εἴτε θάνατος . . . 'whether Paul or Apollos or Cephas or the world or life or death . . .' 1 Cor 3:22; εἴτε γλώσσῃ τις λαλεῖ 'if someone speaks in a tongue' 1 Cor 14:27." Johannes P. Louw and Eugene Albert Nida, *Greek-English Lexicon of the New Testament: Based on Semantic Domains* (New York: United Bible Societies, 1996), 785. I am grateful to Jimmy Akin for this research.

185 Geisler and MacKenzie, *Roman Catholics and Evangelicals*, 188.

186 Geisler *seems* to have this view in mind, but it's not clear.

187 Steve Hays, "Catholic Prooftexts," http://triablogue.blogspot.com/2017/12/catholic-prooftexts.html.

188 See Geisler and MacKenzie, *Roman Catholics and Evangelicals*, 188; Ron Rhodes, *Reasoning from the Scriptures with Catholics*, 79–80.

189 James White gives a similar line of reasoning to a Catholic's appeal to 1 Corinthians 11:2 for biblical support of Sacred Tradition. See James White, "Apolonio Latar and Sola Scriptura I of II," July 5, 2005, https://www.aomin.org/aoblog/misc/apolonio-latar-and-sola-scriptura-i-of-ii/.

190 Clement of Rome, *First Letter to the Corinthians*, Chap. 44, https://www.newadvent.org/fathers/1010.htm.

191 St. Irenaeus, *Against Heresies* III:3:1, https://www.newadvent.org/fathers/0103303.htm.

192 See R.C. Sproul, *Faith Alone: The Evangelical Doctrine of Justification* (Grand Rapids, MI: Baker Books, 1995), 199–200; Ron Rhodes, *Reasoning from the Scriptures with Catholics*, 147–149; James White, *The God Who Justifies* (Minneapolis, MI: Bethany House, 2001), 351–352; John MacArthur, *James*, The MacArthur New Testament Commentary (Chicago: Moody Press, 1998), 137–139;

193 Sproul, *Faith Alone*, 199–200.

194 *A Greek-English Lexicon of the New Testament and Other Early Christian Literature*, 996.

195 Sproul, *Faith Alone*, 200.

196 Ibid.

197 See Jimmy Akin, "Whose Righteousness was Reckoned?" January 3, 2018, www.catholic.com.

198 See Sproul, *Faith Alone*, 200.

199 Ibid.

200 Ibid.

201 Rhodes, *Reasoning from the Scriptures with Catholics*, 150.

202 See Robert N. Wilkin, "Response to Michael P. Barber," in *Four Views on the Role of Works at the Final Judgment*, ed. Alan P. Stanley (Grand Rapids, MI: Zondervan, 2013), 189.

203 Ibid.

204 Ibid.

205 Ibid.

206 Ibid.

207 Geisler and MacKenzie, *Roman Catholics and Evangelicals*, 238.

208 Robert N. Wilkin, "Christians will be Judged According to the Works at the *Rewards* Judgment, but *Not* at the Final Judgment," in *Four Views on the Role of Works at the Final Judgment*, ed. Alan P. Stanley (Grand Rapids, MI: Zondervan, 2013), 39; emphasis in original.

209 Ibid.

210 Joseph Dillow, *The Reign of the Servant Kings: A Study of Eternal Security and the Final Destiny of Man* (Monument, CO: Paniym Group, 2010), Chap.4; Kindle Edition.

211 For further support of this line of argumentation, see Dale Alison, *Constructing Jesus: Memory, Imagination, and History* (Grand Rapids, MI: Baker, 2010), 188–99; Jonathan T. Pennington, *Heaven and Earth in the Gospel of Matthew* (Ada, MI: Baker Academic, 2012).

212 See R.T. France, *The Gospel of Matthew,* The New International Commentary of the New Testament (Grand Rapids, MI: Wm. B. Eerdmans, 2007), 925.

213 D.A. Carson, "Matthew," 21.

214 Ibid.

215 *A Greek-English Lexicon of the New Testament and Other Early Christian Literature,* 189.

216 See John Calvin, *The Gospel according to St. John: Part Two, 11–21 and the First Epistle of John,* trans. T.H.L. Parker (Grand Rapids, MI: Wm. B. Eerdmans, 1959), in loc.; cf. Michael P. Barber, "Response to Robert N. Wilkin," in *Four Views on the Role of Works at the Final Judgment,* 68.

217 Robert Wilkin, "The Gospel According to John," in *The Grace New Testament Commentary,* ed., R.N. Wilkin (Denton, TX: Grace Evangelical Society, 2010), 450.

218 I am grateful to Michael Barber for this line of argumentation. See Barber, "Response to Robert Wilkin," 67.

219 Barber, "Response to Robert Wilkin," 67.

220 See Craig Keener, *The Gospel of John: A Commentary,* Vol. 2 (Peabody, MA: Hendrickson, 2003), 1003; cf. Thomas R. Schreiner, "Justification Apart from and By Works: At the Final Judgment Works will *Confirm* Justification," in *Four Views on the Role of Works at the Final Judgment,* 93.

221 Norman Geisler, "A Moderate Calvinist View," in *Four Views on Eternal Security,* ed. J Matthew Pinson (Grand Rapids, MI: Zondervan, 2002), 97.

222 Ibid.

223 See Ibid.

224 Ibid., 96.

225 Ibid., 100.

226 Ibid.

227 See Mary Healy, *Hebrews,* Catholic Commentary on Sacred Scripture Series (Grand Rapids, MI: Baker Academic, 2016), 217.

228 Geisler, "A Moderate Calvinist View," 100.

229 W. Leonard, "The Epistle to the Hebrews," in *A Catholic Commentary on Holy Scripture,* eds. B. Orchard and E.F. Sutcliffe (New York: Thomas Nelson, 1953), 1,164. Leonard here is referring to those spoken of in Hebrews 6:4–6, but his line of reasoning applies here as well.

230 Patrick Coffin, "The Scourge of Triumphalism," January 13, 2013, https://www.catholic.com/magazine/online-edition/the-scourge-of-triumphalism.

CPSIA information can be obtained
at www.ICGtesting.com
Printed in the USA
LVHW040115170422
716060LV00001B/1